Assets in Action

Assets $_{in}$ *Action*

A Handbook for
Making Communities
Better Places to
Grow Up

Deborah Fisher

Foreword by
Nancy Tellett-Royce
COMMUNITY LIAISON, SEARCH INSTITUTE

SEARCH INSTITUTE

Assets in Action
A Handbook for Making Communities Better Places to Grow Up
Deborah Fisher

Copyright © 2003 by Search Institute

10   9   8   7   6   5   4   3

Search Institute
615 First Avenue NE, Suite 125
Minneapolis, MN 55413
612-376-8955
800-888-7828
www.search-institute.org

ISBN: 978-1-57482-750-7

CREDITS
Editor: Kathryn (Kay) L. Hong
Design: Judy Gilats
Production: Mary Ellen Buscher

About Search Institute
Search Institute is an independent, nonprofit, nonsectarian organization whose mission is to provide leadership, knowledge, and resources to promote healthy children, youth, and communities.

Search Institute's Healthy Communities • Healthy Youth (HC • HY) initiative seeks to motivate and equip individuals, organizations, and their leaders to join together in nurturing competent, caring, and responsible children and adolescents.

Lutheran Brotherhood, now Thrivent Financial for Lutherans, is the founding national sponsor for Healthy Communities • Healthy Youth. The Thrivent Financial for Lutherans Foundation has provided Search Institute with generous support for 2003.

Thrivent Financial *for Lutherans* Foundation

Library of Congress Cataloging-in-Publication Data

Fisher, Deborah, 1951-
   Assets in action : a handbook for making communities better places to grow up / Deborah Fisher ; foreword by Nancy Tellett-Royce.
      p. cm.
   Includes bibliographical references.
   ISBN 1-57482-750-2
   1. Community organization. 2. Young volunteers in social service. 3. Intergenerational relations. 4. Teenagers and adults. I. Title.
HM766.F57 2003
361.8–dc21

                                    2003007388

CONTENTS

PART ONE
Vision, Preparation, and Planning

PART TWO
Making It Happen
Five Action Strategies for Your Asset-Building Initiative

PART THREE
Keeping It Going and Growing

TIPSHEETS

Changing Communities, Changing Lives—Together

I'M WEARING MY "PARENT" HAT this evening, which means I have just driven my 15-year-old son to Circus Juventas and am watching him fly through the air on a trapeze 35 feet above the cement floor. A friend asked me if I worried about him when he was up there, and I said no, that I trusted the rigging and the net to catch him whenever he fell. I can tell that Michael trusts the net, too. He is fearless as he works up there to perfect his skills.

The metaphor of the net reminds me why I do the work I do, to support communities that are working to weave a community-wide net of relationships, opportunities, supports, and experiences—developmental assets—that children and youth need to thrive. No one person or system can create this net. It takes many adults partnering with many youth and organizations and systems to ensure a net strong enough to do the job.

In 1997, Search Institute's president, Peter Benson, wrote in the preface to *All Kids Are Our Kids* that three actions were necessary to create healthy communities for our young people:

1. To meet basic human needs;
2. To target and reduce the risks and deficits that diminish or thwart the healthy development of children and adolescents; and
3. To shift the language about children and adolescents from a preoccupation with problems, deficits, and risks to a vocabulary of what we need to promote.

"The language of developmental assets," he wrote, "is one of positive development, of good things that must be named and promoted in the daily-ness of life." The recent work of Search Institute has largely focused on that third action and what brings it to life.

In 1997 Search Institute launched its Healthy Communities • Healthy Youth (HC • HY) initiative to motivate and equip individuals, organizations, and their leaders to join together in nurturing competent, caring, and responsible children and adolescents.

Now, six years later, we are able to look at the nearly 600 initiatives, encompassing cities, towns, counties, provinces, and school districts across the United States and Canada, and similar work that is bubbling up in Australia, Brazil, and other countries. This book brings you stories from dozens of those community initiatives to show you what it looks like when individuals make a commitment to work together to name, promote, and deliver the positive relationships, experiences, and supports that help young people thrive. Paired with these stories from the communities are some of the framing tools we are using at Search Institute to describe and understand more deeply what we see happening in the field.

Here you will see how young people themselves are powerful change agents in their communities; how professionals working with children and adolescents have transformed their practices by infusing them with asset-building principles; and how citizens of all ages and walks of life are seizing opportunities to create positive connections to the young people who live in their communities. These individuals are working collaboratively to weave this way of thinking and acting into the fabric of their communities. You will hear from them how this work is changing communities and changing lives—the lives of young people and of the adults who engage in this work.

As community liaison at Search Institute for the past four years, it has been my privilege to talk to thousands of adults and youth—many of whose stories and ideas are found in this book—who are working with great enthusiasm to shift the lens through which community members view young people and then interact with them.

As a member of Children First, the first community initiative that formed to take asset building "to scale" across an entire community, I have lived and breathed this work and seen its impact on my own community.

And as the mother of two teenage boys, I have seen the important role that caring adults have played in their lives—whether it is an adult who has mentored them or a stranger who has smiled at them instead of turning away.

People who step up to this work are embarking on a journey of learning and doing, and then learning some more. Asset building is as easy as saying hello to a young person. But that is just a starting point. Once the concept grabs you, you will find yourself asking how to make messages stick in people's minds, how to create events that authentically engage multigenerational groups, how to renew people's commitment to asset building, when to use research and when to use stories to move the work along, and how to determine what is working in your setting.

If you are new to this journey, welcome! I hope this book shows you how individuals can begin to connect in new and more intentional ways with the young people around them and inspires you to find like-minded neighbors and colleagues who care deeply and are willing to join you in working to transform your community.

If you have been on this path for a while, I hope this book provides you with new ideas and renewed inspiration. I applaud you, youth and adults, for your courage and resourcefulness as you help your communities see young people for the treasures they are and continue to invite people to join you in this effort. Together, you are changing the world.

NANCY TELLETT-ROYCE
Community Liaison, Search Institute

Planting the Seeds of Change

This is what we are about.
We plant the seeds that will one day grow.
We water the seeds already planted,
Knowing that they hold future promise.
ARCHBISHOP OSCAR ROMERO

SEARCHING MY LOCAL PAPER for a September 11 anniversary observance that would have meaning for me, I was instantly drawn to an evening multifaith service to be held at a synagogue within walking distance from my home. I loved the idea of a faith coalition composed of Christians, Jews, and Muslims publicly coming together to offer solace and inspiration to one another.

But this single-day event, I discovered, was not just a one-time occurrence. I quickly learned that the five congregations participating in this service had come together the year before, just after the events of 9/11, to find a way to cross the barriers of faith and seek a larger expression of world peace. They had collaboratively created a vision, mission, logo, and dialogue around the idea of building peace in the world together. They intentionally extended their vision by mutually committing their time to building houses for Habitat for Humanity. Fresh from several weeks' work on local building projects, a number of speakers at the event talked about their renewed sense of purpose, including a young Muslim woman who recounted turning away from the fear and mistrust she felt in the days immediately after 9/11 to discover surprising new friendships.

The service ended with young people from each of the five participating congregations lighting candles from a central taper and spreading out through the audience to light the candles that several hundred of us held as we sang.

I felt that I had not only experienced a hopeful, peaceful vision for our community's future, I had also witnessed asset building among youth and adults on many different levels. Among the prayers and songs we shared during this service, the words of Oscar Romero in particular stood out. As community asset builders, we are about the business of planting seeds while we water the ones we have already sown. What could be a simpler, more satisfying, and ultimately more effective approach to growing healthy communities?

This book brings together the best collective ideas from Search Institute and some of the many community asset-building initiatives across the United States and Canada. You will have a chance to read about Search Institute's in-depth research into how four distinct initiatives are transforming their communities and hear from asset builders sharing, in their own voices, what has worked for them.

As an asset builder myself, it has been a gift to me to have the opportunity to work in my community as a nonprofit consultant, helping to infuse developmental assets into several organizations and projects in the Puget Sound region of Washington. As a writer for Search Institute's *Assets* magazine for a number of years, I have had the chance to hear, firsthand, the hundreds of creative ways that people are doing this work all over the country with unfailing enthusiasm.

Now, in this book, I combine my own experiences with insights gleaned from research and with practical tips, stories, and wisdom from dozens of asset-building initiatives. I hope that this resource will inspire you in new ways to put assets in action in your own community.

The Importance and Power of Building Developmental Assets

For many people, the developmental assets have become a source of ideas and inspiration for their work to create healthy communities, even in the face of frustration and despair. With the asset framework, Search Institute has identified 40 positive experiences and qualities that all of us have the power to bring into the lives of children and youth of all cultural backgrounds, from every type and size of community, and in any family of any income level. By focusing on bringing more of the assets to greater numbers of young people, thousands of community activists have found new and effective ways to bring improvements to their larger community as well.

For readers who are new to the developmental assets, a brief review may be helpful here. The asset framework identifies crucial relationships, experiences, opportunities, and personal qualities that help children and adolescents learn to make positive choices and avoid problems. The developmental assets framework encompasses eight broad categories of human development to form a picture of the positive things all young people, from birth to age 18, need to grow up healthy and responsible.

The first four asset categories focus on *external structures, relationships, and activities* that create a positive environment for young people:

- **Support:** Young people need to be surrounded by people who love, care for, appreciate, and accept them.
- **Empowerment:** Young people need to feel valued and valuable. This happens when youth feel safe and respected.
- **Boundaries and Expectations:** Young people need clear rules, consistent consequences for breaking rules, and encouragement to be and do their best.
- **Constructive Use of Time:** Young people need opportunities outside of school to learn and develop new skills and interests with other youth and adults.

The next four categories reflect *internal values, skills, and beliefs* that young people also need to fully engage with and function in the world around them:

- **Commitment to Learning:** Young people need a sense of the lasting importance of learning and a belief in their own abilities.
- **Positive Values:** Young people need strong guiding values or principles to help them make healthy life choices.
- **Social Competencies:** Young people need the skills to interact effectively with others, to make difficult decisions, and to cope with new situations.
- **Positive Identity:** Young people need to believe in their own self-worth and to feel that they have control over the things that happen to them.

Research clearly demonstrates that these assets can have a powerful influence on adolescent behavior—both in protecting young people from many different problem behaviors and in promoting positive attitudes and behaviors. The more assets young people have, the more likely they are to thrive.

Assets can have a powerful positive influence on a young person's life, as demonstrated by the responses of young people to the questions on the *Search Institute Profiles of Student Life: Attitudes and Behaviors* survey, which measures young people's levels of developmental assets, deficits, and thriving behaviors. For example, 53 percent of young people with 0–10 assets report high use of alcohol compared to just 3 percent of young people who report 31–40 assets. More positive behaviors rise with more assets, too. Only 7 percent of young people who report 0–10 assets say they get mostly A's on their report card, compared to 53 percent of young people with 31–40 assets.

But many young people don't experience a high level of assets. Search Institute's surveys of more than a million students in grades 6–12 to measure how many of the assets they experience reveal that students in 6th grade report having an average of 21.5 assets, barely more than half; students in 8th grade report having an average of 17.8 assets; in 10th grade, an average of 16.9 assets; and in 12th grade, an average of 17.2 assets.

The asset approach gives us a framework for shifting how we view young people and a template for what we can do to more fully support all our young people. It represents the good things we do for all young people—common-

40 Developmental Assets

Search Institute has identified the following "building blocks" of healthy development that help young people grow up healthy, caring, and responsible.

External assets

Support

1. **Family support**—Family life provides high levels of love and support.
2. **Positive family communication**—Young person and her or his parent(s) communicate positively, and young person is willing to seek advice and counsel from parents.
3. **Other adult relationships**—Young person receives support from three or more nonparent adults.
4. **Caring neighborhood**—Young person experiences caring neighbors.
5. **Caring school climate**—School provides a caring, encouraging environment.
6. **Parent involvement in schooling**—Parent(s) are actively involved in helping young person succeed in school.

Empowerment

7. **Community values youth**—Young person perceives that adults in the community value youth.
8. **Youth as resources**—Young people are given useful roles in the community.
9. **Service to others**—Young person serves in the community one hour or more per week.
10. **Safety**—Young person feels safe at home, at school, and in the neighborhood.

Boundaries and Expectations

11. **Family boundaries**—Family has clear rules and consequences and monitors the young person's whereabouts.
12. **School boundaries**—School provides clear rules and consequences.
13. **Neighborhood boundaries**—Neighbors take responsibility for monitoring young people's behavior.
14. **Adult role models**—Parent(s) and other adults model positive, responsible behavior.
15. **Positive peer influence**—Young person's best friends model responsible behavior.
16. **High expectations**—Both parent(s) and teachers encourage the young person to do well.

Constructive Use of Time

17. **Creative activities**—Young person spends three or more hours per week in lessons or practice in music, theater, or other arts.
18. **Youth programs**—Young person spends three or more hours per week in sports, clubs, or organizations at school and/or in the community.
19. **Religious community**—Young person spends one or more hours per week in activities in a religious institution.
20. **Time at home**—Young person is out with friends "with nothing special to do" two or fewer nights per week.

Internal assets

Commitment to Learning

21. **Achievement motivation**—Young person is motivated to do well in school.
22. **School engagement**—Young person is actively engaged in learning.
23. **Homework**—Young person reports doing at least one hour of homework every school day.
24. **Bonding to school**—Young person cares about her or his school.
25. **Reading for pleasure**—Young person reads for pleasure three or more hours per week.

Positive Values

26. **Caring**—Young person places high value on helping other people.
27. **Equality and social justice**—Young person places high value on promoting equality and reducing hunger and poverty.
28. **Integrity**—Young person acts on convictions and stands up for her or his beliefs.
29. **Honesty**—Young person "tells the truth even when it is not easy."
30. **Responsibility**—Young person accepts and takes personal responsibility.
31. **Restraint**—Young person believes it is important not to be sexually active or to use alcohol or other drugs.

Social Competencies

32. **Planning and decision making**—Young person knows how to plan ahead and make choices.
33. **Interpersonal competence**—Young person has empathy, sensitivity, and friendship skills.
34. **Cultural competence**—Young person has knowledge of and comfort with people of different cultural/racial/ethnic backgrounds.
35. **Resistance skills**—Young person can resist negative peer pressure and dangerous situations.
36. **Peaceful conflict resolution**—Young person seeks to resolve conflict nonviolently.

Positive Identity

37. **Personal power**—Young person feels he or she has control over "things that happen to me."
38. **Self-esteem**—Young person reports having a high self-esteem.
39. **Sense of purpose**—Young person reports that "my life has a purpose."
40. **Positive view of personal future**—Young person is optimistic about her or his personal future.

40 elementos fundamentales del desarrollo

La investigación realizada por el Instituto Search ha identificado los siguientes elementos fundamentales del desarrollo como instrumentos para ayudar a los jóvenes a crecer sanos, interesados en el bienestar común y a ser responsables.

Elementos fundamentales externos

Apoyo

1. **Apoyo familiar**—La vida familiar brinda altos niveles de amor y apoyo.
2. **Comunicación familiar positiva**—El (La) joven y sus padres se comunican positiva-mente. Los jóvenes están dispuestos a bus-car consejo y consuelo en sus padres.
3. **Otras relaciones con adultos**—Además de sus padres, los jóvenes reciben apoyo de tres o más personas adultas que no son sus parientes.
4. **Una comunidad comprometida**—El (La) joven experimenta el interés de sus vecinos por su bienestar.
5. **Un plantel educativo que se interesa por el (la) joven**—La escuela proporciona un ambi-ente que anima y se preocupa por la juventud.
6. **La participación de los padres en las activi-dades escolares**—Los padres participan acti-vamente ayudando a los jóvenes a tener éxito en la escuela.

Fortalecimiento

7. **La comunidad valora a la juventud**—El (La) joven percibe que los adultos en la comu-nidad valoran a la juventud.
8. **La juventud como un recurso**—Se le brinda a los jóvenes la oportunidad de tomar un papel útil en la comunidad.
9. **Servicio a los demás**—La gente joven partic-ipa brindando servicios a su comunidad una hora o más a la semana.
10. **Seguridad**—Los jóvenes se sienten seguros en casa, en la escuela y en el vecindario.

Límites y expectativas

11. **Límites familiares**—La familia tiene reglas y consecuencias bien claras, además vigila las actividades de los jóvenes.
12. **Límites escolares**—En la escuela propor-ciona reglas y consecuencias bien claras.
13. **Límites vecinales**—Los vecinos asumen la responsabilidad de vigilar el comporta-miento de los jóvenes.
14. **El comportamiento de los adultos como ejemplo**—Los padres y otros adultos tienen un comportamiento positivo y responsable.
15. **Compañeros como influencia positiva**—Los mejores amigos del (la) joven son un buen ejemplo de comportamiento responsable.
16. **Altas expectativas**—Ambos padres y maes-tros motivan a los jóvenes para que tengan éxito.

Uso constructivo del tiempo

17. **Actividades creativas**—Los jóvenes pasan tres horas o más a la semana en lecciones de música, teatro u otras artes.
18. **Programas juveniles**—Los jóvenes pasan tres horas o más a la semana practicando algún deporte, o en organizaciones en la escuela o de la comunidad.
19. **Comunidad religiosa**—Los jóvenes pasan una hora o más a la semana en actividades organizadas por alguna institución religiosa.
20. **Tiempo en casa**—Los jóvenes conviven con sus amigos "sin nada especial que hacer" dos o pocas noches por semana.

Elementos fundamentales internos

Compromiso con el aprendizaje

21. **Motivación por sus logros**—El (La) joven es motivado(a) para que salga bien en la escuela.
22. **Compromiso con la escuela**—El (La) joven participa activamente con el aprendizaje.
23. **Tarea**—El (La) joven debe hacer su tarea escolar por lo menos durante una hora cada día de clases.
24. **Preocuparse por la escuela**—Al (A la) joven debe importarle su escuela.
25. **Leer por placer**—El (La) joven lee por placer tres horas o más por semana.

Valores positivos

26. **Preocuparse por los demás**—El (La) joven valora ayudar a los demás.
27. **Igualdad y justicia social**—Para el (la) joven tiene mucho valor el promover la igualdad y reducir el hambre y la pobreza.
28. **Integridad**—El (La) joven actúa con convicción y defiende sus creencias.
29. **Honestidad**—El (La) joven "dice la verdad aún cuando esto no sea fácil".
30. **Responsabilidad**—El (La) joven acepta y toma responsabilidad por su persona.
31. **Abstinencia**—El (La) joven cree que es importante no estar activo(a) sexualmente, ni usar alcohol u otras drogas.

Capacidad social

32. **Planeación y toma de decisiones**—El (La) joven sabe cómo planear y hacer elecciones.
33. **Capacidad interpersonal**—El (La) joven es sympático, sensible y hábil para hacer amistades.
34. **Capacidad cultural**—El (La) joven tiene conocimiento de y sabe convivir con gente de diferente marco cultural, racial o étnico.
35. **Habilidad de resistencia**—El (La) joven puede resistir la presión negativa de los compañeros así como las situaciones peligrosas.
36. **Solución pacífica de conflictos**—El (La) joven busca resolver los conflictos sin violencia.

Identidad positiva

37. **Poder personal**—El (La) joven siente que él o ella tiene el control de "las cosas que le suceden".
38. **Auto-estima**—El (La) joven afirma tener una alta auto-estima.
39. **Sentido de propósito**—El (La) joven afirma que "mi vida tiene un propósito".
40. **Visión positiva del futuro personal**—El (La) joven es optimista sobre su futuro mismo.

40 Acquis dont les jeunes ont besoin pour réussir

Le Search Institute a défini les pierres angulaires suivantes qui aident les jeunes à devenir des personnes saines, bienveillantes et responsables. Les pourcentages des jeunes détenant chaque acquis sont le fruit d'un sondage mené durant l'année scolaire 1999-2002 auprès de 220 100 jeunes Américains de la 6e à la 12e année.

Acquis externes

Soutien

1. **Soutien familial**—La vie familiale est caractérisée par un degré élevé d'amour et de soutien.
2. **Communication familiale positive**—Le jeune et ses parents communiquent positivement, et le jeune est disposé à leur demander conseil.
3. **Relations avec d'autres adultes**—Le jeune bénéficie de l'appui d'au moins trois adultes autres que ses parents.
4. **Voisinage bienveillant**—Le jeune a des voisins bienveillants.
5. **Milieu scolaire bienveillant**—L'école fournit au jeune un milieu bienveillant et encourageant.
6. **Engagement des parents dans les activités scolaires**—Les parents aident activement le jeune à réussir à l'école.

Prise en charge

7. **Valorisation des jeunes par la communauté**—Le jeune perçoit que les adultes dans la communauté accordent de l'importance aux jeunes.
8. **Rôle des jeunes en tant que ressources**—Le jeune se voit confier des rôles utiles dans la communauté.
9. **Service à son prochain**—Le jeune consacre à sa communauté au moins une heure par semaine.
10. **Sécurité**—Le jeune se sent en sécurité à la maison, à l'école et dans le quartier.

Limites et attentes

11. **Limites dans la famille**—La famille a des règlements clairs accompagnés de conséquences, et elle surveille les comportements du jeune.
12. **Limite à l'école**—L'école a des règlements clairs accompagnés de conséquences.
13. **Limites dans le quartier**—Les voisins assument la responsabilité de surveiller les comportements du jeune.
14. **Adultes servant de modèles**—Les parents et d'autres adultes dans l'entourage du jeune affichent un comportement positif et responsable.
15. **Influence positive des pairs**—Les meilleurs amis du jeune affichent un comportement responsable.
16. **Attentes élevées**—Les parents et les professeurs du jeune l'encouragent à réussir.

Utilisation constructive du temps

17. **Activités créatives**—Le jeune consacre au moins trois heures par semaine à suivre des cours de musique, de théâtre ou autres, et à mettre ses nouvelles connaissances en pratique.
18. **Programmes jeunesse**—Le jeune consacre au moins trois heures par semaine à des activités sportives, des clubs ou des associations à l'école et/ou dans la communauté.
19. **Communauté religieuse**—Le jeune consacre au moins trois heures par semaine à des activités dans une institution religieuse.
20. **Temps à la maison**—Le jeune sort avec des amis sans but particulier deux ou trois soirs par semaine.

Acquis internes

Engagement envers l'apprentissage

21. **Encouragement à la réussite**—Le jeune est encouragé à réussir à l'école.
22. **Engagement à l'école**—Le jeune s'engage activement à apprendre.
23. **Devoirs**—Le jeune consacre au moins une heure par jour à ses devoirs.
24. **Appartenance à l'école**—Le jeune se préoccupe de son école.
25. **Plaisir de lire**—Le jeune lit pour son plaisir au moins trois heures par semaine.

Valeurs positives

26. **Bienveillance**—Le jeune estime qu'il est très important d'aider les autres.
27. **Égalité et justice sociale**—Le jeune accorde beaucoup d'attention à la promotion de l'égalité, et à la réduction de la faim et de la pauvreté.
28. **Intégrité**—Le jeune agit selon ses convictions et défend ses croyances.
29. **Honnêteté**—Le jeune « dit la vérité même si ce n'est pas facile ».
30. **Responsabilité**—Le jeune accepte et assume ses propres responsabilités.
31. **Abstinence**—Le jeune croit qu'il est important d'éviter d'être sexuellement actif et de consommer de l'alcool ou d'autres drogues.

Compétences sociales

32. **Planification et prise de décisions**—Le jeune sait comment planifier à l'avance et faire des choix.
33. **Aptitudes interpersonnelles**—Le jeune fait preuve d'empathie et de sensibilité, et noue des amitiés.
34. **Aptitudes culturelles**—Le jeune connaît des personnes d'autres cultures, races et ethnies, et se sent à l'aise avec elles.
35. **Résistance**—Le jeune est capable de résister à des pressions négatives exercées par ses pairs et à des situations dangereuses.
36. **Résolution pacifique de conflits**—Le jeune tente de résoudre les conflits sans recourir à la violence.

Identité positive

37. **Pouvoir personnel**—Le jeune sent qu'il a le contrôle sur les choses qui lui arrivent.
38. **Estime de soi**—Le jeune affirme avoir un degré élevé d'estime de soi.
39. **Sentiment d'utilité**—Le jeune croit que sa vie a un sens.
40. **Vision positive de l'avenir**—Le jeune est optimiste quant à son avenir personnel.

sense things that can be forgotten in the bombardment of media and research messages about what's *wrong* with young people.

Embracing asset building doesn't mean that we ignore youth who experience difficulties, but it does suggest that we focus instead on seeing young people as resources with strengths to be developed and ideas to contribute. Search Institute calls this intentional effort to help each young person gain a personal web of support "asset building."

Much of society tends to view young people as problems to be solved. But as asset builder Nancy Ashley of Seattle, Washington, has written in her *Heliotrope* newsletter, embracing asset building does not suggest that "we should stop reducing threats such as guns, racism, family violence, or drugs. [Strength-based approaches] do not diminish the need to meet basic needs—economic security, food, shelter, and safety. They do add a powerful route by which we might better reduce risks and help all kids, families, and communities be more successful. They provide us with more strategies and options."

When organized on a larger scale, asset building becomes the basis of a deliberate campaign to make our communities better places for young people to grow up (what some people are beginning to call "developmentally attentive communities"). There are now nearly 600 communities in 42 states and several Canadian provinces working with Search Institute's Healthy Communities • Healthy Youth initiative. As of this writing, 24 statewide networks are operating in the United States, and interest in asset building is growing in Australia, South Africa, and Brazil as well. Instead of focusing only on reducing risks and intervening in problems, these communities are rallying to build the foundation of developmental supports that all young people need—a foundation that is too fragile for too many young people.

What This Book Offers

This book is designed to give you strategies, tactics, and examples to use as you develop and expand a community-wide asset-building initiative. It will take you through the stages of an initiative from the first steps of new efforts to later challenges for maturing initiatives. Along with revealing the key results of Search Institute's latest research into how initiatives work, each chapter is full of examples of how initiatives are creatively transforming their communities to positively support children and youth. This book is not—and cannot be—a one-size-fits-all plan for asset building, because every initiative is particular to its community. Instead, the book will help you discover new ideas for building, energizing, or sustaining any of the many steps toward fulfilling your community's unique vision for young people.

To do this, the book draws from previous Search Institute resources, new research, and the practical experience of many asset builders in the field. Two primary Search Institute publications were used:

- *Cultivating Developmentally Attentive Communities: A Report on the First Wave of the National Asset-Building Case Study Project*, by Marc Mannes, Shenita Lewis, and Nicole Hintz of Search Institute and Karen Foster and Michael Nakkula of Harvard University (2002). This unpublished field study report closely examines the history and day-to-day operations of initiatives in Moorhead, Minnesota; Orlando, Florida; Traverse City, Michigan; and Multnomah County (Portland), Oregon. Successes and challenges faced by these four diverse initiatives are chronicled throughout this book along with key activities, turning points, insights, and promising practices gleaned from each community; and
- *An Asset Approach to Positive Community Change*, by Eugene C. Roehlkepartain (2001). This document provides the structural backbone for this book. In *Assets in Action*, we expand on several significant concepts outlined in this publication—the key principles of asset building, the change pathway, and five key strategies for your initiative to use.

In addition, I've drawn on a wide variety of materials from and about initiatives, including ideas culled from other Search Institute publications, initiative publications such as Assets for Colorado Youth's *Spirit of Culture*, initiative Web sites, and interviews conducted with initiative participants and Search Institute staff. I was also able to glean terrific ideas and observations from grant applications many initiatives had submitted to the Jostens Our Town grant and awards program. The Jostens Foundation brought national attention to asset building by awarding grants to ten HC • HY initiatives over a three-year period (1999–2002). While winners were selected to receive special recognition in this program, all the available grant applications yielded examples of genuine youth engagement, broad involvement of community sectors, significant accomplishments, and innovative strategies that helped make this book richer.

You'll see one staff member of Search Institute quoted especially frequently: Community Liaison Nancy Tellett-Royce. In her position as the "point person" for contact with asset builders out in the field, she talks and emails with hundreds of people each year about every aspect of starting and supporting asset-building initiatives as well as the everyday, informal acts of asset building each adult is called to do. Adding to her experience and wisdom is her long-term volunteering with Children First in St. Louis Park, Minnesota, the very first asset-building initiative.

How This Book Is Organized

The book lays out the fundamentals of how to start, build, and sustain an asset-building initiative. Each chapter gives you information and insight into the tasks and challenges of that effort, while also acknowledging that the work of changing communities for the better is a dynamic process that happens in a unique way in each unique community. There are three sections.

Part One: Vision, Preparation, and Planning

The book's first section describes basic theories and principles to help you lay a firm foundation for your work.

Introduction: The Vision for Asset-Building Communities provides historical background on positive community development that puts your work in context, including a brief history of Search Institute's developmental assets framework and the Healthy Communities • Healthy Youth (HC • HY) initiative. A summary of the National Asset-Building Case Study Project and snapshots of the four participating Wave 1 initiatives are included.

Chapter 1. Beginning the Process of Change describes five phases of change in communities (the change pathway) as well as key shifts in thinking that are elemental to defining asset-building communities. Several initiatives also share their insights about the importance of valuing diversity and building cultural competence into your work from its inception.

Chapter 2. Getting Started: What Needs to Happen First? discusses the conditions and objectives to consider as you prepare to launch an asset-building initiative, including:

- Defining an asset initiative;
- What roles you could take on to get started;
- How to know whom to invite; and
- What information you need and what tasks to begin with.

Some of the basic ideas introduced here, such as how to engage adults and mobilize youth, are explored in detail in Part Two.

Part Two: Making It Happen

Five Action Strategies for Your Asset-Building Initiative introduces five overarching strategies for mobilizing asset builders in your community that will be covered in the subsequent chapters.

Chapter 3. Engage Adults presents tips and ideas for building and sustaining a critical mass of adult engagement and support in the community for asset building.

Chapter 4. Mobilize Young People shares stories from many initiatives on how they are successfully working *with* youth to change their communities on behalf of all youth.

Chapter 5. Activate Sectors and **Invigorate Programs** takes on two related strategies and describes how to enhance programs with the asset framework as well as how to deepen asset-building capacity among schools, congregations, neighborhoods, youth organizations, social service agencies, health-care providers, employers, and other organizations.

Chapter 6. Influence Civic Decisions helps you analyze and shift your initiative's long-term efforts to further embed asset building into policies and practices throughout the community.

Part Three: Keeping It Going and Growing

Chapter 7. Over the Long Haul: Sustaining Your Initiative imparts lessons learned from some of the most mature initiatives to help you sustain, expand, and renew your efforts.

Epilogue: Nourishing the Spirit of the Community Change Leader provides a special section on the inspiration and dedication that asset champions themselves need as they continue their work.

The **Resources** section gives details on books, booklets, posters, trainings, surveys, scholarly articles, and more from Search Institute and from initiatives themselves, organized by the chapters of this book to help you quickly find what you need.

Information in each of the strategy chapters is provided in two parts. The first section of each chapter discusses the relevant themes that emerged from Search Institute's national case study research. These findings are combined with insights and lessons learned from a variety of initiatives to help illuminate the themes. For example, when engaging adults is discussed, the chapter notes that a number of initiatives have found it particularly important to include elders in initiative efforts.

The second part of each strategy chapter is called "Assets in Action." These sections are filled with practical examples of how different initiatives are doing their work on this strategy. These ideas are here for you to borrow, replicate, or redesign in creative ways to help you in your unique initiative.

In these chapters, you'll find sidebars and special features with still more ideas and insights to stimulate your work, such as:

- A short sidebar on the potential barriers you might face in each area along with simple tips and solutions;
- *The Power of One:* short profiles of individuals who've made a difference;
- *Inspired by Assets:* excerpts from essays written by young people involved in the Frisco, Colorado, annual Asset Builders of the Summit Inspired by Assets contest (see the example below);

- Tipsheets with more in-depth information on specific topics;
- Specific advice within each strategy about what it will take to sustain your efforts for the long haul;
- A detailed chart of ideas within each strategy at each stage of the change pathway; and
- A summary of key points.

Whereas books must be laid out in a logical, linear fashion to be useful, the work of asset building is an organic, creative process. The various phases of an asset-building initiative all overlap and recur to varying degrees. Individuals, organizations, and community systems all reflect different levels of commitment to asset building and may be at different phases in the change process. This kind of intentional community change is dynamic, even chaotic at times. Some phases of your initiative are in play simultaneously while specific events transpire in ways that are neither linear nor sequential. Phases and projects wax and wane in importance as you find new opportunities or face new challenges.

This resource is organized sequentially to make it as useful to you as possible, but every initiative will have a unique journey. I encourage you to use *Assets in Action* as a point of departure and to customize the ideas collected here to work for your initiative.

DEBORAH FISHER
Bellevue, Washington

ACKNOWLEDGMENTS

THIS BOOK IS the product of many people, and I'm happy to thank them all not just for their contributions, but because writing this book in collaboration with them was so much fun. I love having a job where I get to call people up, ask them lots of questions, learn about all the wonderful things they're enthusiastically doing, and then give them public recognition for doing it! I also get to work with a wonderful team of editors, writers, researchers, organizers, leaders, trainers, and thinkers, not only at Search Institute, but from around the country who give this work—and me—their best advice, support, and knowledge.

Let me be specific:

My thanks to all of the Healthy Communities • Healthy Youth initiatives that participated in developing the content that forms the basis of this book, through their work to put developmental assets into action, the submission of their grant applications to the Jostens Our Town grant and awards program, contacts with me over the years as I gathered stories for *Assets* magazine, participation in the Search Institute listserv, various conference transcripts, reports, initiative Web sites, and printed materials, and the numerous emails that flew back and forth over the months I've been writing this book.

A special thanks to the four initiatives that became the first wave case study sites—Healthy Community Initiative HC • HY of Central Florida in Orlando, Florida; Moorhead Healthy Community Initiative in Moorhead, Minnesota; the GivEm 40 24.7 Coalition in the Traverse Bay area, Michigan; and the Take the Time Initiative in Multnomah County, Portland, Oregon. They are all teachers, learners, and leaders in this work.

My thanks to the researchers who conducted the National Asset-Building Case Study Project—Marc Mannes, Shenita Lewis, and Nicole Hintz of Search Institute, and Karen Foster and Michael Nakkula of Harvard University. Their insightful work forms the very foundation of this one. I appreciate that the individuals themselves were always accessible and helpful when I had questions.

My thanks to the trainers associated with Search Institute who work with initiatives and inspire them as well as staff. I specifically was able to draw on a great wealth of knowledge from Shelby Andress, Tim Duffey, John Linney, Rick Phillips, and Clay Roberts.

I personally have been privileged to interview many people working on many initiatives, and I would like to thank these individuals for talking with me on more than one occasion and allowing me to share their stories: Mimi Petritz-Appel, Karen Atkinson, Helen Beattie, Becky Beauchamp, Lynn Borud, Maureen McKasy-Donlin, Marilyn Eber, Richard Enfield, Betsy Ferries, Brenda Holben, Raymond Larsen, Nick Lovell, María Guajardo Lucero, Matt McCarter, Chris McMurray, Annie Nelson, Barry Nelson, Tom Osborn, Carmen Patent, Barbara Pearce, Derek Peterson, Marianne Pieper, Lisa Race, Patsy Roybal, James Robinson, Mary Schissel, Mary Scott Singer, Valerie Smith, Joanne Smorgor, Valorie Tanner, Alan VanderPaas, and Paul Vidas,

My special thanks to those initiative members who were willing to go beyond helping me shape the content, to also spend time doing a final—and very important—review of the manuscript before it was published: Swanti Adarkar, Betsy Ferries, Raymond Larsen, María Guajardo Lucero, Chris McMurray, Barry Nelson, Lisa Race, Derek Peterson, and Paul Vidas.

Along with working on this book, I have also had opportunities to work on a variety of projects that bring me in contact with many Search Institute staffers and consultants. Whether directly or indirectly involved in working on this book, the knowledge shared with me has helped me fulfill the vision of this book. My thanks to Mary Ackerman, Joseph Barisonzi, Elizabeth Brekke, Kalisha Davis, Laura Lee Geraghty, Jeffrey Gustafson, Kathleen Kimball-Baker, William Mesaros, Kristie Probst, Jolene Roehlkepartain, Peter Scales, and Terri Sullivan.

My work as a writer has benefited tremendously from two of the finest editors I've ever encountered. I am still quantifying what I have learned from Jacqueline White, my editor for *Assets* magazine these past five years, and Kay Hong, my editor on this book. Both women are consummate professionals and a pleasure to work with.

I have learned much in the last decade since I first heard Peter Benson talk about the asset framework at a National League of Cities conference in what used to be my "home" town of Minneapolis. Embracing asset building has not only changed the course of my work, but my personal life as my husband, Mark, and I have also integrated assets into parenting our son, Mack. I have had special opportunities to have lengthy conversations with a core of Search Institute staff whose work is particularly relevant to mine, including Peter, Eugene Roehlkepartain, Marc Mannes, and Nancy Tellett-Royce. Not only do I learn from these people and enjoy talking with them, but I am humbled by their trust in me to interpret their work in print.

Finally, I would like to acknowledge the young people named in this book. I was able to talk directly with many of these young people for this work (and happily meet some of them at conferences over the years) or I was inspired by what some of them have written. I would also like to thank the parents of these young people who allowed us to quote what their children had to say. While I'm only naming some of the specific youth that are quoted in this book, I wish to acknowledge all the young people I know are deeply involved in all of these initiatives throughout the country. In the unsettled times during which this book has been written, they all give me great hope for the future. My thanks to

Yesenia Becerril, Kristin Bednar, T. J. Berden, Hans Bernard, Emily Enockson, Will Gaines, Ben Hershey, Jessica Higgins, Scott Holbrook, Adam Luck, Harmonie Mason, Molly Miller, Nam Nguyen, Kyle Pfister, Sam Piehl, Ian Rataczak, Sarah Schwartz, Heather Shill, Emily Silberstein, Shawn Smith, Mallory Brandt Steinberg, Roger Stewart, and Jessica Weit.

PART ONE

Vision, Preparation, and Planning

The Vision for Asset-Building Communities

We have in America a fast-growing number of cultivated young people who have no recognized outlet for their active faculties. This paper is an attempt to analyze the motives, which underlie a movement based, not only upon conviction, but upon genuine emotion, wherever educated young people are seeking an outlet for that sentiment for universal brotherhood, which the best spirit of our times is forcing from an emotion into a motive.

JANE ADDAMS, "THE SUBJECTIVE NECESSITY
FOR SOCIAL SETTLEMENTS," FROM HER BOOK
TWENTY YEARS AT HULL-HOUSE, 1910

JANE ADDAMS WAS an educated and restless young woman who left her small-town home in Illinois in 1887 to visit Toynbee Hall, a neighborhood center in the poorest section of London's East End. What she experienced and learned there about community development gave vision and direction to her social concerns, leading her and her colleagues to purchase a mansion in a teeming immigrant neighborhood on Chicago's Near West Side. They invented Hull-House, the first settlement house in the United States.

Addams believed that an action agenda would emerge from living among the poor, sharing their daily life, and building strong relationships. Rooted in the profoundly simple idea of neighborliness, Hull-House became a place where each week, thousands of neighborhood residents participated in activities of interest to them: social and cultural activities, language skills and civics classes, and strategy sessions concerning neighborhood issues. Hull-House tapped a deep desire for connectedness in American society.

Through constant and careful observation, Addams and her colleagues reported on community conditions, becoming pioneering social scientists as well as effective advocates for everything from playgrounds and garbage collections to a progressive service system for juveniles. They also became active leaders in the broader movements for labor rights, women's suffrage, and international peace, linking local concerns with global issues in ways that seem strikingly 21st century. For Addams, the roles of neighbor, policy advocate, and social justice activist reinforced each other in powerful and effective ways, eventually clearing the path for thousands of efforts to replicate the Hull-House experiment.

Many others have since built upon and embellished Addams's vision of community development, including John McKnight and John Kretzmann, who proposed their own ideas about what they called asset-based community development in Chicago in the late 1980s. Veering away from the traditional focus on deficits, problems, and programs, McKnight and Kretzmann based their community revitalization work on identifying and connecting the skills and resources of local citizens with positive, existing efforts in their neighborhoods. They posited that successful community development would emerge from the strengths and relationships of local citizens rather than from institutions.

While the scale, agendas, and players have multiplied, the central thrust of Addams's positive community development approach has endured: a vision of community organizations—owned and directed by local citizens—working together to amplify the power of their voices and efforts for the good of all.

A New Active Ingredient in Community Development: Youth

"When I first started with Search Institute in the 1980s, it was the heyday of evaluation studies," recalls Peter Benson, now the organization's president. "Everyone was trying to figure out what was working in drug and alcohol prevention, teen pregnancy prevention, and violence prevention. I was going to a lot of prevention conferences and over dinner, we evaluators would get together and talk.

"After hearing the same conversation a number of times, a story line registered with me and it was this: someone would say that when they had conducted the pre- and posttests, the kids in the study would all have changed the way they were supposed to, but when they checked back six months later, most kids had fallen back. Everyone would understand that this was because we put the young people back into the culture that raised them and, well, what could you do? I can remember all of a sudden thinking, 'What does that mean?'"

Benson's thinking about changing the larger culture led him to develop a new framework for understanding what all young people need to grow up healthy—the 40 developmental assets. His reflection, experience, and study also led him to think about a new model for how society can provide young people with those developmental assets, a model grounded in the history and best practices of community development. "Most human development policy in America is about economics, service delivery, and risk reduction strategies," says Benson. "All of these are important, but the one missing strategy has been building developmental strengths."

The concept for Search Institute's Healthy Communities • Healthy Youth (HC • HY) initiative grew out of the best practices of community development that have emerged since Addams's pioneering work. By adding a new ingredient—the empowerment and participation of young people—and the accompanying focus on increasing young people's developmental strengths, HC • HY initiatives are a living experiment in the integration of youth into community development.

Search Institute's National Asset-Building Case Study Project

New research in recent years documents the importance of connecting youth to the vital support networks of family, school, and community that can help protect them from risks. By increasing our understanding of exactly how the positive influence of community is created and sustained, the research findings can help community residents conduct the combined work of community development and raising thriving young people more intentionally. In parallel with its work on the asset framework, Search Institute has acted on a deep and abiding interest in studying strength-based community and social change and its impact on positive youth development. The organization is also actively working to be responsive to initiatives that have asked for more information to help them improve their efforts.

With funding from the McKnight Foundation, Thrivent Foundation for Lutherans (formerly the Aid Association for Lutherans and Lutheran Brotherhood), the Donald W. Reynolds Foundation, and the Kansas Health Foundation, Search Institute, together with researchers at Harvard University's School of Education, launched its National Asset-Building Case Study Project in September 2000 to examine more deeply how diverse communities use the asset framework in their strength-based efforts to improve conditions for young people. The first wave of the study focused on understanding how adults and youth in communities build and maintain relationships, how communities organize and act in ways that suggest a social movement, and how a healthier community is established.

> *. . . the research findings can help community residents conduct the combined work of community development and raising thriving young people more intentionally.*

"We want to see how diverse ideas come together within a community around positive youth development," says Marc Mannes, Search Institute's director of applied research and project director for the case study project. "How do communities adopt a vision, build a plan, and then implement a range of activities to foster healthy development? How do groups that don't usually work together become partners in a common mission? How does leadership play out? If we can begin to understand the answers to some of these questions, then we can share that knowledge with others."

During 2001–2, Search Institute researchers Marc Mannes, Ph.D., Shenita Lewis, M.S., and Nicole Hintz worked with Karen Foster, Ph.D., and Michael Nakkula, Ph.D., of the Harvard Graduate School of Education to study the lives of four diverse asset-building initiatives over the course of one year. These four initiatives were selected to represent a balance of factors, including longevity, geographic region, and population size. More mature initiatives were selected because it was assumed that they could offer perspective on a full range of issues. The four initiatives studied in the first wave were:

- **Moorhead Healthy Community Initiative, Moorhead, Minnesota.** Launched in 1994, this citywide initiative grew out of a grassroots organizing effort with a large citizen volunteer base to address problems of underage drinking and youth crime. The initiative started by collaborating closely with the police department to clean up one neighborhood that was heavily trafficked by drug users. Now this neighborhood's previously deserted park is filled with children playing soccer and families having outings. This same neighborhood has an active block club that meets monthly to make neighborhood improvements and promote the community. The initiative is a nonprofit organization staffed by four full-time employees and governed by a volunteer board of directors. The mission of Moorhead's initiative is to mobilize the community to provide developmental assets for every child and youth in the city. The primary focus is on providing free after-school and summer-enrichment programs for all Moorhead youth.

- **Healthy Community Initiative, HC • HY of Central Florida, Orlando, Florida.** The Healthy Communities • Healthy Youth of Central Florida is part of a larger Healthy Community Initiative (HCI) of Greater Orlando begun in 1998 to address the problems brought on by the high mobility of central Florida's population. HCI's focus is on community revitalization provided through training and support of local grassroots initiatives. Asset building is used as a tool to support positive youth development within the larger initiative. HCI is a countywide effort reaching all of Orange County and is staffed by five full-time employees and three community faculty. Ownership and sustainability of the work lie within the local communities. One example: for the Listening Project, one local community's young people interviewed residents of two economically challenged neighborhoods to learn what they'd like to do to improve their community.

- **GivEm 40 Coalition, Traverse City, Michigan.** Launched in 1999, this regional initiative of five rural counties in northwestern Michigan strategically focused on deeply engaging one sector at a time versus spreading the work too thinly across multiple sectors. Starting with the schools, coalition leaders recruited 19 school districts with 4,500 students in grades 7, 9, and 11 to take the *Search Institute Profiles of Student Life: Attitudes and Behaviors* survey, which measures adolescents' levels of developmental assets. They then worked with the schools until the asset model was so infused into policy and procedure that the school district hired an asset development coordinator to maintain its asset work. GivEm 40 is staffed by two employees of United Way and a school district coordinator, with evaluation and support from two researchers at Michigan State University's Institute for Children, Youth and Families, and Outreach Partnerships.

▶ **Take the Time Initiative, Multnomah County, Portland, Oregon.** This initiative was launched in 1997 by the Commission on Children, Families, and Community of Multnomah County (CCFC) and is the only one of the four research sites that is not an independent not-for-profit organization. Four full-time CCFC employees initially staffed this countywide effort. The focus of Take the Time is relationship building, and the initiative has used grassroots methods to engage everyday citizens in the work of positive youth development. In the course of three years, the initiative awarded more than 400 minigrants of $500 or less to asset builders and youth-serving organizations in the community to move the work of asset building forward.

Information was initially gathered through a first round of field visits to the initiatives, neighborhood walks, interviews with various participants, and focus groups conducted at each site. Follow-up contacts were made to get feedback from each initiative on preliminary findings in advance of a second field visit (because of logistics, Portland participated in this second round by phone). The information gathered was focused and structured in such a way as to appreciate the context of each site, delineate noteworthy themes, and gauge how the evolution of each initiative related to Search Institute's change pathway (see Chapter 1 for a discussion of the change pathway). Finally, researchers conducted an analysis of the data to uncover and link critical themes, resulting in a "codebook" of labels, definitions, and examples that could be used to easily identify recurring ideas across all four field study initiatives.

The willingness of these four initiatives to be examined and studied by outsiders has provided a wealth of learning for the researchers involved, for the initiatives themselves, and for other initiatives as well. The second wave of the case study project began in 2002, with additional findings from work with the youth and adults of four more initiatives expected to enrich future publications just as the first wave's findings have enriched this one.

> LEARN MORE: For contact information for the four participating initiatives and for all registered HC • HY initiatives, visit the Search Institute Web site at www.search-institute.org.

CHAPTER 1

Beginning the Process of Change

"I think you have to get people to the point where they're recognizing their own attitudes first, and really saying 'What is my attitude toward youth? Am I afraid of them? Am I willing to meet them on an equal basis?' And we need to begin to tap into what their attitude is. Then you have the ability to change it, and go into transformation."

FOCUS GROUP MEMBER, TAKE THE TIME INITIATIVE,
MULTNOMAH COUNTY, PORTLAND, OREGON

DURING SITE VISITS to the four initiatives for the National Asset-Building Case Study Project's first wave of study, researchers asked the initiatives to describe their work in both words and pictures. When asked to render their initiatives in pictures, a number of participants drew trees and gardens.

"I drew a bunch of trees, and the first tree is really tiny," wrote one youth participant from the GivEm 40 Coalition in Traverse City, Michigan. "They get progressively larger until you can't even see the top of the tree anymore. The reason they're getting larger is all of the GivEm 40 food that is going into the trees."

"This is the foundation here, the ground, and these are little plants with hearts on them," wrote another initiative participant, "because I think love seriously fuels this movement more than anything else."

The initiative participants are not alone in using metaphors of growth and gardening in their descriptions. Other asset builders and community activists have found such metaphors to have a strong resonance, no doubt because starting and supporting a community asset-building initiative really *is* very much like growing a garden.

Before starting a garden, many people spend time dreaming about what they want their garden to look like in a few years. They analyze the local climate and growing conditions. They research different seeds, plants, and tools.

They talk with other gardeners to learn new ideas and to share cuttings and bulbs. They might draw a picture of their ideal garden, then periodically check results and adjust their efforts as they compare their vision with how the garden actually grows.

As gardens vary from little backyard tomato patches to abundantly flowering front flower beds to communal plots shared by a whole neighborhood, the plots in which the seeds of an asset movement are planted and nurtured will vary in size, readiness and richness of the community "soil," the availability of those who will commit to the work, and the history of what has already been planted there. Because of such differences, people who begin asset-building initiatives may organize their efforts to nurture asset building in different ways, depending on the nature of the community in which they seek to build a movement. In fact, the initiative you begin will likely grow at a different pace than one in another county, state, or province; the weather there, the seasons for planting and harvesting, and the "readiness" of seeds to grow will be different.

Before planting begins, you need to "turn and fertilize the soil" to prepare to launch your efforts. To aid you in preparation, this chapter presents:

- Key principles that define an asset-building initiative;
- The importance of incorporating cultural competence into your work at its inception; and
- A theory of community change (the change pathway) that will help you see the phases of change to address throughout your work.

Key Principles for Asset Builders

Asset building can't ignore the need to address risks many young people face, but it does challenge our assumptions about how communities work and it inspires us to realign our focus in some very significant ways. A community initiative begins to become an asset-building initiative when some shifts in people's thinking occur. The most energetic communities craft their initiatives around core asset-building principles that embody those shifts:

- Strengths more than risks or deficits;
- Engagement *with* young people, more than services *for* young people;
- Relationships as well as programs;
- Unleashing, not controlling or directing;
- All adults and youth, not just professionals and parents; and
- Long-term process, not a quick fix.

Strengths More Than Risks or Deficits
Asset building focuses on building strengths instead of just reducing problems, risks, or deficits. Initiatives have a dual role: to bring that strength-based mes-

sage to your community and to help all the sectors in your community shift to strength-oriented action.

"When we began discussing how to create a new sense of community in central Florida," says Raymond Larsen, executive director of the Healthy Community Initiative (HCI) in Orlando, "the solution began with a change of attitude. The stakeholders recognized that they had to become 'community asset builders.' They also began to look for leverage points available in the community that would provide opportunities to change social trends."

While the initial adoption of the asset framework can produce a great rush of energy and activity, the transformation of the entire community takes time. You seek to shift the culture of your community in many complex ways:

- From deficit thinking to an asset approach;
- From focusing on a few youth to recognizing all youth;
- From concentrating just on early childhood to development across the first two decades of life;
- From age segregation to intergenerational community;
- From self-interest to shared responsibility;
- From a narrow focus on programs alone to a focus on building relationships throughout your community;
- From a fragmented agenda to a unifying vision;
- From conflicting and competing signals to consistent and repeated positive messages;
- From youth as objects of programs to youth as actors in building their own assets;
- From short-term priorities to long-term commitment; and
- From civic disengagement to engagement all across the community.

Implementing asset building doesn't eliminate the need to address problems or provide services; rather, it complements those efforts. "I think one very important principle of how we implement all of this," says a Portland initiative member, "is to try to make it relevant to an individual or an organization's unique situation and their own agenda. So [it's a matter of] trying to fit it to their agenda, instead of saying, 'You have to take on our agenda.'"

Ask yourself:
- What are the strong resources for young people that already exist in our community?
- How can they be celebrated and enhanced through asset building?

Engagement with Young People, More Than Services for Young People

One of the most critical shifts you make when you implement asset building is how you interact with young people. Traditional programmatic supports make young people consumers or recipients of services, but asset-building initiatives need to avoid a too-quick focus on how to "serve" youth or "meet young people's needs."

"People get more focused on all the youth than a particular youth," says Director of Child/Youth Advocacy for the Association of Alaska School Boards Derek Peterson, one of the initiators/leaders of Alaska ICE (Alaska Initiative for Community Engagement). "They talk about how to get 'the numbers to go in the right direction.' All the while individual young people are outside, wanting to be noticed, valued, and a part of what is going on. Our work is really about each individual youth we come in contact with."

Recognizing young people as resources, contributors, and leaders makes it possible to fully engage children and adolescents as partners. This also means moving beyond seeing just those young people who may already be visible in the community and engaging young people who may be typically overlooked, such as youth of color, gay, lesbian, bisexual, or transgender youth, youth with disabilities, youth who are shy or troubled, and youth from disadvantaged socioeconomic backgrounds.

Engaging all young people boosts the authenticity and energy needed to start and support an initiative. Adults involved in more balanced, reciprocal relationships with young people also find themselves transformed by the energy, optimism, and creativity that youth contribute to the work.

> **Ask yourself:**
> - Where in our community have young people already been engaged as partners with adults?
> - How can we learn from and build on those efforts?

Relationships as well as Programs

When people first learn about the power of developmental assets, it's sometimes easy for them to think that the only response is to start new programs. The danger in this approach is that people continue to presume that a program alone—not the people or the community—can be responsible for building assets. The truth is that, while a good many of the assets can be built through well-designed and well-implemented programs, many of the assets depend on adults throughout a community noticing and connecting with young people in positive ways over time.

High-quality programs for young people are powerful components of a community's asset-building efforts, equipping people to build assets and strengthening relationships. If young people have few such programs to participate in, creating or encouraging the development of new programs is one of the strategies you'll want to include. Many existing programs in your community have been doing asset building all along without calling it that or recognizing it as that. Such existing programs can become vital allies and partners in your initiative's work. But programs alone cannot replace the power of a community of people who are committed to building assets in all aspects of their daily lives. Both within programs and outside of programs, your main focus should be building strong, healthy relationships.

"At the Summer Urban Academy, we talk about the 40 assets," says Darwin Lee of the Minneapolis-based Calvary Lutheran Church alternative summer school program. "One of the big focuses is that there is another adult who cares about the kids. I run into kids at the mall who know who I am from when I started working with the program seven years ago. The relationships you are building with the kids are much more important than the academics."

Ask yourself:
- How can we help spread innovation through people and their relationships?
- How can we promote an emphasis on strengthening relationships within families, among peers, within schools and other institutions, in programs and outside of programs, and across generations?

Unleashing, Not Controlling or Directing

As an initiative begins to have success in spreading the asset message, individuals and organizations in the community will begin shaping their own approaches and priorities for asset building. Sometimes it may be tempting to control or direct those approaches, especially if an approach isn't quite what members of the initiative think it could or should be. It's important that the initiative not try to control or overmanage the community's many efforts, but instead encourage further understanding and infusing of the asset approach.

As one of the participants in Orlando's Healthy Community Initiative put it, their goal is to bring the idea of asset building to the community, to "try to plant the seeds, and then let other people raise the crop."

Karen Atkinson, coordinator of Children First in St. Louis Park, Minnesota, the first Healthy Communities • Healthy Youth initiative, concurs. "I really feel good when I start picking up newsletters and seeing the asset message and I didn't promote it," she says. "Our role is not to give people permission to do this work, but to give it away. When you get to the point where other people feel like they own it, then you're making some headway."

Building deep and lasting ownership within an initiative begins with valuing everyone's contribution. "We don't have all the answers," says an initiative participant from Portland, Oregon, "but it's important to create an atmosphere of trust and valuing everyone's individual contributions. Then everyone feels like we're in here together."

Ask yourself:
- How will we continually be aware of the need for consistency and coordination among asset-building efforts as well as promoting innovation?
- How will we suggest ideas and guide without constricting others' ownership and creativity?

All Adults and Youth, Not Just Professionals and Parents

Everyone in the community is responsible for supporting young people. Asset building emphasizes inspiring, inviting, and equipping all types of community residents—including young people themselves, professionals, parents, elders, other adults, and business owners—to contribute to the well-being of children and adolescents.

And that means *all* children and adolescents. Not just the young people from low-income families or those who are in trouble, and not just the young people in your own family, neighborhood, or culture.

One key to engaging all types of community residents is to create an initiative that is consistently invitational. "The reason we're easy to walk into," says former Essex (Vermont) CHIPS (Community Helping Inspire People to Succeed) Coordinator Valerie Smith, "is because we're a team. We connect caring adults and youth, and we find ways for people to contribute. We've tried to remain very welcoming, even sort of folksy, even though we've grown quickly and had to become more structured."

> **Ask yourself:**
> - How will an emphasis on engaging everyone influence our priorities and strategies?
> - How can we create a consistently invitational atmosphere so that everyone feels welcome?

Long-Term Process, Not a Quick Fix

Asked how long it takes to build an initiative, Orlando's Raymond Larsen responds with another question and a smile. "How long does it take to grow five feet tall?" The answer? "However long it takes."

The developmental assets provide a framework for long-term action that recognizes the importance of ongoing, positive opportunities and relationships across at least the first two decades of life for all young people. That recognition means that the work of asset building doesn't happen through a single event or program; it needs to keep on happening. Sustaining asset building can be challenging.

"We went slow and built credibility for the concept of a holistic approach to kids," says an asset-building initiative participant in Milton, Oregon. "Finding perceptive players in major areas was key to making inroads into different sectors like the school board and city government. Groping took awhile, but I don't know if there's any way around that."

> **Ask yourself:**
> - What kinds of leadership and support do we need to sustain interest and engagement for long-term, positive change?
> - How can we generate "early successes" without losing sight of the long-term vision?

An asset-building initiative starts and supports a fluid, dynamic process that will take many years to have a broad and deep impact. And if the initiative is successful, asset building will become infused into all the community's systems and relationships, and the initiative itself will ultimately disappear into the fabric of a transformed culture. "Our leaders envision a 20-year plan for a paradigm shift to the assets philosophy," says Matt McCarter, executive director of the Ada County HC • HY initiative in Boise, Idaho. "When we get there, the formal HC • HY initiative will disappear as the community will hold itself in alignment with and live assets every day."

The Importance of Cultural Competence

For a community-wide initiative to enhance the developmental experience of *all* children and adolescents, cultural competence must become just as deeply embedded in asset-building work as a focus on helping young people build developmental assets. Cultural competence differs from the related concepts of diversity and inclusiveness in the following ways:

Diversity refers to the people we as asset builders are trying to reach—the young people we build assets for and with *and* the community members of all ages we invite to become asset builders with us. Diversity includes race and ethnicity, but is more broadly defined to include political, religious, gender, age, sexual orientation, ability, and economic groups as well. The goal is to build bridges of unity and cooperation across the many diverse groups within a community.

Inclusiveness is the process of how initiatives engage audiences. It means involving, reaching, and empowering all members and segments of a community. The lens of inclusivity can be used to examine how decisions are made, who is asked to lead, where dialogues are held, and how resources are distributed. For example, groups with members from a variety of cultural backgrounds often find that using consensus models for decision making, which take time and patience, is more successful overall than using democratic models, where voting processes can lead to "winners and losers" and thus alienate some members from further participation.

To help articulate its vision for participation in the community, the It's About Time for Kids Initiative of Bainbridge Island, Washington, developed this Statement of Inclusion to help communicate that every community member is a part of the asset movement:

> Everyone has a role to play. Parents/guardians are a child's first and most important teachers, but young people need support from other adults. We are not separated in this task by whether or not we have children, by income, age, education, or employment status, gender, or sexual orientation, level of ability or disability, ethnic background, racial background or spiritual tradition, but we are bound together and support each other in our concern for the well-being of our children.

The asset framework works for many individuals of many cultures and is itself an "inclusivity" tool because it invites *everyone* to come together around these common words and concepts and for a common goal: to improve life for all children. Derek Peterson has made assets presentations in southern Mexico, central Mexico, Namibia, Botswana, and to the cultures of the circumpolar north, and, he says, "the message always has resonated."

In the book *Building Assets in Congregations: A Practical Guide for Helping Youth Grow Up Healthy,* then-vice president of the American Muslim Council in Minneapolis, Matthew Ramadan, suggests that the asset message can also resonate across religious divides. "[From a Muslim perspective,] the developmental assets suggest the best possible way to do things," he says. "When people immigrate to this society from other cultures, they don't realize that we're saying some of the same things are important (such as community building and intergenerational relationships) that they thought were old-fashioned in their home country and culture. The assets may offer a way for us to reclaim and rebuild those traditional strengths within the U.S. context."

Cultural competence refers here to the change process that occurs personally and professionally as people are exposed to various cultural strengths and traditions and learn to do things differently as a result. Cultural competence is a topic of special interest and study for Assets for Colorado Youth (ACY) Executive Director María Guajardo Lucero, author of ACY's publication *The Spirit of Culture: Applying Cultural Competency to Strength-based Youth Development.* In that publication she writes:

> I view becoming culturally competent as an unending journey of transformation just like asset building. In this journey, people not only connect with an understanding of different cultural experiences, but also how it shapes our worldviews. The key is that once you absorb that new knowledge, you do something with it. You can absorb a lot of information, but if it doesn't change how you show up, then it's not transformative.
>
> Just as asset builders learn to reach out and connect with youth, culturally competent individuals learn to engage and connect with people of different ethnic and cultural backgrounds. The process is similar and the results are equally as profound. Asset builders who make a conscious effort to give their support to a young person are engaging in behavior similar to a culturally competent individual who asks a person to share the story of her or his cultural background. A combination of these efforts begins to build the relationships that can transform our social fabric.

Asset-building initiatives that emphasize in-depth work in cultural competence find that it involves both behavior (the way that you "show up") and process. Paying attention to everyone's cultural strengths and traditions moves participants from cultural awareness, sensitivity, and valuing, to incorporating this newly appreciated information into one's individual, family, and community experiences, actions, and philosophies. "It acknowledges, not ignores, our differences," explains Guajardo Lucero. "It goes beyond celebrating culture, which is often short-term and time limited, to promoting a new way of thinking that fully embraces diversity. Embracing means getting to know someone, developing a relationship with them, and engaging in a process of sharing with them."

To help people understand exactly what this means, ACY gives participants in trainings and presentations a picture of an iceberg with a small portion visible above the water and a larger portion below. Participants are asked to write in the "visible" 10 percent portion of the iceberg their readily apparent features such as gender, height, and skin color. In the 90 percent that's below water, they list their individual characteristics that aren't so readily apparent, such as values, beliefs, expectations, cultural norms, cultural traditions, and spirituality. ACY uses this exercise with adults to get them thinking about how they often relate only to the obvious 10 percent of other people when it comes to ethnic and racial issues as well as relating only to the top 10 percent when interacting with young people.

"In one of the trainings I did," relates Guajardo Lucero, "I listened to a white woman and a Navajo woman sharing. The white woman said, 'I've never thought about how ethnicity might shape my worldview.' The Navajo woman said, 'I think about it every day.' It was so striking to hear these two women face each other from opposite ends of the continuum, to have this 'aha' experience and begin to learn about the 90 percent."

Embracing means getting to know someone, developing a relationship with them, and engaging in a process of sharing with them.

Many initiatives are finding meaningful ways to become culturally competent. Project Cornerstone in Santa Clara County, California, for example, formed a Diversity Team that is leading a multiwave "Outreach and Listening" campaign. The campaign leads the initiative's outreach to diverse communities by holding focus groups to capture the experiences and traditions of the county's multicultural communities. (See Chapter 5 for more on this group's work.)

Alaska's Derek Peterson calls appreciation for and awareness of diversity one of the foundations of any initiative and notes that in this area, as in so many others, each community has its own unique groups and situations to work within. And timing can be very important. "In Alaska we are fortunate to be working with people from a wide variety of indigenous cultures, and we must move gently and intentionally in order not to offend," he says. "We never exclude but we are always aware of timing and tempo. There are times when the individuals in a group are ready to accept new ideas/people/cultural paradigms and there are times when they are not." Peterson recommends focusing first on forming trusted relationships with members of different community groups and working with those people first to be sure that members of each group will feel safe, welcomed, and accepted in a meeting or at an event.

ACY is working with different community groups that are adapting the asset framework in ways that make it more meaningful for the participants. Here are two examples:

- *Putting the asset framework in a cultural context.* Working with the Denver Indian Center, ACY asked youth of various tribal backgrounds taking part in a mentoring program to more closely tie the entire asset framework to their culture. Beginning with the six support assets, for example, they customized a caring school environment into "My school provides a caring, encouraging environment and supports culturally appropriate ways of learning" and "My school encourages parents and community members to share my American Indian culture and to participate in the school community."
- *Going beyond a literal translation of the asset framework.* A simple literal translation of the assets into Spanish or French or Japanese does not necessarily capture the concepts in a way that works for another culture. A conceptual translation integrates the asset framework and list into a cultural context and allows groups to relate to the framework from their own community's perspective.

  ACY led the work of getting the assets translated into Spanish by having a number of groups of Spanish-speaking community members review the translation. But they haven't stopped there. For example, in a Spanish-language workshop with 60 adults from Mexico and Central and South America, ACY asked participants to create a list of *dichos* or proverbs they had been raised with in their home countries. One example was "Se necesita todo un pueblo para criar a un niño," or "It takes a village to raise a child." A list of 100 *dichos* contained values, expectations, and messages grounded in Spanish-speaking cultures that connected with and validated the asset framework for these participants.

Embracing culture and diversity changes people individually and, consequently, changes the trajectory of initiative work in the community. This is important for all of the young people asset builders seek to develop relationships with. "Young people can better reach their full potential when they achieve a greater understanding of their own cultural heritage and that of others," says Guajardo Lucero in *The Spirit of Culture*. "If you want to build assets, be role models. Begin to have conversations about race and ethnicity with all the youth you come in contact with, not just young people of color. They're learning from you."

Moving along the Change Pathway

When people begin an asset-building initiative, it is often with a simple, clear vision of making their community a better place in which young people can

Seven Habits of Culturally Competent Asset Builders

IN ITS PUBLICATION *The Spirit of Culture,* ACY describes these "Seven Habits of Culturally Competent Asset Builders" for you to use:

1. Name and honor your own cultural heritage.
2. Embrace and honor the diversity of others.
3. Connect assets and culture often.
4. Speak of your own asset-building efforts through a cultural lens.
5. Include diverse perspectives in conversations that silently assume that one size fits all.
6. Be ready to learn by challenging your own assumptions about other people.
7. Reflect on the journey.

grow up. But as the activities of an initiative commence, sometimes that clear vision can be clouded by the myriad details and unexpected events that accompany those activities.

To help describe what initiatives need to do and to guide its own research, Search Institute has reviewed and studied the literature on change and then crafted a theory of change as a cornerstone of its community-based human development work. The change pathway outlines five phases of change, or steps on the journey that people, organizations, and communities commonly take when creating asset-building initiatives. The pathway not only describes change for individuals and groups, it also shows how thinking changes as the framework for positive youth development is infused into a community. Although the pathway indicates a sequence of steps, it's important to remember that the activities of these steps often happen in real life in a much less sequential, more overlapping way.

While it's impossible to predict or plan exactly what will happen as your community embraces asset building, reflecting on where you are (or where one of the sectors you're working with is, or where you want to be) in this change process can help you focus your energies in ways that will help you move toward deeper engagement and commitment.

The five major phases of the change pathway are receptivity, awareness, mobilization, action, and continuity:

- **RECEPTIVITY: Being Open to Change.** For the change process to begin, individuals, organizations, and communities must recognize and acknowledge that their young people are not getting all the help they need to grow up healthy and that things need to be and can be improved. This phase reflects dissatisfaction in one's head and heart—both an understanding and a feeling of dissatisfaction with the status quo—and creates a willingness to consider the need for strengthening the lives of children and youth.

- ▶ **AWARENESS: Understanding the Possibilities of Change.** Before individuals, organizations, or communities take action toward positive youth development, they are likely to need information that helps them think differently about the developmental needs of young people and exposure to situations that move them emotionally and shift the way they feel about meeting the needs of young people. This can either be a change, in which they learn to think and feel differently about youth and child development, or a reinforcement, in which their instincts, beliefs, values, and actions regarding youth and child development are validated. In either instance, they see new possibilities, feel that they can make a difference, and become ready to act accordingly. In this phase, people must be convinced of the benefits of asset building and of their own capacity (time, skills, and opportunities) for personally engaging with young people and for taking social action to better young people's circumstances.

- ▶ **MOBILIZATION: Organizing for Change.** The mobilization phase focuses on heightening individual motivation, and building the team and strategies that will prompt and sustain action to enhance young people's development. A shared vision for positive child and youth development is articulated, and individual and group action plans are created to realize it. As people and organizations commit to and mobilize for promoting healthy development, they may begin connecting with allies through informal networking as well as by establishing more formal coalitions.

- ▶ **ACTION: Making Change Happen.** Bear in mind that receptivity, awareness, and mobilization do not, in and of themselves, automatically translate into intentional, sustained efforts. In the action phase, the emphasis is on the doing. The work here is about establishing a wide range of activities that fill perceived gaps in the landscape of youth development. This occurs by means of individual acts, organizational practices, and community initiatives.

- ▶ **CONTINUITY: Ensuring That Change Becomes a Way of Life.** The continuity phase emphasizes sustaining momentum, energy, and progress toward healthy development for young people so that it becomes woven into the fabric of personal, organizational, and community life. Continuity also addresses the challenges of keeping a developmental focus as the newness of the idea wears off and additional ideas come along. Maintaining a commitment becomes paramount.

You may find that developing an understanding of how communities change will help you make decisions about how to plan your initiative's activities and to measure and evaluate your initiative's outcomes. Search Institute trainer and consultant Shelby Andress often uses the change pathway as a planning tool for organizations and new initiatives to help them identify where they are in the work and where they want to go next.

The pathway is also a tool for helping established initiatives look back, describe what they've done, and see what they've achieved. It can help initiatives see how many publics they serve and where each one of those publics is on the continuum of the pathway, illustrating clearly that the idea of a one-time approach to a whole community is a fiction and that the work always continues. Community Liaison Nancy Tellett-Royce explains: "Sometimes building an initiative is like raising a child. You hit challenges you didn't expect. But if your vision is strong enough and you have good relationships, you'll get through the challenges. The pathway can show you what you've lived through."

Look for the change pathway tipsheets at the end of each of this book's strategy chapters for ideas to help you along in your journey. And see Chapter 7 for an example of a community checklist based on the pathway.

> LEARN MORE: Understanding Change and Measuring Outcomes. For information on understanding the links between change theory and evaluation, we suggest you read *Making Evaluation Integral to Your Asset-Building Initiative: Employing a Theory of Action and Change* by Search Institute's Director of Field Research William Mesaros. (See the Resources listed at the end of this book.)

Beginning the Process of Change

- The principles embodied by asset-building initiatives are:
  - Strengths more than risks or deficits.
  - Engagement *with* youth, more than services *for* youth.
  - Relationships as well as programs.
  - Unleashing, not controlling or directing.
  - All adults and youth, not just professionals and parents.
  - Long-term process, not a quick fix.

- For a community-wide initiative to enhance the developmental experience of all children and adolescents, cultural competence must become just as deeply embedded in our work as the core principles above. The Seven Habits of Culturally Competent Asset Builders are as follows:
  1. Name and honor your own cultural heritage.
  2. Embrace and honor the diversity of others.
  3. Connect assets and culture often.
  4. Speak of your own asset-building efforts through a cultural lens.
  5. Include diverse perspectives in conversations that silently assume that one size fits all.
  6. Be ready to learn by challenging your own assumptions about other people.
  7. Reflect on the journey.

- The change pathway has five stages:
  - **Receptivity** to the potential of change on behalf of positive human development and building assets. People are receptive.
  - **Awareness** of making change in support of positive human development and building assets. People become aware.
  - **Mobilization** of the movement by commitment to action. People mobilize to plan actions.
  - **Action** on behalf of positive human development and building assets. The community engages in action to bring about change.
  - **Continuity** of asset-building action. The community engages in ongoing work to maintain and deepen change.

CHAPTER 2

Getting Started:
What Needs to Happen First?

When I was young I learned to care for only myself, but that was all I could handle. Now that I'm growing, I'm learning how important it is to care for others as well as myself.

SARAH SCHWARTZ, AGE 11, SILVERTHORNE, COLORADO

SPREAD OUT ACROSS the rolling green hills of western Kentucky, rural Ohio County is the fifth largest county in the state, home to 22,000 people. The region has struggled in recent years with economic depression brought on by the demise of its chief industry, coal mining. But it's heart, not money, that drives the Together We Care (TWC) initiative. "People have pretty much lost everything and had to start from scratch, but they're just tough," says TWC's asset mobilizer Marianne Pieper. "The fact that people here have been through so much is why they don't give up, and they're not willing to give up on their young people."

Together We Care started with a series of four meetings in 1997 convened by the Ohio County School Board to consider the broad question of how young people were doing. Forty community leaders, including youth, parents, businesspeople, religious leaders, elders, educators, and others, pored over an extensive collection of existing school and community reports. They found some statistics that alarmed them. For example, 42 percent of the county's children were living in poverty and 48 percent of the area's adults over the age of 25 had not received a high school diploma or GED. The group also saw high rates of drug and alcohol use by young people, teen pregnancy, and violence. Their concerns sparked them to action.

From among the ideas the group members generated for how to respond to their concerns, they selected the developmental assets framework as a starting point and formed their HC • HY coalition. Results of the 1998 administration of the *Search Institute Profiles of Student Life: Attitudes and Behaviors* survey also revealed some of the extraordinary strengths of Ohio County's children—for example, 75 percent of students in grades 6 to 12 reported attending church regularly. Faith and tradition became TWC's foundation says its director, James Robinson. "People here have a lot of faith that things will work out, and they'll help each other out. Our commitment is first, and the money usually comes."

Asset-building initiatives start in many different ways and for many different reasons. Some begin casually and simply; others are more deliberate. Eventually the effort grows and so does interest in creating a more formal structure for moving forward. There is no one right way to grow an asset-building initiative, but there is a balance to be struck between doing so little that efforts flounder or so much that passion and progress are stifled. In fact, many initiatives find that what actually happens is a continuing, swaying rhythm between times of great activity and new ideas and quieter times of reflection and simply "working the action plan" they have under way.

This chapter describes what an initiative looks like when it's getting started and some of the specific steps you can take to get it going. The steps are laid out in a sequence that should prove useful, but don't worry if you've already begun an initiative differently, haven't done some of the steps described, or haven't followed a particular sequence. You, like a number of initiatives before you, may be in the process of what Nancy Tellett-Royce describes as "building an airplane at the same time you're flying it."

Tapping into the Community Impulse for Change

"We started our initiative as so many others do, as a result of problems," says Mason City, Iowa's HC • HY Director Mary Schissel. "Then I went to a conference and heard about this asset model. I came back and said, 'This is it!' We had been struggling with a sense of feeling overwhelmed with problems, but when we found the asset model, then hope came."

The trigger point for beginning an initiative is most likely an individual or small group of community leaders who see the developmental assets framework as an exciting tool for organizing. "Developmental assets provide a common language and a mission," says Nicole Hintz, senior research assistant at Search Institute. "Adopting the language means sharing a culture of intentional behaviors and responsibility for changing community behaviors. The framework provides the simple concepts and doable behaviors that foster cohesion for all of the community-wide efforts."

Search Institute's National Asset-Building Case Study Project discovered two very distinct stages that are often present in initiatives:

▶ **The work starts on a very personal level.** At this initial stage, an individual or group learns about the asset framework, understands it, gains more knowledge about it, and feels passionate about it before promoting it and informing others about it. The Healthy Community Initiative in Orlando, Florida, for example, was sparked by the enthusiasm of an individual. "Someone had heard about assets at a conference and came here to talk about it," says HCI Executive Director Raymond Larsen. "The message really resonated with a principal from one of the local high schools. She got very enthused about it and started generating energy."

▶ **Then the work begins to transition into a larger mission.** The wider circle of participants—both young people and adults—who are attracted to working with the asset framework feel drawn to its special or "larger than everyday life" aspect. Many asset builders who want to spark others to asset building as well have a true passion for this work. It is not unusual to hear them speak of it as a calling, a vocation, a mission, or their life's work.

Inspired individuals who "get it" want to help others "get it," too, as well as helping them believe they can make a difference. These individuals with a mission have used the asset framework to inspire new initiatives and to reinvigorate long-standing ones. The Essex, Vermont CHIPS (Community Helping Inspire People to Succeed) coalition, for example, embraced asset building as a way to rejuvenate existing efforts. "I helped start our original coalition in 1986 when we were searching for ways to respond to community concerns about youth substance abuse," says CHIPS cochair Betsy Ferries. "At one point I left for two years and when I came back, there were very few people at the table and action had stopped. We needed a new focus. We saw asset building as a sensible, logical way of doing what we've always done."

The Power of One in Hamilton, Ontario

PASTOR DAVID BISH of the Stoney Creek United Church of Christ of Canada in Hamilton, Ontario, says the key for them to launch a community-wide asset initiative was finding the right person to endorse it. "In our case, it was a professor of social work at the local university," says Bish. "When we mentioned that he was involved, it was easy to bring other groups on board." After hearing Peter Benson talk at an all-day workshop in Windsor, Ontario, Bish says his church decided to sponsor a local workshop with the school board, organizations, and politicians to share what members learned.

Enthusiastic participants from this local meeting formed the core that led to the formation of an initiative. "We received a grant to get a full-time person to work for the coalition," says Bish. "Then we sponsored a multisector asset workshop at the university that about 300 people attended. We also sponsored a youth symposium. Now we're continuing our work by helping organize the initiative."

What Defines an Asset-Building Initiative?

When a group of residents begins to transition from an interest in the asset framework to an interest in actually building assets, efforts become more intentional. A community asset-building initiative is an organization of people—informal or formal—that helps transform a community using the asset framework.

Think of your role as similar to planting seeds. In some cases, the initiative not only plants the seeds but also tends them as they sprout and mature. In other cases, the initiative may take an even more active role, helping to cross-pollinate by sharing or linking the efforts of one community sector or institution (such as education, government, faith communities, or health care) to those of another. The changes that happen in the community as asset building becomes integrated into the work of organizations and institutions and into the lives of individuals are the *movement* that the initiative seeks to help thrive and expand.

This work of strengthening—and, in some cases, building from scratch—a community's developmental infrastructure is not done by using a "canned" program run by professionals. It's a movement of people across systems that creates a community-wide sense of common purpose. Residents and their leaders, including young people, work on the same team as partners, moving in the same direction to create a new norm in which all residents are expected, by virtue of their membership in the community, to promote the positive development of children and adolescents.

What Is the Role of an Initiative?

An asset-building initiative can germinate and nurture asset-based community change in many ways. In the simplest terms, your role is to:

- Share your energy and enthusiasm by inviting other people to join you in asset building;
- Help them understand the asset approach;
- Be a resource as their commitment grows; and
- Connect them with others when doing so will strengthen their efforts.

An initiative can be an important catalyst and supporter of the movement for positive community change, but be careful not to confuse the actions of the initiative with the transformation of relationships, institutions, policies, and actions within the community itself that will make it more asset rich and asset consistent. That transformation is the real "movement," and an initiative's primary role is to support that movement. Your role at the very beginning of a new initiative is to help guide the development of that support.

Tipsheet #1
Ask Yourself These Questions First

If you call Search Institute and say, "I've just heard about assets and I want to start an initiative, what should I do?" here are some questions you may be asked in return:

1. *Before you start building a community initiative, have you examined your own asset-building interactions with the young people who cross your path? Stretch your efforts.* "You need to be grounded in asset building first," advises Nancy Tellett-Royce, Search Institute's community liaison. "This doesn't just make you credible to others; it also helps you know in your bones what it is you're trying to do."

2. *Who else is interested in doing this with you and who else would you like to invite to the table?* "It's always good to have people within a particular sector talking to each other, but a community-wide initiative needs to engage people from across the community, young and old," Tellett-Royce suggests. Ask yourself: Who is passionate about kids? Who is good at thinking strategically? Who is already deeply connected to young people? Who can influence and shape public opinion and civic decisions?

3. *Have you really imagined what you want your community to look like and feel like to young people who are growing up there?* "If you want an initiative that can make it through the long haul, you need a vision big enough to sustain you."

4. *Do you have young people you can engage to work with you?* "They should be there right from the beginning to help with the visioning process and its implementation."

Suggestions for getting started:

- Pull a diverse group together and review the basic asset-building materials so that all of you will be starting on the same page. See the Resources List at the end of this book for tips and materials available from Search Institute.

- Don't really know any young people? "Talk to two young people on your block or in your building and ask them if they'd be interested in being part of your conversations."

- Get to know what kinds of asset building are already going on in your community. Ask young people to tell you who's building assets; who really knows them and is there for them. You're looking for examples of relationships, not just jobs people are doing. "Adults tend to think of amounts of time or positions as what counts. Asset builders can be in a particular position, like a teacher who directs drama club, but asset building happens when any adults really extend themselves to be in relationships."

- Starting an asset initiative is not primarily about putting more money into programs or finding another place to shelter kids. "You're trying to build a community where all the young people know someone who cares about them, even when they aren't paid to care about them. Asset building is about becoming more invitational to kids, and in the process of learning or relearning that, the community becomes more invitational to everyone."

Avoiding Pitfalls When Getting Started

There is no single way to launch an asset-building initiative. However, watching initiatives get started has led us to see potential pitfalls that grow out of inevitable tensions in an asset-building approach to community change. Here are a few, described in extremes:

	One extreme ⟵⟶ The other extreme	
Structure	Create a structure for the initiative that is rigid, not allowing for creativity, growth, or innovation.	Have no structure so that people do not have ways to get involved or have systems to make things happen.
Turf	Naively believe that there are no turf issues, then become sabotaged by initiatives, organizations, or people who believe their turf has been invaded or that they are not valued.	Obsess about turf issues to the point that the initiative becomes highly political and cannot move forward unless it has everyone on board.
Flair	Put all your energy and resources into packaging assets and the initiative in order to tap people's enthusiasm and emotions, but give the impression that there is no substance or depth to asset building.	Focus so heavily on the science, substance, and strategies of asset building that the initiative never captures the imagination or passions of the leaders and other residents of the community
Control	Presume that all asset-building work in the community must be coordinated by or approved by the initiative.	Presume that once someone or some organization has heard about assets that you don't need to stay in touch or offer guidance.
Leaders	Assume that the leadership for the initiative should only be adults, thus making it a strategy being done to youth.	Assume that all the leadership should be youth, thus limiting adult engagement and responsibility for creating an asset-rich community.
Scope	In order to show "measurable results," design your initiative so narrowly that it actually has little broad impact, engages few people, and touches the lives of relatively few young people.	Create an initiative that is so broad, calls everything asset building, and doesn't have any focus, which makes it difficult to see any progress or sustain commitment.

cont.

Inclusion	Believe that every group of people in the community should be represented in the initiative before anything can be done, thus stalling the initiative, perhaps indefinitely.	Presume that the people and organizations that show up are all that's needed, thus perpetuating power patterns in which structures consistently leave out people, organizations, or groups who may be at the margins and feel unwelcomed.
Programs	Because programs are easier to establish, fund, and monitor, make the initiative little more than a collection of programs that does not engage the community and its residents.	Because asset building is not a program but a philosophy, assume that programs have no role to play in a community's asset-building efforts.
Funding	Put all your energy and focus into ensuring that you have funding so that the initiative becomes purely funder driven and loses its vision.	Ignore the funding needs for coordination, communication, and technical assistance so that the initiative cannot be sustained.

How do you deal with these tensions? Instead of seeing the task like walking on a tightrope (where you must walk carefully or you'll fall) or a balanced scale (which stays static) a better metaphor may be a seesaw, which requires finding the back-and-forth flow that integrates both sides and is always moving.

Who Comes to the Table?

Most initiatives graduate from an individual or small group sparking interest in asset building to the formation of some kind of **initiator group.** Once exposed to the assets and the possibilities of implementing community change, the initiator group agrees to take on the task of getting things up and running.

The first group of 40 students and adults brought together by the school board in Ohio County, for example, were originally asked to commit only to four meetings. They agreed to review a specific set of materials and identify priorities within a set time period. Their final task was to make some recommendations about what to do. Once the asset framework and the Healthy Communities • Healthy Youth initiative model were selected, a series of follow-up meetings was scheduled to flesh out the next steps.

"None of the original 40 participants was pressured to come back," says TWC's James Robinson, "but they all did." The group set up four action teams. Each team focused on a different priority: adult role models, youth as resources, school climate, and community mobilization. Then they began to invite other young people and adults in the community to get involved, too.

Your initiator group will most likely include young people and adults whom you identify as important to invite to the table, as well as those who are attracted to the work as they hear about it. Think creatively and focus on being inclusive. For example, don't assume that people who don't have children at home won't be interested. Some of the biggest supporters of asset building are people with grown children and people who don't have children. Look around your community and invite people from different groups, not just groups with which you're familiar. Think young people, elders, parents, and nonparents. Think diversity. Think media and community funders. Think organizations, neighbors, and grassroots. And think decision makers.

Don't think small. Invite the mayor, the police chief, the head of social services. Who doesn't stand to gain by working with youth in a positive, proactive way?

"You have to think outside of the box and identify potential stakeholders early on," says Moorhead (Minnesota) Youth Initiative Executive Director Barry Nelson. "So many times when a movement starts, you're dealing with the non-decision makers. Sometimes the grassroots can really push the momentum and get leaders to listen, but if you get the leaders to catch the vision with you, then you can get that inspiration that will put you over the top. Don't think small. Invite the mayor, the police chief, the head of social services. Who doesn't stand to gain by working with youth in a positive, proactive way? They may surprise you."

As you get started, look for those individuals and groups whose enthusiasm is sparked. "When you're a new initiative, it's a delicate, fledgling kind of time," says Mimi Petritz-Appel of the Michigan GivEm 40 coalition. Petritz-Appel was GivEm 40's first coordinator and now serves as the schools asset development coordinator. "It's important to figure out which organizations, people, and players are really going to authentically support the initiative. People aren't used to thinking about movements, so it can be hard for them to participate in an organization that's bigger than them. We looked for people who saw this as enhancing their work instead of diminishing it."

Eventually, the initiator group will probably establish a **leadership group** that will take on more responsibility for designing and implementing a community-wide plan. Think about who you want to have involved and how to organize them, placing a premium on keeping your structure simple, informal, and as voluntary as possible. Try to avoid becoming too bureaucratic; instead, keep it easy for people to access.

Some initiatives have a larger, policy-oriented committee that oversees plans with smaller committees focused on specific tasks. Many initiatives have specific asset-action committees that concentrate on projects clustered around a single asset. Still other initiatives eventually set themselves up as nonprofit organizations to manage activities. Some initiatives have no formal leadership structure at all, relying instead on a network of community-based committees to continually move the work forward.

Chapters 3 and 4 provide more specific tips and ideas about how to involve individuals, but for now, keep in mind some of the following ideas to help you get started:

- **Recognize that asset builders come in all shapes and sizes.** Some are visionaries who can see the big picture and communicate the asset vision to others. Many are those who daily enact the asset message in small ways that affect the lives of children and youth with whom they have contact. Being an asset builder may have nothing to do with your job description or your place in the community. It's all about having a passion for infusing assets within the lives of young people. Your role is to identify, celebrate, and link all these asset builders together.
- **Have young people at the table from the beginning.** You can't really implement a community-wide initiative to change conditions for young people without *involving* young people. "You can't build a future for youth without them," says Paul Vidas, director of the Fox Cities, Wisconsin, United with Youth initiative. "After all, we adults won't be there. If youth don't build their own future, they won't like it."
- **Seek diversity at all levels.** A community-wide initiative is intended to touch the developmental experience of all children and adolescents. This goal requires ongoing, deliberate attention to involving, reaching, and empowering all segments of a community, building bridges of unity and cooperation, through the common language and concepts of the developmental assets, across political, racial, gender, sexual orientation, ethnic, religious, and economic lines.

> LEARN MORE: For more on getting started and for descriptions of Search Institute trainings that can jump-start your initiative and help you present the asset framework to diverse audiences, see the Resources section.

What Are Your First Tasks?

Your first tasks will involve gathering information about your community. Sharing what you've learned will help you start raising awareness of issues and assets in a broader context. Eventually, this information gathering will also form the basis for setting priorities and making an action plan. There's no one right way to get started here. It just has to fit your community and your vision.

Here are some key questions to consider:

- Where do we live and what type of community do we have?
- What issues are important in our community?
- What's already working?
- How do we organize our initiative?
- Should we administer a Search Institute survey to measure assets?

Where Do We Live and What Type of Community Do We Have?

Considering your local geography is important; much of the energy that can be mobilized for children and youth resides in overlapping systems of neighborhoods, schools, youth organizations, parks, and religious institutions within a legally defined locality such as a town, city, county, state, or province.

Community is more complicated than just a physical geography. It is a **geography of influence** with some definable boundaries. Systems can overlap or combine, bringing several cities, counties, or areas together. Schools can draw from multiple suburbs or towns can share a school district. A rural community is very different from a large urban one.

How you define your community from the outset is important. That definition will help you design the best strategies for implementing asset building where you live. For example:

- A **rural** community may choose to design an initiative that empowers many small towns to launch and support a series of initiatives together, with one overall vision team playing a coordinating role.
- A **suburban** community might want to also develop and coordinate initiatives across multiple places, perhaps working with school districts or other social institutions that cut across multiple boundaries and municipalities.
- An **urban** community might initiate simultaneously citywide and neighborhood efforts. Citywide strategies can provide overarching supports such as long-term public education with many media and communications partners as well as with technical assistance, training, and speakers. Initiatives can then target efforts at the neighborhood or association level.

What Issues Are Important in Our Community?

An assessment of the issues facing your community may help you decide how to shape your initiative for the long term. What are the important political, economic, social, and health issues that are of particular concern to your residents, especially in regard to how they affect your young people?

Here are a few examples of how an understanding of local issues has helped start and shape an asset initiative:

- *The Healthy Community Initiative of Greater Orlando* examined the profound impact of growth in its region. High rates of population and employment growth have contributed to central Florida's economy, but schools and other public institutions have had trouble keeping pace, making it difficult to maintain a consistent quality of life for families. Also, high rates of family mobility impact the education system: In one year an estimated 44 percent of the region's elementary school children did not finish the year in the school in which they started. Many of HCI's priorities revolve around helping local communities build and maintain their own capacities to support their residents.

➤ Residents who initiated the *Moorhead Healthy Community Initiative* in Minnesota first gathered as the result of concerns over news reports that certain crimes were escalating among youth. A focus for this initiative became the development of a strong network of after-school programs for Moorhead's young people.

➤ The mayor and city manager of Hampton, Virginia, convened a group to discuss an economic development initiative. The *Mobilization for Youth initiative* grew out of a group of residents exploring questions about the future of the community's workforce. Broader civic engagement was identified as a way to strengthen Hampton's support for youth and families so that young people would feel invested in the future of the community.

You don't need to spend a lot of money to get the information needed for an initial review. Many initiatives begin by pulling together existing information. Together We Care's initiator group, for example, reviewed a "Profile of Ohio County" prepared by a representative of the state board of education that was culled from existing local school and health reports. The Youth Plus Initiative in Union County, Iowa, found that a student health survey measuring youth risk behavior had been conducted in the state for many years but it had never been widely shared. An initiator group presented the data along with the developmental assets model at a community meeting; fifty residents there signed a pledge to participate in the new HC • HY initiative.

What's Already Working?

Another important area to explore in gathering information is **what's working.** No doubt, many youth-serving organizations, congregations, school programs, and individuals are already doing many great things for and with young people in your community. Knowing what these resources are will not only keep you from expending energy on reinventing the wheel but also give you a foundation to build on. Many of these groups are already doing asset building even if they don't call it that. Recognizing, publicizing, and affirming these efforts and the professionals and volunteers who work on behalf of positive youth development helps to reinforce their commitment and inspires others to take similar action.

Longtime initiative coordinator Karen Atkinson of Children First in St. Louis Park, Minnesota, affirms this emphasis on recognizing what's already working.

"This is very important because some people will feel as if you are laying claim to something new that they've been doing all along," she says. "You need to recognize what they've done, introduce the asset language, and let them know that you are trying to get others on board to support the good things they have been doing."

How Do We Organize Our Initiative?

It's important to openly address how you will organize your initiative because your structure will have an impact on how you work. Intentionally selecting a structure leads to less confusion among your participants. New structures or approaches may evolve as an initiative works over time.

At least three specific ways of organizing have been used by initiatives:

- **The "bubble-up" approach.** This is one of the least formal ways to organize an initiative and can be very creative and effective. In this case, the primary role of the initiative is a bit like *scattering seeds and waiting to see what grows or bubbles up;* some people term it an "organic" approach. The initiative encourages organizations and sectors to take action, but does not attempt to provide any formal linkage across the community. It may also work to draw attention to what is happening as a way to encourage others.

  Example: Jerry Mogul of the Mayor's Office on Community Partnerships in Boston says, "I've been very reluctant to formalize some kind of citywide coalition. . . . Then you start dealing with organizations, rules, who's in, who's out, and roles." Instead, Mogul has focused on encouraging organizations and sectors that take action. "It's just starting to bubble up, and we'll see where it goes," he says.

- **The "attach it" approach.** This approach concentrates on infusing asset building into existing programs and organizations that focus on young people. It will likely involve identifying current asset-building activity, naming it as asset building, and then supporting its growth. In this case, the primary role of the initiative is to *"cross-pollinate" the asset approach into what is already growing in the field.* Although this approach is not geared to creating a formal coalition, the asset framework provides informal linkages by introducing a common language and focus around which groups can unite.

  Example: When Sharon Rodine began exploring how to promote asset building in Oklahoma City, she quickly heard that the community didn't want another single-issue coalition. So they created a "barnacle coalition" and began infusing asset building into the work of several existing coalitions. "The asset approach is . . . an anchor that a lot of different groups can attach to," Rodine says. "It's not a competitor, but it's value-added."

- **The community-wide coalition.** This approach organizes the initiative's work through forming a community-wide coalition or integrating asset building into the mission of an existing coalition. The primary role of the ini-

Discussion Guide: Next Steps

Use these questions to help you and your group think about the next steps you need to take to get started. This tipsheet is not intended as a long-range planning tool, but rather to help you take the pulse of the asset-building work in your community and commit to a direction and plan for the immediate future.

1. What is the current state of your initiative? Just starting? Been around but needs a jump start? Established community player? Other? What strengths and resources do you have?

2. What is the current awareness level of your community regarding the existence and goals of your initiative?

    Unaware   1   2   3   4   5   Very aware

3. What is the current awareness level of your community regarding the developmental assets framework?

    Unaware   1   2   3   4   5   Very aware

4. How would you describe the current status of your community with regard to the asset-building principles for community change: strengths more than risks or deficits; engagement *with* young people, more than services *for* young people; relationships as well as programs; unleashing, not controlling or directing; all adults and youth, not just professionals and parents; and long-term process, not a quick fix. (Make a general statement.)

5. What are the three steps that you can take immediately to support an asset-building movement in your community?

Adapted from the *Starting and Supporting Asset Building in Communities* training in *Essentials of Asset Building: A Curriculum for Trainers,* copyright © 2002 by Search Institute, Minneapolis, MN; 800-888-7828; www.search-institute.org. See the Resources section at the end of this book for more on how Search Institute trainings can assist you in your asset-building initiative work.

tiative is to *help build and maintain a more formal structure* that seeks to plant and nurture seeds of change in a more systematic way by linking all sectors of the community in the effort. This approach generally includes a more formal leadership structure in which all major sectors are represented and provide staffing and operating support.

Example: Boise, Idaho, created a strategic plan and a formal structure to support asset building. Five founding agencies (the city, YMCA, United Way, the major medical center, and the school district) are providing ongoing support, with each providing staffing and operating support for a three-year period.

There are many ways to organize an initiative, each with its own advantages and challenges. Less formal approaches are more easily instituted but may not provide the kind of networks that will allow you to clearly track the progress of your initiative's work. More formal approaches may involve the community in a more systematic and thorough fashion but are harder to build. In fact, one risk with building a more formal coalition is the danger of spending too much time and energy just on establishing and maintaining the structure of the coalition.

Should We Administer a Search Institute Survey to Measure Assets?

Some HC • HY initiatives start or further their work by conducting the *Search Institute Profiles of Student Life: Attitudes and Behaviors* survey, which gives a snapshot of the asset levels of the community's young people (grades 6–12). Although the institute has published results from an aggregate sample of more than 200,000 young people surveyed during the 1999–2000 school year, many communities find it important to do their own survey. "We had to have local research or people wouldn't believe it," says United Way Executive Director Becky Beauchamp of the GivEm 40 Coalition in Traverse City, Michigan. "We wanted to use the survey as a catalyst for action and substantive change."

GivEm 40, for example, spent two years making sure all 19 school districts in its region were on board before doing the survey, with the provision of Search Institute trainings for educators as an important part of the preparation. Some communities find it useful to concentrate on building the infrastructure of their initiative before doing the survey. Whether and when you do the survey depend on the needs of your community.

Often, the release of survey data to the local community is the centerpiece to a series of events that formally launches an initiative. The survey results also become the basis of the initiative's action plan. Some communities spend considerable time laying the groundwork for their initiative before conducting the survey. "The release of data is a step in the process, not an end in itself," cautions Karen Foster, one of the lead researchers on the case study project. "Your leadership group needs to develop a formal plan that is really clear about what they hope will happen as a result of the survey data release."

Foster suggests that initiatives pay particular attention to several factors when planning for their survey data release:

▶ **Define critical mass.** Determine up front who your core leadership group needs to be and who will be recruited later. This core group needs to be excited and committed enough to push your plans past the initial rollout.
▶ **Maintain constant communication.** "You can never overcommunicate the nature and purpose of the survey," says Foster. "Everyone involved needs to be kept connected every step of the way."
▶ **Consider the variables.** Think about how you will handle both positive and negative reactions to the survey data. Do you have the capacity to handle an overwhelming demand for information? What will you do if the local media characterize some groups as having let youth down?

> LEARN MORE: See the Resources listed at the end of this book for more on the *Search Institute Profiles of Student Life: Attitudes and Behaviors* survey for students in grades 6–12, as well as the *About Me and My World* survey for students in grades 4–6.

Framing Your Asset Initiative

You've now laid the groundwork for starting a community-wide asset-building initiative. You have:

- Defined your community;
- Clarified the initiative's role;
- Convened an initiator group and/or a leadership group;
- Conducted preliminary research into local issues, existing community resources, and what's already working in the community; and
- Decided whether and how to administer the *Search Institute Profiles of Student Life: Attitudes and Behaviors* survey.

Now you're ready for your next set of tasks. Focus on:

- Developing a vision and mission for your initiative;
- Designing an action plan; and
- Setting goals and objectives.

Developing the Vision and Mission

It's important for your initiative to develop a shared vision and mission that describe your picture for engaging all residents in asset building. The vision and mission will help you center your work, but you should recognize that both will likely change as new participants embrace the asset framework and join in your efforts. The job of the initiative is not to protect its own picture of what an asset-building community might look like but rather to show that vision to others and actively encourage them to help cultivate it so that it is truly shared by the community.

For asset building to be fully realized, an initiative engages committed residents to act at three different levels:

- **Individual:** Perhaps more than half a community's asset-building potential resides in daily relationships—some fleeting, some sustained—between youth and adults and between adolescents and younger children. A major long-term target is to encourage the growth of this relational power.
- **Organizational:** All socializing systems of a community—including families, schools, congregations, youth organizations, media, employers, neighborhoods, and health-care providers—become intentional about growing their relational and programmatic capacity to build assets.
- **Community-wide:** Underlying the long-term asset-building efforts of residents and organizations is an infrastructure of norms, values, supports, policies, and resources that energize, unite, and sustain the initiative.

Broaden your vision and mission to encompass all three of these levels of involvement, but first (and continually) focus on individual relationships. "Strengthening the asset foundation for all kids," says Search Institute's Special Advisor Eugene C. Roehlkepartain, "has to do with unleashing the asset-building capacities of a community's people and doing it in all of the settings in which the lives of adults and youth intersect."

And remember that your vision needs to remain open to change as more and more people come on board with your initiative.

What Is the Difference between a Vision and a Mission? The Alliance for Non-profit Management defines vision this way: "A vision is a *guiding image of success formed in terms of a contribution to society*. If a strategic plan is the 'blueprint' for an organization's work, then the vision is the 'artist's rendering' of the achievement of that plan. It is a description in words that conjures up a similar picture for each member of the group of the destination of the group's work together."

For example, those attending the first set of community meetings held by local stakeholders in the Healthy Community Initiative (HCI) in Florida were asked to consider "What if?" as a way to help them begin the visioning process. One question was, "What if you could help to create an environment where all children and youth have the opportunity to reach their full potential—physically, mentally, emotionally, and spiritually?" As HCI's Raymond Larsen recounts, "Our stakeholders recognized that the shared dream and plan that came from answering that question would be powerful and motivating." HCI's entire action plan now flows from the "how" answer to that initial "what if?"

HCI's vision statement says: "Greater Orlando, in the 21st century, is a place where individuals are valued and encouraged to use their unique talents and gifts to create an outstanding community. Our community proudly serves as an example of what is possible when people find common ground and work together."

An example of a community vision statement that more explicitly focuses on young people comes from Georgetown, Texas: "A community where no child is hungry, hurt, alone, or rejected and where all children and youth believe they are loved, respected, and treated with dignity."

A mission statement, on the other hand, *communicates the essence of your organization, network, or coalition to your stakeholders and to the public.* It says more about who you are, what you're doing, and why you're doing it. HCI's mission statement is "to create a new sense of community which leads to an environment where all individuals and families flourish."

Designing an Action Plan

To know where you're going, you need a logical set of steps, clearly tied to your vision and mission, that helps you actualize your vision for a healthier community. An action plan also helps maintain momentum later on. "People need a structured way to move forward," says Joanne Smogor, former coordinator of New Hampshire's Makin' It Happen Coalition for Resilient Youth. "You can't just 'meet' and talk about building assets."

A clearly written plan helps you assess your progress, improve your plans, and garner resources as you move forward. An initiative's plan is not a rigid set of steps but an organized way of helping you tie a series of actions together.

Here are some of the major actions to include in your initial plan:

▶ **Establish an identity for the initiative.** Many initiatives feel that it's critical to develop a distinct identity. Designing the components of this identity— a name, a logo, a tag line—inspires participants to articulate what their community initiative means to them. It also helps the community begin to recognize the initiative as you move forward in your promotion and marketing efforts. In addition, having an umbrella identity makes it easier for some organizations to join in.

"When we started our coalition," says GivEm 40's school coordinator Mimi Petritz-Appel, "our three founding organizations said they wanted the coalition to be 'real,' so we took the time and worked with a husband-and-wife graphics team to develop a logo that would help build our movement. We wanted something edgy, that kids could relate to, that spills off the

G j v E m 4o
24.7

tongue. It needed to have meaning but be cryptic enough so that people would ask what it is. It also had to be fun and fluid and flexible so it wouldn't sound like a deadly bureaucracy. Now it's recognizable."

At the same time, you may not want to *rush* to establish an identity, Derek Peterson of the Alaska ICE initiative cautions. "There is some timing to developing an identity, and it is usually when you get enough of the right people at the table, and they begin asking for it because they are actually needing it. Don't do this too quickly, or you may end up 'selling' your initiative rather than 'selling' the message about young people."

▶ **Figure out how you will communicate what you are doing.** One of the most critical aspects of your initiative is how you educate the community and keep it updated on your progress and accomplishments. Communications may require a plan of its own that includes specific tasks and tools like newsletters, town meetings, public service announcements, and working with local media. (See Chapter 6, "Influence Civic Decisions," for a wealth of communication techniques and ideas.)

▶ **Develop a system for learning and changing as you go.** Think early about what your process will be for learning and incorporating lessons as you go. How can you tap into people's insights and wisdom to help you grow? How will you gather the stories you'll need to share with the community as well as potential funders and supporters? How will you network existing efforts? What kinds of learning loops can you establish to keep useful information constantly flowing through your initiative? How will you continue to build awareness, recruit new members, sustain mobilization, and continue on your action plan? How will you build time for reflection into your meetings?

Setting Short-Term and Long-Term Goals and Objectives

Once you've affirmed the initiative's vision and mission and drafted your larger action plan, it's time to figure out *what* to do and *how* to do it. The strategies you choose should be the broad approaches you plan to take; your goals and objectives then are the general and specific results you're after. Strategies, goals, and objectives can be developed in a variety of ways, including individual inspiration, group discussion, formal decision-making techniques, and so on. Try to strike a balance between being optimistic and realistic. It's best to start small, pick a focus, and celebrate your successes along the way.

Here's an example of one strategy with a goal and several objectives flowing from the Orlando, Florida, HCI's vision and mission:

Tipsheet #4
Planning with Your Vision in Mind

This exercise comes from the Alaska Initiative for Community Empowerment. Participants in community workshops write answers to the following questions as one of a series of steps to create a short, easy-to-do plan for getting started in asset building.

- State our goal. (A goal sets direction, but is never fully achieved. It is not objectively measurable but is more like a direction or a concept—broad and subjective. We'll feel it as we move toward it.)

- What need does our goal address?

- How can we create or intensify people's awareness of this need?

- Who are the people who will be involved in implementing our proposed change?

- How can we involve them meaningfully?

- What are the values cherished by the people of the community that we should address when seeking their support for our initiative?

- Who are the key opinion makers whose approval or endorsement we need?

- How can we involve these key opinion makers meaningfully?

- What small-scale efforts (e.g., pilots, field tests) would demonstrate viable ways of achieving our goal?

- How can we assure success for our first effort?

- What skills need to be developed for maintaining the sustained change?

- What feedback procedures would assure periodic evaluation for improvement?

- What kinds of resistance ought we to expect?

- What supportive forces are helping us?

- What concrete actions could we take to overcome resistance?

- What concrete action could we take to use supportive forces?

The strategy: To empower local communities to build their own assets.

The goal: HCI seeks to help communities build their local capacity so they can sustain asset building on their own. That might mean recommending a member of their Community Faculty (volunteers with specific skills who are also trained in asset building) who is available to help a community with its first round of meetings, information gathering, priority setting, etc.

The objectives: To reach this goal, HCI might do any of the following:

1. Initiate and facilitate local community projects to mobilize the community to build assets.
2. Host and facilitate the Community Asset Network to support and deepen asset-building initiatives and champions.
3. Publish weekly FYI newsletters to inform and encourage asset building in the community.

You can imagine the number of specific activities that HCI might initiate to move it toward achieving each objective: doing research on current community projects; asking initiative members to list their contacts in such projects and then getting in touch with each one; recruiting volunteers to gather information and write the articles for the newsletters, and so on. But before you move ahead to create specific activities, consider taking your action plan one step further by creating a "results map" to help you ensure that the activities will really contribute to the achievement of your goals and objectives. There are organizing techniques that can guide you in taking a structured look at your goals and objectives to help you surface the assumptions embedded in your plan and analyze whether your planned activities are likely to achieve your goals.

LEARN MORE: Two resources from Search Institute can help you with your planning: *First Steps in Evaluation: Basic Tools for Asset-Building Initiatives* and *Making Evaluation Integral to Your Asset-Building Initiative: Employing a Theory of Action and Change.* See the Resources listed at the end of this book to find out how to obtain them.

Creating, planning, and sustaining an asset-building initiative constitute a dynamic and exciting process filled with both rewards and challenges. One of the main pitfalls to avoid is having your initiative become another "program" in the community. "When we began our initiative," says Ada County HC • HY Executive Director Matt McCarter of Boise, Idaho, "we agreed we would not become one more 'thing.'"

Other pitfalls to avoid include:

- Promoting the initiative instead of promoting asset building;
- Equating asset building with volunteering to run the initiative;
- Asset building *for* young people but not asset building *with* young people;
- Limiting asset building to one or two activities;
- Associating activity with progress;

Letting Things Happen instead of Making Things Happen: Some Tips for Going with the Flow

By Eugene C. Roehlkepartain, senior advisor at Search Institute and member of the Children First initiative, St. Louis Park, Minnesota

WE LIVE IN A CULTURE and society where strategic plans, checklists, and clear objectives rule the day. You have to have them for funding, for boards, and, often, just to get anything done. We need some steps to follow, some signs of progress, some nudges to keep us on task. So we sell ideas, push agendas, seek out surefire strategies. We need to be efficient.

Many of those are vital impulses, and they can be key to maintaining our focus. Yet we also know there's another side to community change and community building. It's more organic, more fluid, more unpredictable. Here are some tips, based on a more organic, less mechanistic understanding of how complex change occurs:

- Listen a lot. Find out what people care about. Then unleash people's passions, commitments, and interests for building an asset-rich community, whether or not they are part of a structured strategic plan.
- Watch for and embrace creativity and innovation on the edges—outside of existing power systems and institutional structures. They may be pointing the way.
- Encourage and celebrate small steps that are moving in the direction of big change.
- Give lasting change time to take root, emerge, and grow within individuals, groups, and systems within your community. Don't push too hard. Don't give up too soon.

You may be tempted to think that these approaches mean that you don't have to be thoughtful or focused or that you won't need to work hard. In fact, the opposite may be true. You may actually end up working harder (though you won't be pushing harder). But in the process, you may find that creative, important, and transforming change occurs that's better than you could ever have planned for.

> **LEARN MORE:** For more information on change strategies based on chaos theory and organic (instead of mechanistic) understandings of systems and organizations (with a focus on business), see *Surfing the Edge of Chaos: The Laws of Nature and the New Laws of Business*, by Richard T. Pascale, Mark Millemann, and Linda Gioja (Crown, 2000). Or read the story "The Garden" in Arnold Lobel's children's book *Frog and Toad Together* (HarperCollins, 1979).

- Equating asset building with volunteering in a youth program or school;
- Getting many people energized without providing them with something to do.

This chapter does not present a definitive list of steps or instructions on how to start your community initiative, nor is it meant to. It paints instead in broad strokes the big-picture tasks that most initiatives have found important as they began their work. But don't let the details of structure, group membership, and planning keep you from getting started with other kinds of action. "Sometimes initiatives get too focused on how things will be structured or funded or what goes into a work plan," says Search Institute's Nancy Tellett-Royce. "The primary role of an initiative is to keep reaching out and sparking asset building in the community."

Where to Now?

As your initiative moves forward, you'll be thinking and learning about ways of bringing new people on board, monitoring your progress, making course corrections, celebrating successes, broadening and deepening your work, and keeping things going. The next chapters of this book contain lots of information and ideas to help you reach out to your entire community to inspire, engage, and link people in asset building.

Keep these underlying points in mind as you proceed:

- Projects work best when they are locally owned and operated and dedicated from the start to being inclusive.
- Deepening relationships is central to growing an initiative.
- Young people need to be involved in meaningful and effective ways to forge a new norm for youth-adult partnerships.
- Available resources need to be identified and eventually connected to one another to multiply the power and effectiveness of the community's work.
- Growing a healthy community is a long-term process that requires constant nurturing and vigilance.
- Don't be afraid to try new, unusual ideas.

No matter how your asset-building initiative is organized, its role is to plant and nurture the seeds that will yield an asset-building community change "movement." With no seed-packet picture of what that movement will look like once it's grown, it will likely take on an image of its own shaped by the community in which it grows. Be ready for the unexpected: you may think you're planting corn seeds, but a sunflower may sprout instead.

The initiative's strength and direction will come, in part, from continually seeking to understand the context from which your initiative springs, that unique collection of ideas, individuals, orientation, and structure that is your community. "An initiative has energy like a wave," says GivEm 40's schools asset development coordinator Mimi Petritz-Appel. "Some people are ready to ride it, some aren't. Our job is to honor both while balancing limited resources, always providing opportunities for others to jump on when they're ready."

Lessons Learned from Fox Cities, Wisconsin, United with Youth Initiative

Lesson #1:
Responding to human needs in the context of community is what works.

There must be a constant review of "where are we going and why?" This allows people to see the big picture as they focus on the details. It means that everyone must study all the time in order to keep current. Doing what was done before may work, but there is no guarantee.

Lesson #2:
Initiatives initiate.

Building on Lesson #1, initiatives must take the first steps as communities move toward progress. Getting people to abandon the status quo is difficult at times. Persistence is the key. Be like flowing water. It is going where it must. Water goes around obstructions or eventually obstructions are worn away, not through strength but persistence.

Lesson #3:
Empowerment is the glue that holds groups together.

People want to help, but will not waste their time. This is especially true of youth.

Lesson #4:
The process is more important than the finished product.

If the process is flawed, the product will be flawed. There are many tried-and-true examples of processes for just about any task one might undertake to draw from. It is tempting to cut steps in any given process in order to save time, but avoid that temptation.

Lesson #5:
Give your best guess.

There is little that is actually known. As humans, we are constantly giving our best guess as though we do know. Young people are sometimes very shy about giving their opinions. "I don't know" is heard often. It's not about being right or wrong. Make sure everyone understands that adults in the group are sharing opinions and that the opinions of youth are needed to give the group balance.

—PAUL VIDAS, DIRECTOR, UNITED WITH YOUTH

Getting Started: What Needs to Happen First?

- Asset building can start in many ways but usually begins on a personal level and then transitions into a shared mission within a group.

- Asset building becomes an initiative when it moves into becoming an *intentional strategy* for helping transform a community around the developmental assets framework. The changes that happen in the community as a result become the *movement*.

- The initiative's primary role is to support the movement toward positive community change and positive youth development.

- It is vital to have young people, along with many diverse community members, at the table from the very beginning.

- Begin your work by gathering information about your community, important issues, the resources you already have, and what's already working in the community.

- If you choose to conduct the *Search Institute Profiles of Student Life: Attitudes and Behaviors* survey, remember that it is one step in the process of developing your initiative, not an end in itself.

- There are many different ways to organize your initiative, but keeping it less formal in the beginning will make it easier to get started.

- Developing a simple action plan allows you to bring together your initiative's vision, mission, strategies, goals, and objectives into a fluid, logical document that will help you move forward and adjust as you grow.

- Figure out not only how to communicate what you are doing to the wider community but also how to gather feedback on what you're doing so that the initiative can grow and flourish.

- Keep reaching out and sparking asset building.

PART TWO

Making It Happen

Five Action
Strategies for Your
Asset-Building Inititative

AT EVERY COMMUNITY ORIENTATION for volunteers presented by Hampton, Virginia's Mobilization for Youth, a cake shaped like an elephant is served. "It's based on the old joke 'How do you eat an elephant?'" says Director Cindy Carlson. "One bite at a time." Elephant cake reminds everybody, on a regular basis, that the process of creating an asset-building community is a long-term, multistep process. The chapters in this section are intended to help you get into that process "one bite at a time."

The four chapters in this section focus on illuminating overarching strategies that are needed to transform your community with and for youth. Although these strategies are laid out in separate chapters, keep in mind that, as with many other phases of your work, your use of these strategies will overlap and flow together, as your community initiative twists and turns but generally moves forward.

- **Engage adults** from all walks of life to develop sustained, strength-building relationships with children and adolescents, both within families and in neighborhoods.
- **Mobilize young people** to use their power as asset builders and change agents.
- **Activate sectors** of the community—such as schools, congregations, businesses, and youth, human service, and health-care organizations—to create an asset-building culture and to contribute fully to young people's healthy development.
- **Invigorate programs** to become more asset rich and to be available to and accessed by all children and youth.
- **Influence civic decisions**—Influence decision makers and opinion leaders to leverage financial, media, and policy resources in support of this positive transformation of communities and society.

The five interrelated action strategies can be visualized in this way:

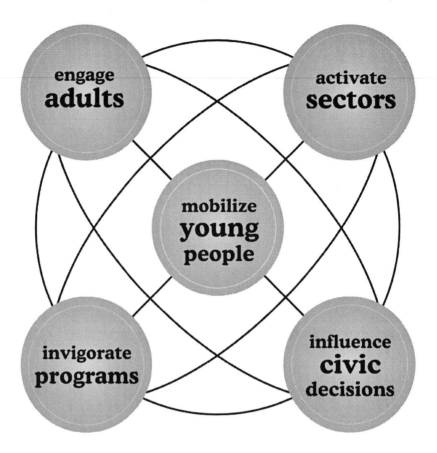

These five action strategies are needed to transform your community into a place where young people have access to and experience more developmental assets. The two lower circles represent the traditional ways in which communities have gone about this work, with a focus on the "three Ps" of policy, programs, and professionals. But those two strategies are not enough. We can't transform our communities and society without also focusing on activating the asset-building capacities of a community's members in all of the settings where the lives of adults and youth intersect. It is the combination of all five strategies that creates the overarching picture of what an asset-building initiative aims to do.

Each of the strategy chapters explains what you need to know to build your efforts in that area. The first part of each chapter offers key themes and tactics gleaned from field study research to help you fulfill the vision of your initiative in each of the five strategies. The second part of each chapter offers "Assets in Action"—practical wisdom, lessons learned, and activities and ideas, gathered from asset-building initiatives across the United States and Canada, that you can borrow and customize to the needs of your initiative.

CHAPTER 3

Engage Adults

There are many people in your life that make a difference in what kind of person you turn out to be. These people are the kind of people that are the true heroes of this life. I know it sounds kind of corny, your parents being your heroes and all, but thanks to my parents, my life is better in many ways.

YESENIA BECERRIL, 16 YEARS OLD
SUMMIT HIGH SCHOOL, DILLON, COLORADO

POSITIVE RELATIONSHIPS with adults are fundamental to asset building in the lives of young people. Writing about life's real teachers for the Inspired by Assets writing contest in Dillon, Colorado, Becerril identifies her relationship with her parents as an asset-building one. But young people need more than that. Each young person needs support from and positive interactions with neighbors, teachers, businesspeople, and doctors and nurses, too. One key step to mobilizing a community is to begin inspiring all of its adults to be asset builders.

The most basic "unit of change" in your initiative is each individual who lives in your community. While your initiative will include parents and professionals who work with children and youth, an important challenge will be to reach *other* adults who haven't been expected—or invited—to be resources for young people. Some of these adults won't even be aware that they *can* be resources in this way.

"Your role is to empower people to connect with young people no matter what their experience or training," says Search Institute's Nancy Tellett-Royce. "You're showing every adult that he or she is important and has a role to play in the life of a young person. When it comes to raising a healthy community for youth, willingness is the most important credential."

Engaging a wide range of adults on behalf of children yields many benefits. More people in the community begin to recognize and act upon their responsibility to contribute to young people's well-being. Young people feel more valued, and parents feel more supported. At Horace Mann Middle School in Denver, Colorado, for example, Asset Teams of students, parents, and staff are working together to use developmental assets as a way of boosting student success. "The asset framework can be a unifying force for change," says Principal Jim Trevino, "because it provides concrete, tangible roles and actions for stakeholders." Parents, teachers, and school staff are a logical place to start, but this strategy is about engaging a much wider range of adults on behalf of children.

Fulfilling the Vision

When the researchers on Search Institute's National Asset-Building Case Study Project analyzed how the four participant initiatives engaged adults, several key themes emerged. Think about these points as you launch your own efforts.

Speak the same language. Use the asset framework to provide a common language that helps everyone understand the goal of an initiative. Think of it as a set of simple goals and doable behaviors to share with as many adults in the community in as many ways as you can.

Use the framework to:

- *Define your initiative's work.* "We've formatted our structures, our planning, our evaluation, everything, around the asset model," says Mason City, Iowa's Youth Task Force Director Mary Schissel.
- *Activate and connect others.* Orlando's Healthy Community Initiative acts as a knowledge center, for example, making its members and consultants available to help local communities get their initiatives started. "Winter Park and West Orange 'own' their initiatives," says Raymond Larsen. "We just help weave them together."
- *Validate what's already being done.* When Derek Peterson, director of child/youth advocacy for the Association of Alaska School Boards, talks with groups about the asset framework for the first time, he doesn't start by talking about the assets. He first asks everyone to name what he or she thinks young people need to grow up healthy. Then he invites them to look at the framework and recognize what's already there.

Find ways to reduce barriers between adults and youth. Polls remind us that young people fear rejection by adults, but adults can fear being rejected by young people, too. "Find simple, structured ways for adults to be in the presence of young people," advises Tellett-Royce. For example, congregations can include young people among their greeters, and youth organizations can pass

The Power of One in Lone Rock, Wisconsin

NOVEMBER 12, 2002
DEAR SEARCH INSTITUTE

This should be a happy letter for you to read because it describes a success story. It all started a few years ago when our circuit court judge invited one of your eloquent speakers to come to Richland County and enlighten us. I was an unsuspecting member of the audience.

Afterward, I decided to try asset building in my own rural, isolated valley, inhabited by a few active farm families and three or four nonfarming households.

Accustomed to walking for exercise every early morning, I started to time my walks to coincide with the arrival of the school bus picking up the neighborhood kids. Before long, I knew all four children by name, they knew me, and we had a pleasant exchange of small talk and body language.

When I started looking to expand the asset building, I hit upon the idea of attending the local high school varsity soccer games. Soccer was the only game I knew because I grew up in Holland where football and baseball were unknown. To my surprise, I discovered that only family members of players attended the games. I was the only nonfamily member on the bleachers. To this day, four years later, that is still the case.

But being the only "outside" fan brought unique advantages for asset building because, before long, I got to know all 18 families on the benches and, through them, all 18 members of the team. Now, whenever I go shopping in our small town, a current or past soccer player invariably changes my oil, checks my groceries, or waves at me while mowing the right-of-way. I have been invited to graduation parties and notified of hospitalizations or successful college entrances. I really got to know a lot of teenagers, and they got to know me. Assets were being built en masse while having fun.

Last night was the night of the annual soccer banquet. As usual, I was the only nonfamily member enjoying the accolades the soccer players received from their coaches and the generous applause from their parents and grandparents. At the end of the evening, the player who had received the highest award was asked to say a few words. He hesitantly rose, straightened himself, and said: "I want to thank Henk for coming to all our games. It meant a lot to me."

I was moved. Driving home, I realized how much this statement meant to me and how it all started with learning about asset building.

From the bottom of my heart, thanks.

HENK NEWENHOUSE, LONE ROCK, WISCONSIN

out "conversation cards" to adults printed with three questions they can ask young people who've been invited to join them at a meeting.

You may find yourself needing to (tactfully) help some adults change their attitudes about young people. "I think the biggest thing young people need is to know that adults see them as complete human beings," says Union Hill Alliance Church Senior Pastor Tom Osborn in Redmond, Washington. "The biggest rap against kids is that someday they're going to grow up. Someday, they'll *be*

Youth members of Florida's Healthy Community Initiative work with an adult participant on initiative action planning at the Sage-ing Center of the Winter Park Health Foundation.

something. Young people need to know *now* that they have something to offer. Then they'll grow into their potential."

And don't forget to share with reluctant or fearful adults that there are benefits to *them* when they become asset builders for and with young people, too. As they say in the Alaska ICE initiative's book, "Every adult needs a child to guide; that's how adults learn."

> LEARN MORE: For ideas about connecting with young people, take a look at *Tag, You're It! 50 Easy Ways to Connect with Young People.* See the Resources listed at the end of this book for details.

Call on your elders. Both youth and elders have become segregated by age in modern society. A vital aspect of asset building is to bring youth and elders back into the same circle. Many initiatives are rediscovering the power (and benefits for all participants!) of bringing youth and seniors together in intergenerational dialogues, mentoring programs, and oral history projects—as well as in initiative teams (see Chapter 5 for a wealth of examples).

Build assets for and with adults, too. Many initiatives are also discovering that if adults are going to excel in building assets, they need assets, too. In the Healthy

Community Initiative of Greater Orlando, they sometimes say, "You cannot give what you do not have." For them, the idea of grown-ups needing assets is a continuing issue, and they work to consider how to provide support and encouragement to teachers, to health-care givers, and to parents, among others.

Identify existing asset builders. "Name adults in the community who are already asset builders," says Nancy Tellett-Royce. "By showing all the small and large ways in which they are asset builders, you make it easier for people to hop on a train that's already moving instead of having to push to get it started."

Making It Happen

When you begin recruiting and engaging adults, you're looking for "the people that stick to you," as one Florida initiative participant describes it. "The crucial asset to any neighborhood is the people who live there, so if we're going to have an initiative, it needs to be 'owned' by people and not by an agency. In local communities, we send somebody in whose job is to build capacity for an initiative. We tell them to look for the people that stick to them and when there's nine or ten of them, bring them into one room and call them the Leadership Committee. It becomes theirs."

There's a delicate balance to be struck, however. You'll be looking for ways to support and move adults at their own pace and comfort level from learning about asset building to doing something about it. Not everyone will respond to

What Barriers Might Prevent Adults from Getting More Involved with Youth?

1. **Adults think they don't have enough time.**
   Try this: "Name the smallest molecules of what it takes to get involved so adults won't think it takes years," says Nancy Tellett-Royce. "Say hi to the young person bagging your groceries. Make the intermediate steps count."

2. **Adults might not feel comfortable with young people or tend to think of them only in terms of problems.**
   Try this: "Adults have trouble trusting kids because I think a lot of adults forget how it was to be a kid," says Redmond (Washington) police officer Nick Lovell. "A teenager is just a young person learning how to be an adult."

3. **Adults think it's not worth doing unless they can sign up for an important-sounding job.**
   Try this: It's enough to watch for and act on the potential asset-building moments. Remind adults to think of the times in their own childhood when a kind word or a simple gesture from an adult made a difference to *them*.

the same tactics. What one person finds refreshingly direct, another might find pushy. Your job is to listen, watch, ponder, and gather information about the adults you come in contact with. Combine that with your own knowledge to find the optimal ways to invite them to participate meaningfully.

And don't be overconcerned with getting everyone on board right away. In examining how communities respond to long-term innovation in health care and social services, sociologist, teacher, and researcher Everett Rogers has documented that it takes some people longer than others to get on board. There may be a significant time lag between people who get involved early on with a change and those who respond later. Rogers identifies a "diffusion of innovation" curve for how people typically get involved this way:

- **Innovators** (2.5%)—This small group represents those folks who are ready for change. They may seek out change, and they are usually years ahead of others in embracing and trying new ideas.
- **Early adopters** (13.5%)—These people are enthusiastic about new ideas and willing to try something new even if it hasn't been fully tested or implemented.
- **Early majority** (34%)—This group will stay on the sidelines at first, but once it sees that a new idea is working, it'll willingly come on board.
- **Late majority** (34%)—The folks in this group will often be oblivious to the changes occurring around them, and no matter how much you may think you've let them know about it, they will often "discover" the new idea only after three or four years. When they see that it's working and has been adopted by others, they too will accept the idea or innovation.
- **Laggards** (16%)—This group may never come on board and will tend to resist adopting any new way of thinking.

To bring the theory into the everyday world, a creative Portland, Oregon, initiative participant described it in terms of handheld personal organizers: "The innovators bought them when they cost $500; the early adopters tried them out and a number of early majority folks began to buy them when the cost came down; the late majority will finally get them when the software is on version 5.0; and the laggards may not even want a computer at home, let alone a small portable version to carry around."

Because of the varying rates at which people in a community accept change, whether the change is technological innovation or a new framework for how to interact with young people, it is important to remember that change takes time and not everyone will eventually come on board. Rogers suggests that simply having a new idea adopted by the first three groups may take three to four years.

Because asset building marks a significant departure from the societal norm, it may take even longer than Rogers's theory suggests. You may want to hurry, especially since asset building involves the vital work of creating a more sup-

Raising Expectations about Adults' Interactions with Young People

ONE OF THE MAJOR CHALLENGES in mobilizing adults as asset builders with young people outside their own family is that we live in a society that doesn't really expect adults to take responsibility for "other people's kids."

In the *Grading Grown-Ups 2002* national telephone survey (supported by Thrivent Financial for Lutherans), Search Institute found that most adults and youth believe it's important for adults to connect with children and youth outside their family in many positive ways, such as encouraging school success, teaching shared values, and teaching respect for cultural differences. Yet both young people and adults agree that most adults don't do these positive things regularly.

The study also found that some things make a difference. Adults are more likely to be engaged with young people when they experience a strong social expectation to be involved; when they talk with parents and other adults about how to be involved; and when they are involved in their community. Each of these findings suggests strategies for ways communities can more effectively mobilize adults, including:

- Use media, public meetings, and other communication strategies to highlight the importance of adults getting involved, the positive impact they can make, and how it benefits them, too. Have adults who have gotten involved tell their stories.
- Provide easy ways for parents to talk about how other adults can share a little of the fun and responsibility of building assets with their children. Encourage other adults to approach parents.
- Start with people who are already active in the community. Encourage them to get more connected and to influence their friends and neighbors to get involved.

> **LEARN MORE:** For more about social norms in regard to young people, see *Grading Grown-Ups 2002*, as well as the previous 2000 study, *Grading Grown-Ups*, at www.search-institute.org.

portive community for all youth. When things seem to be moving slowly, it can be encouraging to remember the magnitude of the innovation that asset building introduces. It's important, too, to remember that the small things begin making a difference right away, even though large-scale change takes time. For example, getting individual adults to start smiling more at children and youth makes a difference to those young people—and those adults!—and that doesn't take three years.

The next section of this chapter presents tips and ideas for engaging adults. This large ongoing task is discussed in terms of four smaller steps:

- **Building awareness.** Ideas for how to inform and educate adults in your community about asset building.
- **First steps.** Simple actions for people to start building assets.

- **Taking action.** More concrete ideas for engaging adults.
- **Making asset building a way of life.** Deeper, larger ideas for making asset building a continually renewing activity.

Assets in Action

1. Building Awareness: Informing and Educating Adults in Your Community

Starting the conversation that will never stop. To mobilize others for asset building, you must first raise their awareness and help them learn. Many initiatives design and distribute a never-ending flow of brochures, fact sheets, survey results, and other printed materials to repeatedly inform both long-standing and new community residents. Over the life of your initiative, you need to continually invite adults to start their efforts by listening to a conversation about asset building, then thinking about what they can do. The rest of your efforts are spent in helping them do all the creative things they think of!

Many resources are available from Search Institute (see this book's Resources section for examples) or out in your community to help you develop the materials you need. You may want to ask other initiatives to share with you some of the materials they're using. Regardless of the resources you access, keep these general tips in mind when you do get started:

- *Keep things simple.* Skip getting an expensive toll-free phone number and instead put inexpensive printed materials about your initiative—with reply cards and drop boxes—wherever people wait (doctors' offices, car repair shops, hair salons).
- *Think twice.* Teach teachers about assets, but also distribute information through schools to parents. Also look for ways to "seep" asset information into organizations through their newsletters and bulletins.
- *Make it personal.* The more you can have community people talking to each other about their personal involvement with asset building, the more impact you'll have among friends and neighbors.

> LEARN MORE: *Pass It On!* is a relatively low-cost book available from Search Institute that is filled with handouts for you to copy and distribute to everyone from parents and teachers to coaches, clergy, and law enforcement officers. See the Resources listed at the end of this book for details.

Mapping. Mapping is an activity in which you can ask young people to help document community resources that support asset building, and then use the results in ways that are meaningful to them. In the Waupaca Healthy Communities • Healthy Youth initiative in Wisconsin, the mapping project was an eye-opening experience for adults and youth, who had very different pictures of their community. Adults identified area parks, congregations, schools, and the

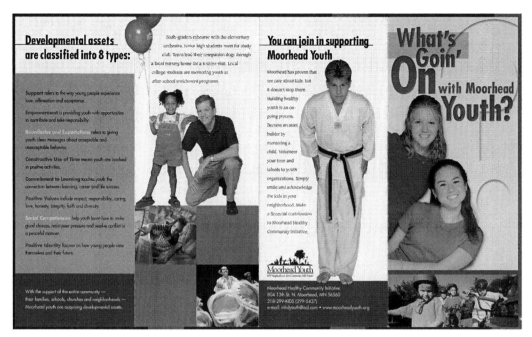

One side of an eight-panel brochure created by the Moorhead Healthy Community Initiative shows an "engaging" resource for engaging adults in asset building.

library as places where people meet. Youth said they gathered at the local truck stop and area parking lots. The results galvanized the community: students are now able to get free help with their math homework from caring adults at the truck stop most evenings, and skateboarders now enjoy their sport at a new skate park located in a city park.

Directories and handbooks. Many communities are inserting asset messages into existing publications or developing productive publishing partnerships with organizations whose mission is compatible with asset building. For example:

- Region A Family Preservation/Family Support in Bryson City, North Carolina, collaborated with Ohio State University's Department of Family and Consumer Services to produce a **calendar** that featured asset-building tips throughout the year.
- It's About Time for Kids in Bellevue, Washington, works with the city's Parks and Recreation Department to publish asset messages in **program catalogs** mailed quarterly to all city residents.
- HC • HY of Ada County in Boise, Idaho, helps publish a youth sports **coach's manual** full of asset tips concurrent with a tip guide for parents of participating athletes.
- The Monroe County Asset Partner Network in Rochester, New York, highlighted a year's successes in asset building in a **community yearbook**, which was distributed to local schools, libraries, and organizations.

One neighborhood at a time. Many initiatives are using different neighborhood strategies such as block parties to engage adults. They not only provide opportunities to educate citizens but also are great ways for adults and youth to have a chance to get acquainted.

The Watertown Healthy Youth Initiative in South Dakota, for example, organized **a series of citywide block parties** that encouraged neighbors and youth to mix and helped increase a sense of safety as well.

Members of the Mason City, Iowa, HC • HY initiative, the Mason City Youth Task Force, are involved in **a multiyear effort to engage adults** from five neighborhoods, five service clubs, five business, and six schools in asset building. Organized groups of youth fan out through the community, asking adults in neighborhoods to get to know the names of children, service clubs to involve youth in community projects, businesses to find ways to support youth, and everyone in schools from teachers to janitors to develop individual relationships with youth. Youth are holding adults accountable by asking them to sign an Our Town Partnership Agreement in which they commit to asset building. "Adults may not know the best way to relate to youth," says Emily Silberstein, a high school member of the Youth Task Force when the partnership effort was launched. "We're teaching them how to build assets with youth because we know firsthand what works, just from living."

2. First Steps: Simple Actions for People to Start Building Assets

Create special events. Waupaca, Wisconsin, has many organizations, foundations, and civic groups that provide opportunities for the whole community, but had no centralized networking event for those organizations to share information. The Waupaca HC • HY held a Community Resource Fair at a local school. Service groups, Scouting organizations, sports representatives, school activity leaders, social, civic, and faith-based agencies, and others set up displays in the gym so that youth and adults could explore opportunities at one location. Middle school students, coached by their teachers to look for new opportunities, visited the fair during the school day. Contact information for all of the participating organizations was gathered into a booklet that was distributed at the fair. The connections made at the fair resulted in new volunteers and members for organizations, families participating in library activities, and the kickoff of a new annual event.

A variation on this event: Mature initiatives can take advantage of the resource fair idea as well. A "Support Moorhead Youth" event was staged to help revitalize the efforts of 11 area congregations that had long been involved in the initiative but had run out of steam. A multicultural open house was announced during services several weeks in advance. Fifteen organizations were involved in a day full of fun and entertainment for the entire community.

What Makes You an Asset Builder?

All kinds of people are asset builders: parents and nonparents, youth workers and neighbors and teachers and bus drivers, adults and young people and elders, those who are outgoing and quiet, wealthy and just getting by, city people and small-town residents and farm families. Although most asset builders don't have all the characteristics listed below, all the strengths you have (or that you develop) will help you as you work at being an asset builder in the lives of young people in your community.

Who You Are or Could Be

- Open and honest.
- An active listener.
- Committed to integrity, responsibility, helping others, and promoting positive change in the world.
- Hopeful and optimistic about young people and the future.
- Self-aware and committed to personal growth.
- Appreciative of others' strengths and uniqueness. Striving to be a caring and supportive friend and colleague.
- Reliable and trustworthy.
- Willing to share your "assets" (time, knowledge, caring, experience, and wisdom) with young people.

What You Do or Could Begin to Do

- Say hello, wave, or ask a simple question to take the initiative in building relationships with youth and younger children.
- Respect and affirm youth and children, seek to understand them, and expect respect in return.
- Believe in and take good care of yourself.
- Attend young people's sports events, poetry readings, concerts, plays, or other performances.

- Look for the good in others and seek common ground with them.
- Engage in healthy relationships with young people, elders, and neighbors.
- If you are a parent, you invite other caring, responsible adults to be part of your children's lives.
- Talk with young people about personal values, beliefs, decision making, and cultural differences.
- Model positive behaviors, including kindness, lifelong learning, voting, and self-restraint.
- Forgive people when they make mistakes, yet hold them accountable. Know how to apologize, explain, negotiate, and resolve conflicts peacefully.
- Encourage young people to succeed in school, serve their community, and be valuable resources, through both your words and your actions.
- Use the asset framework to guide your interactions with young people and to check on your own healthy development.

Adapted from a handout in the *Everyone's an Asset Builder* training in Search Institute's *Essentials of Asset Building*. See the Resources listed at the back of this book for more Search Institute trainings.

Grow new friendships. "My daughter's school has a yearly fund-raiser where they sell annual plants," says Patricia Jones of the Minneapolis Friends (Quaker) meeting. "Lots of other kids in the meeting go to the school and many adults arrange to pick up their plants at the meeting. But one couple in their 80s from the meeting went to the school to pick up their own plants. It made such a nice connection for the kids that these people came to their school.

"People from the meeting are starting to volunteer more at the schools because children from the meeting attend those schools. One man went to a kindergarten to read to kids and teach Spanish. Another woman who does puppets volunteered to do puppet shows at the school. It lets the kids know there are real people who care about them when they show up at their school."

St. Anthony's volunteer "parks and recreation department." "Since we are a small city [in the Twin Cities metro area], we don't have a parks and recreation program," says Amy Sparks of HC • HY ACTION (Adults and Children Together in Our Neighborhoods) in St. Anthony, Minnesota. "We have a volunteer group of students, parents, city council members, school board members, and the school district wellness coordinator that meets to create safe and affordable activities for the youth of the community. One summer, for three days, we laid enormous plastic sheets (100 feet long) down a big hill in the park. The fire department pulled out their hoses to douse the sheets with a flood of ongoing water, making a great water slide. Older students volunteered to keep the younger children safe. The kids knew it was fun. *We* knew they were developing a sense of connection with peers and parents."

> *"The kids knew it was fun. We knew they were developing a sense of connection with peers and parents."*

Neighborhood asset pledges. Youth in the primarily Hispanic San Jose/Quail Valley neighborhood in Georgetown, Texas, planned and organized a march in their neighborhood for National Night Out in conjunction with the police department. Fifteen youth canvassed the neighborhood with materials about the developmental assets and asked people to sign an asset pledge card to place in their window to show support for the children of their community.

Finding more ways to share the news. Cary, North Carolina, city council members set aside a **Youth Matter to Cary Day** to celebrate the talents and achievements of the community's young people. The daylong celebration featured youth theater productions and a jamfest. Stories of outstanding young people were disseminated in the media. These included articles about several young people involved in raising money for breast cancer research (and cutting their hair to donate for wigs), teens working on building a local skate park, and

Cary Teen Council members who received recognition for volunteering almost 2,000 hours in one year.

3. Taking Action: More Concrete Ideas for Engaging Adults

Reconnecting generations. When senior citizens from the Clarkston 50s and Up Club in Michigan were asked to consider how they could help youth feel valued, they came up with a fun, creative way to recognize youth in the community. For years these elders had enjoyed attending the annual high school musical drama production. Now when they attend, they go with a camera in hand. They take and develop pictures from the play, then send them along with notes of encouragement to the students involved. The senior citizens also notice positive stories about youth in the paper and drop kids a note in the mail. Ideas from other communities:

- Students in Orlando, Florida, interviewed elders for the Carver Court **Oral History Report.** The interviews were developed into a book, and a documentary film was made of this experience.
- Mason City, Iowa's HC • HY Initiative sponsors **SAY-IT! (Seniors and Youth Intergenerational Talks)** at which high school students involved in the Youth Task Force high school Action Teams have the opportunity to build relationships with senior citizens in the community. Students from Newman Catholic, Alternative, and Mason City high schools as well as the juvenile detention center take turns having lunch at the Senior Citizen Center one day each month, where discussion focuses on a specific issue. Youth prepared sample conversation-starter tipsheets on topics such as safety and hobbies prior to launching the project.

  This project has yielded some surprising results. First of all, while the tipsheets were initially helpful in making youth feel comfortable and prepared for their visit, once the young people and elders got together, very little structure was needed—people just talk and elders especially look forward to return visits by "their" student. Second, the first high school group scheduled to visit the Senior Center when the project started couldn't make it, so youth from the detention center actually kicked off the project by taking May baskets full of flowers. "We were originally concerned," says Initiative Director Mary Schissel, "but we adults found we were caught up in our own stereotyping. We were suitably humbled by the enthusiasm of the youth and seniors at that first session, and now it's one of our most dynamic groups."
- Adults at the Bethlehem Lutheran Church in Kalispell, Montana, rediscovered how much positive energy is produced when generations come together. The congregation decided to redesign its **rally day for Sunday school** with asset building in mind. Typically this event separated youth from adults in worship. Instead, the church hosted an intergenerational information fair that included organized activities for young people. They sold T-shirts,

The Power of One in Hartford, Kentucky

DORIS INHULSEN with the Together We Care HC • HY initiative in Hartford, Kentucky, knows clothes—she's helped give away almost 3,000 outfits during the past year. As a TWC coalition member and a person who loves kids, she felt that the extreme poverty of some young people in Ohio County affected their self-esteem. She helped conceive the TWC Clothes Closet and a voucher system for families to receive needed clothing. She did this as a volunteer initially and now receives a small salary from United Way to help support her work. She still goes the extra mile, taking donated clothes home to launder for children in need.

had lattes, and held Sunday school sign-up at the same time. "Part of the excitement is having the kids be right there under your feet," says church member Michelle Brown.

Speaking of asset building. Training, supporting, and organizing adults to talk about the assets in different formats—as asset storytellers, presenters, and members of **speakers bureaus**—allows community members to feel ownership and investment in the initiative while cultivating receptivity in others.

Orlando, Florida's Healthy Community Initiative takes this one step further with its **community faculty** who act as peer consultants, helping others develop their asset-building work. "We identify people who are 'connectors' in their neighborhoods," says HCI's Raymond Larsen, "people who have knowledge, skills, and experience. We don't have enough staff to support every community that calls asking for help, but we can send our community faculty members to do some informal consulting to help get that group started. We've even gotten a small grant to pay them."

Working together. Teamwork is the key to asset building in communities like Frisco, Colorado, and Moorhead, Minnesota. In Frisco, teams are organized around specific assets. The local sheriff, for example, works on asset 14, adult role models. In Moorhead, seven asset teams address the many sectors of the community. The "neighborhoods" team works with police to integrate asset building into neighborhood block clubs and the "parenting" team works on introducing assets to parents in small groups.

Mentoring. Mentoring has long been a popular way for adults to interact positively with young people. Variations include:

- In Bellevue, Washington, adult **lunch buddies** meet regularly with elementary school kids to work on reading and just hang out.
- The Winter Park (Florida) Health Foundation's **Sage-ing™ Center** helps prepare older adults for the experience of mentoring, and then assists in placing participants in established mentoring programs.
- Aunts and uncles in Clarkston, Michigan, can participate in an intergenerational **cousins' camp** with nieces and nephews in their families.

- Adults identified by youth in Essex, Vermont, as **natural mentors** were honored for their work with a poster designed by high school students. Many of those identified then went on to form the core group of volunteers in a new mentoring project in that community.
- **College students** in Moorhead, Minnesota, are getting training and community service credit for mentoring high school students.

Invisible mentoring. Bob Tift, former principal and now president of Benilde-St. Margaret's, a Catholic school of more than 1,000 students in grades 7 to 12 in St. Louis Park, Minnesota, runs an "invisible mentoring program" called The Student Support Team. The principal, counselors, deans, and school psychologist identify students who they feel would especially benefit from mentoring; many of these are students with whom the adults already have a working relationship. Faculty and staff interested in mentoring are matched with students—unbeknownst to the students. The adults then form relationships with the students quietly and casually. Over time, with assets in mind, they assertively pursue improving these relationships.

4. Making Asset Building a Way of Life: Deeper Ideas for Helping Adults Adopt Asset Building

Hispanic Task Force. An outgrowth of Healthy Community Initiative's outreach, the Hispanic Task Force was a logical extension of asset building in Winter Park, Florida. Kicked off by initiative member Luz Rivera, also a member of the Mental Health Association, the task force assembled Spanish-speaking leaders and Hispanic youth from the community to learn about assets, established its own leadership committee, and surveyed Hispanic youth throughout the county to help develop strategies to mobilize the Hispanic community for asset building.

Telling everyone's stories. One way Alaska ICE, the Alaska Initiative for Community Engagement, mobilized adults across the state was to publish its own version of a best-selling Search Institute book: *Helping Kids Succeed—Alaskan Style*. Representatives and elders from diverse communities and tribes were asked to bring to special three-day retreats their stories—and the stories of three other people—about significant people in their lives. Each attendee got five minutes to tell her or his story while everyone else listened and wrote down the assets they heard. Three rounds of storytelling were conducted to make sure all the stories were heard, and then everyone split up into small groups. As each group talked about what they heard, the assets and descriptions were put on charts, capturing the essence and traditional voices that were eventually included in the book.

> LEARN MORE: For information on how to order *Helping Kids Succeed—Alaskan Style,* see the Resources listed at the end of this book.

Supporting parents. The Arleta Elementary School in Portland, Oregon, supports parents in a number of ways. There's the Family Room, a **resource room** where parents can come, check out reading materials, use the computer, or share a quiet cup of tea with another adult. Parents created their own **community empowerment team** that works within the school and fans out to share asset information with other folks in the neighborhood in an effort to widen the support network for the school. This group also received a grant to work on small projects including a cleanup campaign developed by Arleta students to make their neighborhood feel like a more caring place. Other ideas:

▶ The Colorado Statewide Parent Coalition sponsors a course called **"Los Padres"** that is taught by dads for dads. Dads learn about asset building, communication and leadership skills, and child development, and then help recruit and train other dads to become peer trainers.

▶ Parents in Ada County, Boise, Idaho, have their own gathering place called **Bridges, a Parent Resource Center.** The center, located in the Children's Home, serves as a central location for parents to take classes and access medical services and information resources. Parents also create their own informal events where parents and young people can talk, eat, and learn together.

The power of one neighborhood. After receiving a federal "Weed and Seed" grant, two longtime residents and developmental asset activists focused on improving living conditions for low-income youth in the Greenwood Mobile Home Park in Moorhead, Minnesota. Joe and Cory Bennett partnered with the parks and recreation department to upgrade equipment and supplies for youth in "forgotten" neighborhoods like Greenwood. Joe, a small business owner, also uses his annual Christmas party to promote asset building, garnering sneakers for the soccer team from his business sponsors and bike helmets for kids in the area. Impressed by such results, the local chief of police, a strong contributor to Moorhead's initiative through his community-policing program, helped secure ongoing funds for positions in the neighborhood when the grant money ended.

Sustaining Your Efforts

Make asset building personal. The more personal you can make the invitation to adults to participate, the more effective you'll be. "I believe the asset message cuts across cultures," says Assets for Colorado Youth education consultant Patsy Roybal. "It doesn't matter what language we speak or our ethnicity. The bottom line is we all want our kids to be successful. When we work with parents, for example, we really take the time to reach out to them over and beyond just sending a flyer. We try to model the assets and build relationships."

Listen, then lead. To get adults in your community interested in asset building, you take steps to introduce them to it. To *keep* them involved, you need to lis-

Supporting and Engaging Parents in Your Community

SOMETIMES COMMUNITY networks get frustrated because they have trouble getting parents involved. Indeed, parents are more often perceived to be part of the problem than part of the solution. Yet the vast majority of parents are working hard to raise healthy, caring, and responsible children and teenagers—often with little support from their communities, friends, neighbors, and extended families.

That is a key message in a recent study of 1,000 parents by Search Institute and YMCA of the USA. Here are five key findings from the study that can set the stage for dialogue and planning for how your community can mobilize, support, and encourage parents as asset builders:

1. A majority of the parents surveyed receive little support from their family, friends, and community in the vital and challenging task of raising children and teenagers.
2. A key—but often lacking—resource for parents is a strong relationship with their spouse or partner.
3. Most parents who were interviewed generally feel successful as parents most of the time. They do many things to help their children grow up strong and healthy.
4. Though most of these parents generally feel successful, they still face obstacles and challenges, such as job demands, sibling rivalries, overscheduling, and the family's financial situation.
5. Simple things they say would really help them as parents include being affirmed for their parenting, having opportunities to talk with other parents, and having other trusted adults spend more time with their children.

How true are these findings for parents in your community? What differences might you see? How can your initiative build on these findings to engage parents (and other adults) as asset builders and leaders?

LEARN MORE: For information on the Building Strong Families study, including ideas for communities and organizations to support parents, visit www.search-institute.org/families.

ten to what they're interested in and then offer a wide variety of simple, doable, inexpensive activities to match their interests. It will be important to monitor people's satisfaction with their asset-building experiences to make sure their expectations are being met so they don't get disillusioned or burned out. Also, keep in mind that not everyone wants to be involved in the same way. Just as it takes many kinds of plants to make a beautiful garden, it takes all kinds of asset builders to make a community, and every act of asset building counts.

Surround asset builders with asset builders. Sometimes participants can get discouraged if they experience negative reactions from others about what they're doing. Employers might complain about the time put into volunteer work; friends might question why all that time is being spent with young people. An asset-building initiative can help with encouragement and by continuing to reach out and gain the support of influencers in the community who will reinforce individuals' commitments.

Go slow. "If you're really excited, you need to do a reality check," says one Chicago organizer. "If you think everyone will jump right on, you'll get disappointed and burned out. Slow and steady—and not giving up—wins the race."

Reflect and learn. An initiative must periodically provide opportunities for participants to reflect on and learn from experiences while also learning new skills. Help people feel successful, share what they've learned, and celebrate their work together. Recognition, awards, gifts, discounts, contests, and other incentives can also help keep people motivated.

"You don't have to tell every adult how to build assets or what to do," says Nancy Tellett-Royce. "It's very powerful to share information about assets and then invite people to do what they choose to do. Your role in engaging adults is to always keep inviting, informing, and circulating ideas."

Ideas on the Change Pathway for Engaging Adults

PATHWAY	TIPS/ADVICE
Receptivity: being open to change	The coordinator of the Central Bucks 40 Assets Project in Doylestown, Pennsylvania, regularly holds asset information meetings on the first Thursday of each month at the public library for people interested in learning more.
Awareness: understanding possibilities	"Raising awareness can never stop," says Nancy Tellett-Royce. "It's at least 50 percent of what an initiative does." Use innovative techniques to reach more adults. For example, Asset Builders of the Summit in Frisco, Colorado, helped the county produce a new human services directory based on assets.
Mobilization: organizing for change	Building on the idea of the "tipping point" (small changes can have a dramatic effect; from Malcolm Gladwell's book of that name), Florida's Healthy Communities Initiative encourages community members to invite ten of their friends to an informal meeting or a meal to learn about assets and how to be asset builders. Meetings can be with friends from the neighborhood, faith communities, or civic clubs.
Action: making change happen	The principal of Our Lady of Perpetual Help, a private middle school in the Lehigh Valley, Bethlehem, Pennsylvania, got asset training from the HC • HY initiative and then met regularly with students to discuss and help implement their priorities such as a revised lunch menu.
Continuity: ensuring change becomes a way of life	After learning about assets from Project Cornerstone, the Mexican American Community Services Agency in Santa Clara County, California, adopted asset building as part of the foundation of two new charter schools.

Engage Adults

- The most basic "unit of change" in your initiative is each individual who lives in your community.

- Use the developmental assets framework in a variety of ways: to provide a common language that helps everyone understand the goals of the initiative, to guide your interactions with young people, and to help organize your efforts.

- Find ways to reduce barriers between adults and youth so they can work together in meaningful ways. Inviting elders to participate in the initiative's work is vital.

- Build assets for and with adults, too, so they can build assets for and with youth.

- Remember that not everyone will get involved right away or want to do the same things.

- Take steps in the beginning to help sustain your efforts to engage adults throughout your initiative, including:

  1. Make asset building personal.
  2. Listen, then lead.
  3. Surround asset builders with asset builders.
  4. Go slow.
  5. Reflect and learn.

- Keep inviting, informing, and circulating ideas.

CHAPTER 4

Mobilize Young People

I see more need for teenagers to get involved at the community level where they can practice leadership skills and help in some of the decisions that are made. I hope students throughout the community can help in the planning that affects our lives. It makes us feel like a part of the community and that our opinions are respected.

SCOTT HOLBROOK, SENIOR,
NAMPA HIGH SCHOOL, NAMPA, IDAHO

THE NORTHWESTERN RURAL VERMONT communities of Essex, Essex Junction, and Westford found it easy to rally support when concerned adults first started a substance abuse prevention coalition back in 1986. Federal dollars flowed into efforts to launch a curriculum in the schools and a teen center. But by the early 1990s, the group's energy had flagged. "There were very few people at the table and there were no kids at all," recalls longtime community activist Betsy Ferries. "The kids who started the teen center had graduated and moved on. Action had stopped."

Adopting the asset model allowed the former prevention coalition to transform itself into the more proactive Essex CHIPS (Community Helping to Inspire People to Succeed). Step one was changing youth involvement from attending adult-run functions to recruiting youth leaders to set and implement the initiative's new agenda. "The biggest mistake for a community initiative to make," says Ferries, who now cochairs CHIPS with high school student Adam Luck, "is to develop a youth initiative without youth. We needed to get students totally engaged on our boards, creating and implementing projects."

When Luck attended his first CHIPS meeting, he knew something was different from other community projects he'd worked on. "You don't always get adults that are so welcoming to youth. Right away, I liked the setting and the things they were trying to do. It was easy to be heard there because the adults seemed really excited to have youth at the table. My first time, anything I said was taken seriously and put under consideration. Youth are there to spark a lot of ideas. The adults spark ideas, too, but they're there mainly to help us get our ideas accomplished."

Young people have tremendous potential as asset builders by engaging in asset-promoting activities and relationships, through nurturing their peers' assets, and by reaching out to younger children to build their assets. Your initiative's role in this area will be to provide young people with the encouragement, skills, and opportunities to be proactive asset builders themselves. At the same time, you'll be facilitating the development of new relationships between youth and adults and assisting adults in learning how to work with young people. When adults *and* youth begin to truly understand the implications of a dynamic new relationship, real change begins.

The broad strategy of mobilizing youth has three main components:

1. **Young people building their own assets.** Young people can take responsibility for building many of their own assets through the choices they make, the relationships they have and build, and the personal values, skills, and qualities they develop.
2. **Young people as asset builders for their peers.** Young people have tremendous potential to be asset builders by engaging in asset-promoting activities and relationships, through nurturing their peers' assets, and by reaching out to younger children to build their assets. This component emphasizes providing young people with the encouragement, skills, and opportunities to proactively build assets themselves.
3. **Young people as active partners in communities and organizations.** Asset-building efforts are greatly strengthened when young people are mobilized to be active partners in the change efforts. Viewing youth as resources means opening up opportunities for them to lead and contribute to all the activities of your initiative.

Keith Pattinson, the regional director of Boys and Girls Clubs of British Columbia, relates a moving story that clearly demonstrates that young people want to be and can be asset builders in all three of these ways:

> During the course of Drug Awareness Week in Kamloops, British Columbia, the local Phoenix Centre and the Boys and Girls Club of Kamloops joined forces to host the first-ever asset-building workshop for grades 6 and 7 students in Canada. The organizers initially expected an attendance of around 40 young people, but were forced to change venues when four local schools registered 330 students for the 1½-hour event.
>
> The workshop was designed to introduce young people to their potential to build assets in the lives of others. During the workshop, participants were asked

to think about what they would do after leaving the workshop to help kids their own age and younger. Each was given a sheet of paper with six blank lines on it to write down her or his ideas. When the young people indicated at the end of five minutes that they needed more time, we allowed another five, thinking the students were having trouble grasping the concept. When they begged for another two minutes, we concluded that our approach was off the mark.

How wrong we were! In the end, 27 boys and girls volunteered to come on stage to read their commitments. Due to time and space limitations, we were compelled to narrow the report-back to those who had compiled 20 or more individual ideas in the allocated 12 minutes; in total, the 330 youngsters documented more than 2,500 ways in which they intended to make a difference. Here is a sampling of the responses:

- I'll go to school and help some people who don't understand questions.
- I'll tie little kids' shoelaces.
- I'll give them a "putup" instead of a putdown.
- I'll stick up for someone younger.
- Even if another person is an adult, I'll try and help.
- I'll help others learn to do what they can do to be asset builders.
- I'll let them borrow something if they need it.
- I'll never say rude comments.
- I'll help those who are crying at school.
- I'll say hi when I pass by.

Those of us who worry about the lack of values, innovation, and sense of responsibility among our future leaders should be heartened.

And those of us involved in or beginning asset-building initiatives can remember that when we want to improve our communities for all young people, we need to have those young people right beside us.

Fulfilling the Vision

"You want to have young people be part of the visioning process at the very beginning," says Search Institute's Nancy Tellett-Royce. "Have them name what it looks like and feels like to them when their community cares about them."

When National Asset-Building Case Study Project researchers analyzed how the four participating initiatives mobilized youth, several key themes emerged. Think about these points as you launch your own efforts:

▶ **Learn to work "with" young people rather than conducting activities "for" them.** The most fundamental shift in *authentically* involving youth in all aspects of asset building is to stop thinking in terms of doing things "for" them and become fully immersed in doing things "with" them. Youth become equal partners in the work, not just recipients of services and activities. As mentioned before, the key is getting young people involved from the beginning. "I think it's important to get youth involved in developing ideas," says 16-year-old Emily Enockson with the High Expectations Initiative of Dodge and Jefferson Counties in Wisconsin. "You need a youth perspective because adults don't understand what will attract kids."

▶ **Create an atmosphere that sparks young people's aspirations.** The initiative can play an important role in supporting young people in their discovery of new things about themselves. "Don't just ask youth to come in, do a task, and then go away," advises Tellett-Royce. "Get them talking about their dreams." Then help them learn how to fulfill their dreams. As you facilitate the development of a knowledge base for young people, you also facilitate their learning about asset building, encouraging them to integrate it into their life's work.

Kristen Bednar, for example, joined the Essex, Vermont, CHIPS Middle School Initiative, a governance group, when she was in grade 6 because it "sounded like fun." Now entering high school, she stayed because she liked the chance to meet and work with so many different people. The experience changed her view of life. "This has really shaped the way I'm going to be the rest of my life," says Bednar. "Now I have lots of people to fall back on, to help me move on. I have lots of dreams."

▶ **Dig deep and incorporate key elements of authentic youth involvement.** Youth involvement in initiatives takes on many forms, from one child participating in a single event to a young person growing up in a leadership position for an entire initiative. Initiatives that have successfully mobilized young people have demonstrated genuineness in their efforts. That genuineness is marked by empowering, listening, valuing, soliciting, and respecting youth's opinions, ideas, feedback, and contributions. Among the most common elements of authentic youth involvement are the following principles:

- *Youth are valued and heard.* Young people know adults genuinely regard them because adults truly listen, their ideas and opinions are actively sought, and they see their suggestions put into action. "Adults take the extra mile," says Ben Hershey, who got involved with the St. Louis Park, Minnesota, Children First Initiative as a teenager. "If you say something, they don't blow you off with a 'but.' They say, 'Maybe this is the way to go' or 'That's what we needed.'"

- *Youth shape the action agenda.* Young people's ideas guide an initiative's overall strategy. Their unique perspective shapes what the initiative does. For example, when youth involved in Portland, Oregon's Take the Time Initiative were asked where they wanted to concentrate their energies, they decided to tackle negative coverage of teens in the local media.

What Barriers Might Come between Young People and Adults Trying to Work Together?

1. **Both adults and youth hold stereotypes about each other.**
   Try this: Stay positive and resolute, sharing positive examples of youth and adults working together.

2. **Adults assume young people have no interest in getting involved in the process.**
   Try this: "Youth want to participate in the governance of their communities," says Hans Bernard. "Sell the benefits of involvement and assign youth to meaningful and needed tasks.

3. **The process appears boring or slow, making it difficult for youth to want to get involved.**
   Try this: Find ways to facilitate interesting and fun youth-adult involvement. St. Louis Park always uses icebreakers at its meetings. Essex CHIPS always takes time for everyone to check in.

Possible solutions drawn from *The Power of an Untapped Resource: Exploring Youth Representation on Your Board or Committee,* by Alaskan youth Hans Bernard.

Among their many accomplishments: The *Oregonian* hired a reporter dedicated to covering a broad range of youth stories and instituted a weekly youth-issues column called "The Zone."

- *Youth build assets for and with each other.* Another aspect of authentic youth involvement is that young people work to build assets for and with each other. Later in this chapter you'll find many creative examples of projects in which young people mentor each other or younger children, thereby spreading the asset message and building assets at the same time. Says Emily Enockson of what she learned from her opportunity during middle school to design and implement a mentoring project at a nearby elementary school, "I've always been a leader, but I always wanted someone to lead *with* me. Having built a successful program has really increased my confidence. I feel like I can do anything." (Read more about the project in the Assets in Action section of this chapter.)

Making It Happen

Engaging youth in an asset-building initiative requires strategic thinking. Adults need to be clear about what they want young people to do. Many initiatives realize it's important to train youth to prepare them to participate and take on

One important aspect of youth and adults working together is also playing together, as this photograph from an Essex, Vermont, CHIPS celebration event illustrates.

leadership roles in the work. What adults sometimes don't realize initially, however, is that it's often more important to train the *adults* so they know how to really listen to and discuss issues with young people.

"Actively engaging youth to work alongside adults requires that adults relinquish control and exercise patience," says Nicole Hintz, Search Institute's senior research assistant on the case study project. "Adults who did this successfully in the initiatives we studied often functioned as mentors who modeled leadership, as well as allowed themselves to be transformed by the energy, optimism, and creativity that the youth contributed to the work."

Of course, when you genuinely partner with young people, the need for patience goes both ways. As Karen Atkinson of Children First in St. Louis Park, Minnesota, points out, "I'm finding the youth mentoring us and young people needing to exercise patience with adults. We have a lot to learn from them!"

Other ideas to keep in mind when you're thinking about strategies for mobilizing young people:

▶ **Don't expect one young person to represent all youth.** "I've been at meetings where the adults wanted the 'youth' point of view," reported Ben Hershey of Children First in St. Louis Park, Minnesota, of other community efforts he'd attended. "Suddenly, all the eyes would look at me." Hershey, then a 17-year-old initiative participant, is now a student at the University of

North Dakota. To avoid the kind of token youth representation he experienced, ask each adult and young person involved in your efforts to recruit one young person to participate.

- **Consider your logistics.** Be strategic about when and where you hold meetings to maximize youth involvement. For example, consider scheduling meetings at schools youth attend and at times compatible with their schedules.
- **Recognize the young people who attend.** "When youth come to a meeting," says Nancy Tellett-Royce, "don't spend time talking about all the youth who aren't there. It's important to value the youth *and* adults who do attend instead of bemoaning the people who didn't."
- **Be relational.** At the beginning of meetings that include young people, "check in" on a personal level. Have each person at the table chat a little about his or her weekend plans, for example. It takes a bit of time, but the check-in helps participants "warm up" and be ready to focus and share ideas.
- **Provide coaching.** Young people may need some pointers on how to be part of a meeting or group, especially if you're asking them to get involved in leadership. Designate coaches to prepare them to shine. And remember that education, training, and coaching of *adults* on working as partners with young people will likely be necessary, too.
- **Keep tasks doable.** Instead of asking youth who attend to "bring more friends," ask each one to bring one more friend. Specific tasks are easier to manage.

Finally, think about ways to make your meetings interesting. "This is important for retaining everybody, not just youth," says Nancy Tellett-Royce. "If a youth doesn't return, you'll assume he or she got bored, but odds are, adults will

The Power of One in Butler, Georgia

SEVENTEEN-YEAR-OLD GERICA McCRARY decided to go against 31 years of tradition in Butler, Georgia, when she suggested that her 2002 junior prom at Taylor County High School be integrated. Even though the community was legally integrated, parents and students had been holding two separate proms—one for whites and one for blacks—for many years. McCrary asked her fellow classmates to "stand for what is right" and vote to hold one prom that year for students of all races. "At first, I was standing alone," said McCrary. "Some thought it was absurd. I wanted unity, diversity, equality. The kids got together. Now, I walk through the halls of the school and people are smiling." Nearly 75% of the school's juniors and seniors supported the proposal.

This story, an Associated Press piece written by Elliott Minor, ran in the Sunday, April 21, 2002, *Seattle Times.*

leave for the same reason. Have food, do icebreakers, break into smaller groups for discussions, get people up and moving."

The next section of this chapter is filled with tips and ideas for engaging youth.

> **LEARN MORE:** For asset-building icebreakers and group activities, take a look at *Get Things Going!, Building Assets Together,* and *More Building Assets Together.* (See the Resources listed at the end of this book.)

Assets in Action

This group of ideas and activities is organized in two segments:

1. *Ways for young people to participate.* A range of activities youth have designed, organized, or participated in. These include creative activities, ways to nurture safe, caring environments, youth-led mentoring, and service-learning opportunities.
2. *Ways for young people to lead.* A range of leadership opportunities involving youth. This section highlights several different models of youth leadership, including youth leaders working side-by-side with adult leaders or on separate youth-led leadership groups.

Ways for Youth to Participate

HAVING FUN BEING CREATIVE

First Night. The Boise City Arts Commission has organized a New Year's celebration for six years, but in 2001, it joined with the HC • HY of Ada County (Idaho) and local youth for the first time to plan and organize the event. Teens worked with local artists to develop a **Garage Party,** held on the second-floor parking lot of Boise's City Hall. More than 1,000 young people attended the safe, drug-free event, which included a dance, games, an interactive arts mural, sumo wrestling, a Battle of the Bands, and a People's Procession—led by Boise's own dancing group, Rhythm Pups and Dogs—in front of City Hall for the New Year's Eve countdown.

Acting out assets. The **Teen Theatre Troupe** associated with the GivEm 40 Coalition in Traverse City, Michigan, uses the developmental assets model to educate teens and adults about the issues critical to teens. The troupe brings to life the difficult choices teens face each day, performing for peer groups as well as fraternal and community organizations around the Traverse Bay area.

A synagogue community. Many congregations are experimenting with creative ways to integrate asset building into their youth activities.

North Shore Synagogue in Syosset, New York, has a large youth program

Tipsheet #7

One Initiative's Experience with Youth Involvement

Paul Vidas was teen program director for the Fox Cities YMCA when the organization received funding from its national office to do a "large event for teens" in 1999. He had been intrigued by asset building in various trainings and decided to infuse developmental assets into the Teen Symposium 2000 he put together. The symposium exposed local youth to the asset model, gave them a chance to go over their *Search Institute Profiles of Student Life: Attitudes and Behaviors* survey results, and put out a call to action. "The symposium was really the spark that started the fire," says Vidas, who was immediately reassigned to head the new initiative that came out of the event. "The fire's still going really well."

United with Youth has built a strong and diverse youth board tightly involved with United Way and responsible for minigrants among its many activities. These practical suggestions drawn from Vidas's experience will help any initiative effectively mobilize young people:

1. **Share a vision.** Vidas suggests jump-starting your efforts by getting all existing youth groups and youth-serving organizations together to share ideas and strategies. "They already have youth involved. You're asking them to help you create more opportunities for other youth."

2. **Get things done.** Just like many adults, youth won't join or stick around if nothing's happening. "You work for your youth. Do your best to see what's feasible when they make suggestions and then make it happen."

3. **Stop and say "wow."** Set some short-term milestones that aren't too far into the future, then take a moment to celebrate as you reach them. This keeps everyone motivated.

4. **Empower others.** "Our mission is to 'enhance other people's efforts,' not run programs. We initiate so that others will take over the job for the long haul."

5. **See youth as experts.** "I don't know what's cool, but they do. If you want to appeal to any given group of young people, you have to ask them what they want."

6. **Keep expanding opportunities.** "Start with the young people you've got and make it a part of their job to increase opportunities for others. If you do that, you'll always have youth involved." Vidas also advises making sure that your initiative has many different things for young people to do, so that the youth who normally try to do it all, can't. That ensures that there is plenty of room for others to get involved.

Finally, Vidas shares an example of how he talks to potential funders about the worth of asset building: "Ask this question: 'How much do we spend on football games to get youth to compete?' Then ask, 'What do we do to teach young people how to cooperate? What will really make a difference in young people's lives in 10 years?' I say, 'Give me the budget for one football game and see what I could do!' "

that serves close to 400 young people in a congregation of 900 families. As a result, a lot of Youth Director Jeff Green's job is keeping track of schedules, going to meetings, and dealing with paperwork.

But even with the large size, the synagogue seeks to be a warm, close community for young people. "We want everyone to be part of the community and to feel comfortable in this environment," he says. All the activities and opportunities are designed for young people to "learn from one another and grow with one another."

A lot of the youth-to-youth relationships are formed in the congregation's youth lounge, which is designed with relationship building in mind. For example, all the games in the lounge are for at least two people to play together. And the youth group programming is planned and led by young people.

Green summarizes: "We are a community at the synagogue. We want to teach these kids where they can belong in the overall community."

Skate parks. Youth in Nampa, Idaho, who attended a "Youth and Adults: Unity in the Community" conference developed an action plan to build their own skate park. Over the next few months, they talked to city officials, then researched and suggested a design, worked with adults to help solve design issues, developed use guidelines, and secured a location. Adults rallied to the cause by donating land and funds. "This was the first student-led initiative of its kind in the city and the first one to cross generations in a mutual effort to address youth issues of concern in a tangible way," says Healthy Nampa, Healthy Youth initiative participant Lynn Borud, who helped coordinate the skate park meetings. "It demonstrated to youth that adults do listen when young people speak."

CREATING MORE SAFE, CARING ENVIRONMENTS

Getting Handz-On. Teens at Winter Park High School in Florida decided to reestablish a more inviting atmosphere at their school by creating murals in hallways and adopting and painting bathrooms. Young people involved in Handz-On say they're committed to getting things done. "I love working on Handz-On," says high school student Sean Smith, "because it not only helps the school and community, it's fun."

Helping spread the message. When students and parents from Abraham Lincoln High School's bilingual Parent Advisory Committee in Denver, Colorado, attended an asset training, students got fired up about wanting to help spread the message. They worked with bilingual teacher Martha Montijo to **recruit other students and secure a youth role** in an upcoming asset presentation for Lincoln and two of its "feeder" schools. The eight Lincoln students were the highlight of a Saturday morning parent event that drew 100 participants. They passed out **flyers** listing the names of Spanish-speaking staff who help parents and helped draft a pledge that parents were encouraged to sign.

One team at a time. High school athletes took the lead in telling players, parents, and coaches about asset building in Naperville, Illinois. The folks with the Kids ROCK (Reaching Our Community's Kids) HC • HY initiative created 3-x-5 **cards with reminders** about what it takes to be an asset builder in sports. Each card had five bullet points and a short message about asset building on the front plus the local initiative's information on the back. Separate sets were created for coaches, parents, and players.

High school athletes then attended Little League games all over town at the

Asset Parent Pledge from Abraham Lincoln High School, Denver, Colorado

STUDENTS ASKED PARENTS TO COMMIT TO:

1. Talking to high school staff every two weeks about their child's progress.
2. Talking to their child daily about the child's interests, dreams, and goals.
3. Attending school functions that their child is interested in or participating in.
4. Getting to know their child's friends and helping their child to build positive relationships.

beginning of the season (no small feat in a big town) and gave a two-minute speech. It took some effort to recruit and coordinate all the speakers, but the cards were inexpensive, and the project was extremely well received.

Places to hang out. Many initiatives are working with youth to develop and run teen centers, which allows many other segments of the community to get involved, too. The Ohio County Sheriff's Department Office Band sponsors and plays at Youth Talent Nights at **the Blender** in Hartford, Kentucky. In Essex, Vermont, high school and middle school **governance teams** run the local teen center, planning fun and fund-raising activities that involve youth and the community.

The Wadena, Minnesota, County Youth Asset Program found an opportunity to build assets while renovating its youth-oriented activities and technology center, **the Cyber Café.** Twenty Native American youth, ages 18–24, from the Tribal Civilian Community Corps volunteered to help on a remodeling project. New friendships were created. When one of the TCCC volunteers commented that he wanted to attend college in the future but wasn't sure how to begin, a local teen who had finished one year of college helped him navigate the system to take his college entrance test and get started on gathering college applications.

Learning together. The Vibe Youth Ministry in St. Paul, Minnesota, puts assets into action through **a camping program for urban youth** that builds relationships, teaches social justice, and provides young people with an opportunity to explore their spirituality. The camp is structured around family groups, with elders and youth from twelve different urban congregations participating in experiential learning activities. To avoid cliques, the groups start by going through a series of trust-building exercises so that adults and youth get to know new people right away.

"Igniting relationships and communications was the key for working through all aspects of the social justice piece," says Vibe's John Holt. Activities include learning exercises and discussions about hunger, racism, prejudice, and religious persecution. "The social justice emphasis gives the campers a place to begin discussion about faith and difficult questions," says Holt. "When we focused on social justice, we had a clear identity and more relationships built, especially among youth who wouldn't have otherwise connected."

YOUTH-LED MENTORING

Screaming Eagles. Students who have special needs at Ohio County High School in Hartford, Kentucky, wanted more of a chance to practice their academic and communications skills, so they formed the Screaming Eagles Academic Team. Sponsored in part by the Together We Care Initiative, this creative community service project brings 20–30 team members into local elementary schools where they get to read to and mentor younger children. One of the Eagles' favorite projects is its monthly date to read to students ages 5–8 at the local McDonald's Playspace in the restaurant's Reading Buddies program. These collaborations emphasize reading for pleasure and also give the Eagles team members a chance to be leaders and mentor others. "I love reading to the little kids," says Roger Stewart, an ardent team member who has cerebral palsy, "and they really seem to like it, too!"

Silent Asset Mentoring (SAM). In the HC • HY Initiative in Mason City, Iowa, middle and high school students picked teachers and staff to support, rather than the more common silent mentoring in which adults pick students to mentor. About 100 students met monthly to create small themed craft projects with messages for their secret staff pals. The school year ended with a party at which youth revealed their identities to their pals, although some adults had guessed along the way. "This really opened a door and created more communication between students and teachers," says 17-year-old Jessica Higgins from Newman Catholic High School. "Students learned that a lot of teachers really are there to teach. Teachers learned that lots of students really do care about them."

That was important to other staff members, too. "I was going through a rough time in my life while Jessica was leaving Hershey's kisses and notes on my desk," says Newman staff member Carolyn Hill. "What she did was just like a ray of sunshine. It meant a lot to me."

The InterNAT Project. The Intergenerational Network of Adults and Teens is a creative collaboration of the Healthy Communities Initiative in South Bend, Indiana. During eight-week-long courses taught at local community centers, youth teach elders how to navigate around a computer and use the Internet. In return, youth learn valuable life lessons from their senior partners. The course begins with sensitivity training for the young people, who put on gloves and goggles to help them understand the kind of visual problems and agility difficulties experienced by many elderly people, but quickly graduates to weekly topical themes and practical lessons on how to use computers for research.

"We advertise this as a computer class," says initiative Director Marilyn Eber, "but our emphasis is on building relationships. At one mixer, when everyone did introductions, one young man said, 'I'm from Adams High School.' The woman sitting next to him said, 'I graduated from Adams 50 years ago.' They started talking immediately and a nice bond was formed."

Feed Your Brain. Feed Your Brain was dreamed up by four middle school students in Watertown, Wisconsin, who were searching for a community service project. It's now cosponsored by the High Expectations Initiative in Dodge and Jefferson Counties. "We knew teachers had tried an after-school homework program at Schurz Elementary, but it didn't work," says Emily Enockson, now 16, one of the Riverside Middle School grade 8 students who designed the project. "It was set up too much like detention. The adults ran it and it was very boring."

Emily and her partners infused asset building into their new design for the homework club, making it more kid-friendly by using youth as mentors and offering games and nutritious snacks. Teachers report that some students' grades went up, as well as other meaningful results. "One little boy wouldn't start his homework until I got there," says 18-year-old Kyle Pfister. "His eyes would brighten. He had something to look forward to every afternoon, and I had the opportunity to touch someone's life."

TAKING UP THE CHALLENGE OF SERVICE

Youth making a critical difference. Coordinators with the Fairborn Cares Project in Fairborn, Ohio, eagerly launched their Summer Lunch and Enrichment Program. The initiative chose a neighborhood that was on the edge of town with a lot of low-income families, but after a week of very low attendance, coordinators were ready to cancel the program. Two teenage babysitters found out about the program and saved the day. The two girls joined with another family to invite neighbors to daily activities, which included lunch, sports, reading, and projects with volunteers from the police and fire department and local 4-H. By the end of the summer, 90 children and youth were involved. Initiative coordinators found that lunch was the reason for starting the program and why many children and youth came, but the relationships that developed between adults and young people were the reason children kept coming.

A "kool" place. Partners for Ottawa County Youth (POCY) helped middle school students in Commerce, Oklahoma, form Klub Kool—a safe place for students to go to interact with adults and experience a caring environment. Kids meet once a week and work on projects like antitobacco campaigns and putting on a monthly Family Movie Night for the community. With Klub Kool in place, the local police reported fewer vandalism calls than the previous year. The initiative is supporting Klub Kool launches in other communities and is working with Native American community members interested in the concept as well.

Teen Service Database. Maintained by United with Youth (UWY) in Fox Cities, Wisconsin, the Teen Service Database is a way to help youth find volunteer opportunities in the community. The original database was formed from UWY's first Teen Symposium. Four hundred young people filled out Call to Action forms, sharing information about what kinds of activities they'd like to be involved in, what organizations they're connected to, and what special skills they have. The local Volunteer Center staff members maintain the database. As service opportunities come up, the center notifies individual youth and sends emails to tell groups about special events. Youth can tap into the database for information about volunteering, scholarship and award programs, rallies, and lobbying efforts. The initiative can also use the database to poll youth on their current priorities or opinions about current community issues. The initiative is working with volunteers from another youth-focused initiative, America's Promise, to update the database and has a goal of involving 4,000 Fox Cities youth.

Teen service challenge. Each spring, students from the Boise, Meridian, and Kuna school districts and from various county youth organizations in Idaho compete for the most volunteer service hours. Before beginning the challenge, teams identify a service project that they wish to complete with their sponsoring school or organization. Individual and team "prizes" are awarded for completing the most service hours during the month. Team prizes go to fund service projects identified by the winning teams. The ultimate goal is to creatively engage people in service and perpetuate the cycle of service with the incentives that lead to more service. In 2002, nearly 1,000 participants served a total of 5,816 hours.

Ways for Youth to Lead

Young people can exercise leadership in an initiative in many ways (running committees, supervising specific activities, serving on boards). Various models show how to facilitate that level of involvement. All the models require commitment from youth and adults to make them work.

Essex CHIPS: side by side. Essex CHIPS recruits youth to cochair its coalition and all subcommittees in partnership with adults. Teens make up the majority of the coalition's membership, which gives them many opportunities to shape and implement all of the initiative's activities. Middle and high school governance teams not only run the Essex Teen Center but also interview, hire, and participate in the performance evaluations for the center's director, assistant director, and coordinators for specific programs such as Community Tobacco Prevention. Youth also are active in the development of all funding activities, including grant writing.

One example of how youth input customized what might have remained a fairly traditional project is the Connections Mentoring Project. Initially, a group of high school students were invited to come together to select a mentoring program. After reviewing the available models, the young people decided to dream up their own model program, which would be based on youth interest first, rather than the more typical way of adults matching their preferences to youth. Young people wanted to learn a variety of things, from how to fish or snowboard to how to put a stereo in their car. The design group kicked off its efforts by asking students to identify adults who had already had a significant impact in their lives and featuring those adults on a poster to publicize the new mentoring project.

One key to Essex CHIPS ongoing youth involvement is constant recruitment at the middle school level. Says CHIPS cochair Betsy Ferries, "You need to get students totally engaged on governance boards, creating and implementing the projects, but you also have to constantly pull them in from the middle schools to keep feeding into the high schools. That way you have the student power and they know what they want." "I was pretty nervous at my first meeting because I didn't know anyone," says high school student Kristin Bednar, recruited to the governance board in 6th grade. "But it was easy to catch on. The 7th- and 8th-grade students showed me how things should go. I liked how it was pretty out in the open. Everyone was an individual and you could say what you really thought. With everyone working together, we got a lot done."

> *"Everyone was an individual and you could say what you really thought. With everyone working together, we got a lot done."*

Hampton Mobilization for Youth: parallel process. The Hampton Mobilization for Youth Initiative in Virginia has been experimenting with ways to more deeply incorporate a true youth voice into every system in its community. Youth serve on city entities such as the arts commissions, school climate evaluation team, and the Parks and Recreation Advisory Board. There is a youth advisory group for the superintendent of schools as well as a group called Youth Environmental Action of Hampton (YEAH), which advises the Environmental Relations office of the city's Department of Public Works. Two high

Tipsheet #8
Leading Successful Meetings with Young People and Adults

Part of "walking the assets talk" is having both youth and adults participate in leadership and decision making. But how do you make sure this is a good experience for everyone involved?

Getting Started

- Be creative and sensitive about meeting times and places. For example, if evening meeting times interfere with teenagers' after-school jobs and Saturday times are bad for Jewish youth, meet on a weekday at lunchtime in the school cafeteria. Identify group members who can offer rides to others who need them.

- Understand the needs of youth participants. If they come to a meeting straight from school, you might need to serve snacks. Most youth don't carry calendars with them, so you might need to make reminder phone calls a day or two before each meeting. (If you don't know the young people's needs, ask them. Then ask again after you've had a meeting or two.)

- Include at least two young people. Avoid the temptation of thinking that one young person can represent all young people.

Communication and Language Issues

- Talk openly about language issues. Will you go by first names? Is the term "kids" offensive to some participants? What about statements like "You're too young to understand" or "you're too old to understand"?

- Become aware of and confront adult bias. Watch for unconscious stereotyping of young people by age, by appearance or clothing style, by gender, race, or economic status.

- Give each participant—youth and adult—a chance to talk, and give each speaker your full attention.

- Be intentional about taking young people seriously and be ready to redirect the conversation if adult participants talk too much, interrupt or ignore young people, or are critical or scolding.

- If young people are hesitant to speak up or tend to respond "I don't know" to questions you're sure they have an answer for, help them identify the reasons for their reticence (e.g., fear of put-downs, difficulty telling when people are done talking). Be encouraging when young people do speak up.

Training, Support, and Process

- Make sure to bring new people—young people and adults—up to speed. Review the group's goals and provide pre-meeting training for newcomers about basics such as meeting structures, discussion ground rules, and agendas and reports.

- Be aware of the developmental needs of young people and accommodate the preferred learning styles of all group members. This may mean adding more experiential meeting elements, augmenting written and verbal communication with

cont.

visual aids, and breaking into small groups.

- Start off with a game or other fun activity that helps all participants with the transition from other activities to the meeting.
- Plan concrete projects, give youth responsibilities early, and expect achievement. Let young people learn from their own mistakes, too.
- Be clear about each participant's role and level of authority, the time and number of meetings, and the expected duration of the commitment.
- Have youth and adults periodically evaluate the role of young people (e.g., are young people being given only insignificant or peripheral tasks?).

From *Assets* magazine, autumn 1997, copyright © Search Institute, Minneapolis, MN; 800-888-7828; www.search-institute.org.

school students hold paid positions in the planning department as youth planners.

Hampton has tackled the intricacies of a "parallel process" for youth involvement and leadership, in which youth and adults first address a problem among their peers rather than in mixed-age groups. Initiative participants liken the model to an accordion—work gets done by the two sides separately, but the hands come back together to keep the music going. The Hampton Youth Commission, which oversees the city's comprehensive plan and distributes funds for youth development projects, uses this model. The model fits the developmental needs of both youth and adults. Young people find youth-only meetings meaningful, fun, and interesting. Adults can work in their own modes.

This process worked successfully early in Hampton's strategic planning efforts. Youth and adult groups brainstormed separately, then prioritized the needs of the city. Some interesting differences in priorities resulted. For example, though the racial mix of the adult and youth groups was similar, youth ranked race relations a top priority, while the adults didn't even list the issue. Youth input was quickly recognized and incorporated into the final plan.

"This accordion-style process of going into one's own world and then returning for dialogue is both educational and affirming for youth and adults," says initiative coordinator Cindy Carlson. "It also helps break down stereotypes and communication barriers. When we've used it, it results in richer dialogue and a better product."

Carlson cautions, however, that the process can be very staff intensive. "On the youth side, it requires a skilled adult facilitator, well versed in youth development theory, who can help a diverse group of youth stay engaged, reach consensus, and develop skills to communicate in the adult world."

Other initiative ideas for implementing youth leadership. Here's a sampling of how other initiatives are experimenting creatively and successfully with youth leadership:

- **The Summit High School Diversity Club** in Frisco, Colorado, has two of its members on the Asset Builders of the Summit HC • HY Initiative steering committee. Youth also serve as the Action Team leadership for the initiative's work on asset 34, cultural competence. Summit Middle School youth also serve as an advisory board for the initiative and design and implement asset projects.

- Greater Orlando's Healthy Community Initiative established the **Legacy Venture Team** in which youth are trained in all aspects of philanthropy, including reviewing grant applications for asset-building projects and awarding funds. Different teams award funds focused on a specific area. For example, the Jewish Community Center Team's focus is diversity, the Boone High School Team's is sustainability, and the Winter Park High Team focused on using all 40 assets. The Youth Philanthropy Team awarded $75,000 one year to youth initiatives supporting developmental assets.

- Iowa's Mason City High School, Newman Catholic High School, Mason City Alternative High School, and Mason City middle schools all have **youth action teams** that are responsible for a variety of service programs, including Government Day, Truth Squads (groups available for public speaking about youth issues), Holiday Helpers, and the SAY-IT! Intergenerational Dialogues. In addition, representatives from each of the school's action teams serve on the local initiative's planning council, the Mason City Youth Task Force. Youth Task Force members, in turn, serve on the Executive Committee with adults.

In 2001, 1,200 Youth in Action members contributed an astounding 12,000 hours of community service!

- Ohio County's Together We Care Initiative in Hartford, Kentucky, has a **Youth Ambassador Council** (YAC) that involves middle and high school students in decision making, public relations, and program design. They meet separately from the initiative's board of directors to accommodate school schedules, but the two groups work on the same issues. Youth have developed a process to recognize asset-building efforts conducted by faith groups, businesses, and individuals. YAC, along with other youth, has a media team that produces public service announcements, skits, and other asset messages. YAC also manages the local teen center, the Blender, and helps coordinate activities with the youth volunteer service group called Youth in Action. In 2001, 1,200 Youth in Action members contributed an astounding 12,000 hours of community service!

- United with Youth in Fox Cities of Wisconsin, has 35 students on its **Youth Board** representing a dozen different high schools and a broad spectrum of ethnic and cultural diversity. In addition to advising the initiative, this group developed its own vision and set of priorities, including the distribution of $3,000–$6,000 in youth-oriented minigrants every year. Two Youth Board members are also voting members of the Fox Cities United Way Board.

- At Children First in St. Louis Park, Minnesota, the initiative's **Vision Team** (approximately 40 people) now has more students at meetings than adults. A great deal of the credit goes to cochair Luke Johnson, a high school sophomore. Initiative coordinator Karen Atkinson reports one result of this high level of youth involvement: "When our city manager left the last meeting, he was amazed and heartened. He has been involved with Children First from the beginning and loves the energy that a throng of young people brings. He said that now, when we ask for volunteers, *many* hands go up."

- Bellevue, Washington, takes a lead role in the community's It's About Time for Kids' Initiative by working to infuse youth voices into all the city's activities. A prime venue is the city's **Youth Link Involvement Conference.** Bellevue Youth Link is a youth empowerment program cosponsored by the city of Bellevue and Bellevue Public Schools for teens from middle and high school. Every two years, members of the Bellevue Youth Council work side by side with adult staff to plan a daylong, all-city Youth Involvement Conference at which teens identify and prioritize their prime issues and concerns. More than 300 young people from 14 schools attended the city's most recent conference, and the school district sanctions the event by giving participants an excused absence for the day. Youth can take workshops on topics such as legal rights, new laws of interest to teens, and how to develop leadership skills or find a job. A sign of the event's importance is the presence of city officials as well as members of Washington's congressional delegation, who meet in afternoon workshops with young people. Youth plan, run, and evaluate the conference.

  Recommendations for youth priorities that come out of the conference are forwarded to the city council for action. A Youth Link Board of six youth and six adults appointed by the city manager allocates funds for youth projects and programs that come out of the conference action slate. Previous conferences have resulted in the development of a teen center, a late-night Safe Rides program, and Teen Job Ready project. You can find out more at www.youthlink.com.

- Examples of two different ways initiatives are working to infuse youth more broadly into community leadership include HC • HY of Ada County (Idaho) and Essex CHIPS (Vermont). Ada County HC • HY is working with community groups to get **youth on every board and commission**. The city of Boise has already added young people to all of its boards and commissions. The Essex CHIPS Youth Initiative Committee succeeded in having **legislation** introduced in Vermont that would enable students under 18 to become voting members of school boards. While they continue pushing for passage of that law, youth are using the bill as leverage for getting young people involved with school board committees in nonvoting capacities.

Sustaining Your Efforts

Think "different." Building an asset initiative that is truly engaged in working with youth and not doing things "for" them requires that adults make significant attitudinal shifts. From examining personal biases to restructuring how groups work together, "walking the talk" of authentic youth engagement requires that adults relinquish some of their control and power.

Take risks. True partnership with young people is different—and more difficult—than just providing services and activities for them. Partnership involves allowing youth to participate in decision making and countering the prevailing beliefs that they are disinterested, irresponsible, and socially unaware.

Model and coach. Initiatives that mentor youth in leadership roles find that young people are highly motivated to serve their communities and to contribute their ideas and energy when they feel it is genuinely invited. Adults who really open up to working with youth find that young people rise to higher expectations and trust and *want* to work more closely with adults. "I've always had a good connection with adults," says Mason City, Iowa, Youth Task Force member Jessica Higgins, "but by being on the Youth Task Force, I got to be more open to more adults and them to me. Sometimes there's a bar between the two. They're the brains and the youth usually do the work, but without the connection between the two, without understanding, you've got nothing."

Be prepared to be surprised. "When my niece turned 11," says Nancy Tellett-Royce, "I invited her to join me in my volunteer work with the Children First initiative in St. Louis Park, a suburb of Minneapolis. Her first question was, 'May I bring my three friends?' Now we call them the Fabulous Four. They come prepared. They've really changed people's minds about the age at which young people can contribute. The high school students in the group also connect with them, which thrills my niece and her friends. It reminds me that fostering generational diversity among young people is important, too.

"Don't underestimate young people," concludes Tellett-Royce. "And don't stop recruiting."

> LEARN MORE: To help your initiative mobilize young people, Search Institute offers a variety of youth-oriented trainings. See the Resources listed at the back of this book for details on many of the trainings currently offered. Also in that section are resources from initiatives in Alaska and Iowa for involving youth.

Ideas on the Change Pathway
for Mobilizing Young People

PATHWAY	TIPS/ADVICE
Receptivity: being open to change	To get youth involved, be specific. "If someone had just asked me to get involved in asset building," says Jessica Higgins of her decision to become a Silent Asset Mentor in Mason City, Iowa, "it wouldn't have gotten my attention. Being asked to work on a project where I would get to know a teacher better was much more appealing."
Awareness: understanding possibilities	"When you first invite youth to be involved," says GivEm 40's T. J. Berden in Michigan, "bring them up to date on everything that's going on. Help them get familiar with things and put it all into context so they don't feel thrown in."
Mobilization: organizing for change	Challenge and rethink assumptions. In *The Power of an Untapped Resource: Exploring Youth Representation on Your Board or Committee*, Alaska youth school board representative Hans Bernard suggests that adults learn to be flexible about meeting times to accommodate school schedules, slow down while new youth members are learning the ropes, and make some adjustments like paying young people's expenses for attending meetings and providing snacks.
Action: making change happen	Don't ask a question unless you're prepared to deal with the answers. "Young people are action oriented," says Annie Nelson, executive director for the Minneapolis Youth Coordinating Board. "If you ask a question, they expect you to follow through."
Continuity: ensuring change becomes a way of life	Build relationships. "Everything we've been able to accomplish is because of youth and adults working together," says Essex CHIPS cochair Adam Luck. "We can't do anything without the other." Involving young people as early as middle school allows for a continuous stream of young people involved in the initiative as some young people graduate from high school or move out of the area.

Mobilize Young People

- The broad strategy of mobilizing young people has three main components:
  1. Young people building their own assets;
  2. Young people as asset builders for their peers; and
  3. Young people as active partners in communities and organizations.

- Bring young people into the earliest visioning stages of your work.

- Learn to work "with" youth rather than conducting activities "for" them.

- Create an atmosphere that sparks young people's aspirations.

- Dig deep and incorporate key elements of authentic youth involvement so that young people feel valued and heard, participate fully in shaping the initiative's agenda, and build assets for and with each other.

- Don't expect one young person to represent all youth.

- Consider the logistics of how you work and make changes that make it easier for youth to participate.

- Recognize the youth who show up.

- Provide coaching so that youth can shine.

- Keep tasks doable.

- Don't be afraid to change your thinking and expectations about young people.

- Be open to seeing young people rise to higher expectations and trust.

- Take risks.

- Develop relationships.

- Be prepared to be surprised.

- Don't stop recruiting.

CHAPTER 5

Activate Sectors
and Invigorate Programs

My experience ever since Project Cornerstone reached out to me and got me involved has given me tremendous growth in the way I and others have gotten to serve the community. My peer-counseling group has been inspired to take the initiative in their fellow brothers and sisters' lives. Assets give youth powerful opportunities. The possibilities are endless.

NAM NGUYEN, YOUTH COCHAIR, STEERING COMMITTEE,
PROJECT CORNERSTONE, SAN JOSE, CALIFORNIA

THE HEADLINES IN 1994 in Moorhead, Minnesota, had begun to take an alarming turn—juvenile crime was going up. More children 10 and younger were committing larceny and vandalism. Among the increasing number of burglaries, auto thefts, and assaults, there was one rape and one murder. A small group of community leaders, including parents, law enforcement, and school representatives, decided to ask more questions about what was going on and see what answers would emerge.

"When people first came together to talk, the solutions went down traditional routes," says Moorhead Healthy Community Initiative (MHCI) Executive Director Barry Nelson of their initiative's history. "They were discussing how to stop the trend in terms of consequences and punishment until somebody said, 'Is there another way we can look at this?'"

The superintendent of schools had heard about Search Institute's work and a connection was made. An early partnership of citizens, law enforcement, city officials, social services, health care, and local colleges came together to help mobilize the community. Students took the *Search Institute Profiles of Student Life: Attitudes and Behaviors* survey in 1994, leading Moorhead to become the second asset-building initiative in the United States.

Diverse groups of volunteers used the survey to help set priorities for established Asset Teams to focus on different tasks. The After-School Hours Asset Team, for example, focused on the needs of young people in grades 4–8, asking students what activities they wanted, then developing a plan to implement "Moorhead Youth's Top 20 Activity Choices."

The Moorhead initiative has been successful at developing youth-serving resources, launching programs where none existed, and assuring access to those resources for all youth—particularly youth of color. Their list of achievements—including awarding Youth of Color Scholarships, establishing a Raices de Mexico After-School Enrichment program, an American Indian Youth Leadership Camp, and the Quinceanera Club for preteen and teenage girls—reflects their commitment to diversity.

As a new director coming into the leadership of the eight-year-old MHCI, Barry Nelson says it's apparent to him in talking with people that the depth and breadth of partnerships are what make the initiative work. "Early on, people caught a vision. The charter members were highly visible, legitimate leaders of the community, but they weren't there just for their names, but to actually get things working. Now whenever I go to a meeting and youth issues come up, someone will always say, 'Has anybody talked to MHCI?' The initiative has credibility and legitimacy."

All organizations and sectors in a community—including schools, congregations, neighborhoods, youth organizations, social service agencies, health-care providers, employers, and more—have potential for asset building.

The third and fourth strategies for developing a community asset-building initiative are related: to activate sectors by mobilizing, equipping, and supporting organizations, institutions, and individuals to become stronger resources and allies for asset building, and to invigorate the programs of those organizations and institutions, making them accessible asset-building resources for all community young people.

All organizations and sectors in a community—including schools, congregations, neighborhoods, youth organizations, social service agencies, health-care providers, employers, and more—have potential for asset building. The activation of many sectors, in fact, is crucial to realizing the larger vision of an asset-building community. Networks of people acting as ambassadors for assets provide the encouragement, information, language, and resources organizations need to shift their culture, programs, and practices.

Involving organizations doesn't mean they *have* to collaborate on programming or even be part of the community-wide planning, though they may want to be. Rather, you're calling on them to:

- Play up their own strengths;
- Develop asset-building strategies within their own arenas of work;

- Add their own improvements to the vision; and
- Take a lead role where and when it's appropriate.

Your role is to find ways to inspire and assist organizations to infuse asset building into their culture, programs, and practices. You'll want to employ techniques that will prompt and sustain action, like informal networking and team building. You want to connect the initiative with allies not only in different sectors but also within and across sectors to build and strengthen your community's entire network. Many communities have found it important—as Moorhead has—to start or run programs needed to fill gaps in supports for youth.

Initiative participants have used various ways to infuse asset-building practices into programs, organizations, and sectors, including:

- **Showing organizations and sectors how to enhance the asset-building potential of existing programs.** The YMCA of Westfield, New Jersey, recognizing the value of increasing the time young people spend with caring adults, set an asset-building goal that two-thirds of all new activities would be intergenerational. And Jorge Perez, executive director for the Urban Mission YMCA in Indianapolis, uses the asset framework to assess every decision he makes. He writes grants using the asset language and framework and revamps programs when they build only a few assets so that they build even more.

- **Inspiring organizations and sectors to mobilize their own internal asset-building capacities.** The Teen Volunteer Corps coordinator for the Carmel Clay Public Library in Indiana builds asset by providing volunteer activities for more than 100 teens. And in New Richmond, Wisconsin, high school students assemble cardboard building blocks labeled with the eight asset categories. These blocks and a handout on assets become part of a gift pack given to all new parents at the local hospital.

- **Helping organizations and sectors to create family-friendly policies, systems, and structures.** Bunn-O-Matic, a coffeemaker assembly plant in Union County, Iowa, that is committed to the local Youth Plus initiative, has embraced the developmental assets model and used it to change the culture of its plant environment. For example, the company lets its employees slice up four vacation days into convenient, family-friendly chunks of time off to attend school or sporting events.

- **Creating networks among organizations in the community.** Fox Cities, Wisconsin's United With Youth initiative cochairs a special project called Operation MENTOR, a coalition of agencies specializing in mentoring. The group meets regularly to brainstorm ideas for promoting everyone's mentoring projects.

The rest of this chapter will give you more ideas from initiatives about creative and inspiring ways they're finding to infuse asset building into community sectors, including education, business, youth-serving organizations, and juvenile justice.

Fulfilling the Vision

When the researchers on the National Asset-Building Case Study Project analyzed how the four participating initiatives infused asset building into programs, organizations, and sectors, several key themes emerged. Think about these themes as you launch your own efforts in these areas.

Look for any avenue to infuse, connect, and expand. You want to activate both intentional and informal ways of spreading assets into the community. You can facilitate the process by sponsoring specific actions and events to help raise awareness and grow the initiative.

You may develop deliberate education, public relations, and marketing campaigns, for example, to promote the idea of asset building and increase participation in the initiative. Many initiatives "piggyback" their messages about asset building on existing communications, like newsletters and radio shows. Others include a focus on recognizing the asset-building programs and activities that take place in the community, honoring the good work already being done but naming it and associating it in people's minds with the concept of asset building. Eventually, as the saturation spreads, people will hear about asset building and participate in it without someone from the initiative directly facilitating the process.

As asset building becomes more visible in communities, opportunities may also arise to respond to events with an asset emphasis. In the wake of the Columbine, Colorado, school shootings, Team Winslow, the association of downtown business retailers in Bainbridge Island, Washington, wanted to host community and high school dialogues to give people a chance to talk about what had happened. Because they were aware of the work that the It's About Time for Kids initiative was doing, Team Winslow partnered with the initiative to conduct the dialogues. As a side benefit, the business group invited a young person to serve on their advisory board to help strengthen business-youth relationships.

Develop strategies for uniquely adapting assets one sector at a time. Each sector has its own sphere of influence, its own language, its own way of working, and will approach asset building in its own way as well. Schools will understand, translate, and use the asset framework differently than the business community will. Youth organizations are likely to use the asset framework initially as a way to enhance the quality of their programs. Your role will be to negotiate a good fit between the framework and an existing sector while recognizing and respecting that system's way of doing things.

A good instance of adapting asset building to the needs of sectors comes from Georgetown, Texas. There, the organizers of the Georgetown police summer program for young people began viewing the program through an asset lens and found ways to enhance the program through asset-building contributions from numerous other community sectors. For example, they connected with a local candle-making company to provide opportunities and training for creative activities, set up a service project to benefit the Parks and Recreation Department's baseball fields, and built in special efforts to reach out to parents during pickup and drop-off times.

Another tactic for working with a specific sector is to **identify a sector champion** who will help you expand your efforts. Many initiatives have found that a school district administrator or executive director of a youth-serving agency who gets excited about assets is willing to be the point person on introducing the framework in her or his own spheres of influence. For example, a Hispanic member of Florida's Healthy Community Initiative leadership team involved with the regional Chamber of Commerce has helped establish working groups in both the business community and the Spanish-speaking community.

Find ways to help different sectors connect. In addition to helping a particular sector or group infuse assets within its programs and organizations, look for ways to connect efforts across sectors. This could mean networking all of the youth-serving agencies in your area (focusing on one sector) or developing relationships between different sectors, like helping libraries and congregations work together (networking across sectors). Your task will be to identify and bridge gaps among and between groups and by encouraging the sharing of perspectives, information, resources, and opportunities. "That can be as simple as having ten $50 sponsors of an event instead of one $500 sponsor," suggests Search Institute's Nancy Tellett-Royce. "Or bring together all the youth-serving agencies—with youth involved—and name all the resources housed across the agencies. See where the gaps are. Then the group can figure out how to funnel resources where they're needed."

A number of initiatives help different sectors connect in these common ways:

- **Rally different sectors around the common vision and mission of asset building.** The Bainbridge Island It's About Time for Kids initiative has involved members of many different groups on behalf of young people, including the Multicultural Advisory Council to the schools, the board of the Indian Education Council, members of the gay/lesbian community and PFLAG (Parents and Friends of Lesbians and Gays), and the local Interfaith Council.
- **Connect asset building with existing strength-building efforts in the community.** Many initiatives have been successful in jointly accomplishing a defined task. In Frisco, Colorado, the Asset Builders of the Summit initiative work with local America's Promise fellows to help infuse assets through youth and family agency service plans and conduct joint projects such as creating an asset kit for early childhood providers.

➧ **Look for opportunities to build key bridges.** At times, the extraordinary efforts of a key individual, organization, or group can facilitate vital connections across or within sectors. For example, Moorhead businessman Steve Scheels, who had given large grants to the community for a number of years, struck upon the idea of sponsoring a matching grant to encourage other local businesses to contribute to the initiative and stimulate community ownership.

In Union County, Iowa, the Iowa Savings Bank has become an asset bridge builder. The bank's executive vice president wanted to give out awards to outstanding people in the community. The bank joined forces with the county's Youth Plus initiative to recognize a wider array of asset builders, including day-care providers, teachers, students, and parents. The bank and initiative have also presented together a daylong symposium on building assets in the workplace, with an evening banquet for Excellence in Education Award winners.

What Are the Barriers to Activating Sectors?

WHAT BARRIERS MIGHT KEEP VARIOUS SECTORS FROM ADOPTING ASSET BUILDING?

1. **People perceive that you're only working with "bad kids."**
   Try this: Have youth-adult teams explain the needs all kids have for asset builders in their lives.

2. **Groups perceive that you are telling them they've done a "bad job."**
   Try this: Learn what they do well and share with the groups how their good work is already asset building. Then encourage them to take their efforts to the next level.

3. **Groups think you just want them to give you money.**
   Try this: Share the stories of how businesses, for example, have contributed significantly to asset building through networking, changes in policy, and other measures that don't cost money.

WHAT BARRIERS MIGHT KEEP DIFFERENT SECTORS FROM WORKING WITH EACH OTHER?

1. **Groups see themselves as dissimilar with different goals.**
   Try this: Use the asset framework to provide groups with a common language and common set of large goals.

2. **Groups don't normally share information, perspectives, or resources.**
   Try this: Suggest as a starter activity that several groups assemble information on programs offered for youth across many different agencies and promote them through a joint booklet or an information fair.

3. **Groups must compete for resources or territory.**
   Try this: Point out how sharing resources strategically can help groups meet their own goals and that collaborative efforts have a strong appeal to many grantmakers.

Making It Happen

The success of GivEm 40's school engagement drives home a key point about infusing assets into programs, organizations, and sectors: long-term sustainability of your initiative comes through deeply embedded community ownership.

When initiative organizers approached school principals about conducting the *Search Institute Profiles of Student Life: Attitudes and Behaviors* survey, they were met with two reservations: (1) that youth wouldn't take it seriously and hence skew the results, and (2) that local media would use the results to rank schools in competition with one another. Over the course of a year, Youth Advisory Council members prepared their peers for the survey, and initiative organizers educated the media in advance. All 19 school districts in the five-county region did the survey during the same week. Very soon after, all superintendents committed to implementing the asset framework with action plans in their districts. Not a single negative story or comparison appeared in the local media.

"The school sector took ownership, responsibility, and the practice of asset building in its environment," says GivEm 40 Coordinator Alan VanderPaas. "This ownership came about only with a depth-oriented strategy. We tend to think of it as drilling deep, so deep that when you reach the aquifer at the core, the energy comes streaming out and there is no stopping the momentum."

GivEm 40 highlights these key components that contributed to its success in the education sector. Consider them as you proceed to infuse assets into various sectors of your community:

- Use a messenger who speaks the unique language of that sector and can help translate the asset message into relevant benefits and practices for that sector.
- The messenger will help sector members see the link between asset development and the sector's core mission.
- The messenger or someone else the sector members trust must be present to plant the seeds of change and perhaps do some "hand-holding" along the way.
- Encourage the messenger to include the voices of young people in delivering the asset message.
- Capitalize on that sector's strengths in ways that have an asset-impact in that community.
- During the first year or two, let the initiative take the risks while crediting the good outcomes to sector leaders.

A graphic depiction of how Wisconsin's United with Youth sees many sectors of the community playing their part in youth-focused community development.

Assets in Action

The following section gives a broad range of ideas for infusing asset building into existing programs, for connecting organizations within a particular sector, and for connecting groups and organizations across different systems. The ideas are organized by sector.

Youth-Serving Organizations and Programs: A Common Goal

Many youth-serving organizations are already deeply engaged in building assets for and with youth whether they've called it that or not. Many asset-building initiatives partner with these already-active community organizations. But there can be barriers to overcome. Sometimes organizations fear that initiative efforts will further strain local funding or that they're being told they have somehow not done a good enough job.

"There's a big shift that happens when we start thinking of someone who does the same work we do as a partner rather than a competitor," says Search Institute's Nancy Tellett-Royce. "We tend to hunker down and forget that we all have a common goal about young people. The YMCA has a common goal with the YWCA, Boys & Girls Clubs, 4-H, Campfire USA, and Scouts. Your initiative is looking for ways to communicate that common goal and provide opportunities for people to act."

The Moorhead Healthy Community Initiative provides a variety of examples about how to successfully activate youth organizations. When MHCI's After-School Hours Asset Team reviewed local and Search Institute survey data, the needs of students in grades 4 to 8 clearly emerged. Young people in this age group felt too old for day care, but were too young to be left unsupervised. A list of 20 top activity choices came out of conversations with youth, and MHCI made the decision not just to support the work of existing organizations but also to start new programs where gaps were most obvious. "The board debated this because they felt being a change agent was their original mission," says MHCI Director Barry Nelson. "They were afraid that if they got into programs, they'd lose sight of their primary function."

Ultimately, the initiative decided that programmatic support was necessary to uphold a clearly identified priority that would also strengthen adult engagement. MHCI has been successful in getting state dollars targeted for after-school enrichment and then managing a grant process within the community. The initiative infuses asset building into its entire process of contracting out, training, monitoring, and reporting. An important goal is for any program that MHCI launches to become self-sufficient. Youth are involved at every level.

The initiative also looks for creative ways to infuse asset building into local programs as well as encouraging partnerships among local organizations:

- **Mentor Link.** MHCI serves as the training and connecting source for local mentoring programs. The initiative recruits interested mentors (including

Enhancing Out-of-School Programs to Build Assets

PROGRAMS ARE VITAL LINKS in the web of support that asset-building initiatives are forging in their communities. High-quality programs already make a strong contribution by providing young people with help in areas such as constructive use of their time and increasing their commitment to learning, and that contribution can be strengthened when programs view their work through an asset-building lens. For example:

- Programs cannot order up for every child a loving, supportive parent, but they can commit to **promoting family support** and positive family communication. Intentional efforts to have staff meet and greet parents when they come to pick up a participating child can do wonders at fostering relationship between staff and parents. And when staff make a point of telling each parent something positive about her or his child's time in the program that day, or invite parents to volunteer in the program, those are steps toward weaving the web of support young people need to thrive.
- Programs, like parents and volunteers and neighbors, can't build every asset for every child every day, but sometimes a simple asset-inspired addition to a program can **boost the program's asset-building capacity.** Take the common example of an after-school basketball program; it's healthy and fun for young people to have the chance to play, and when the coaches and supervisors emphasize good sportsmanship and relationship building, it's an asset-building activity. How could it build even more assets? How about: recruiting parents to be "cheerleaders" at pickup games? Adding a small library of books and magazines about sports to encourage reading during breaks? Implementing a rotating position of team captain to empower players and teach them about leadership? Setting up a mentoring segment of the time in which better players work one-on-one with less experienced players?
- **Increasing access** to programs is another way to enhance asset building. Consider these questions: Are programs available in my community for all young people, or for only certain "target" groups? What barriers, such as transportation needs or lack of awareness of activities, are affecting participation? How could partnering with other organizations or agencies extend our mutual ability to reach and involve more young people?

> **LEARN MORE:** Search Institute resources for youth-serving organizations and programs include *Walking Your Talk: Building Assets in Organizations That Serve Youth* and a number of mentoring resources. See the Resources section for details.

many college students), conducts four 2-hour training courses a year, then refers mentors to organizations that need them, like Big Brothers & Big Sisters. United Way is developing outcome measures to determine the value of the trainings for the individuals and organizations involved.

- **Support Moorhead Youth**. This community event celebrated all the organizations that are working on behalf of youth, including 11 congregations that had been with the initiative from the beginning. Fifteen organizations, including the Girl Scouts, YWCA, and Native American Youth Center, set up booths and the entertainment was multicultural.

▶ **After-School Enrichment Program Scholarships.** One of the biggest barriers to young people being involved in existing programs, the group found, was cost. Funds from the state's Department of Children, Families and Learning support scholarships so that young people can participate in any activity in which they're interested. Youth review the scholarship requests, keeping in mind the requirement that each activity be skill building (learning to do something vs. just roller skating for the afternoon). Emphasis is placed on supporting youth from diverse cultures.

Other organizations have implemented some of the following ideas:

▶ **Sports tips.** Concerned about an overemphasis on winning in local youth sports programs, the HC • HY of Ada County, Idaho, convened a group of people to design asset-based tips for coaches, instructors, and parents. Among the tips are such suggestions as aiming for participation from every player, encouraging positive communication between players and family, and having fun. "Remember," says tip #18, "you are developing good human beings first; developing performers is secondary." The tipsheets are circulated among the county's many sports programs.

▶ **Partnering to meet needs.** The First Baptist Church of Los Angeles, California, decided to set up a recreation and arts center in its neighborhood. The congregation wanted to offer a safe place for youth along with constructive ways to spend their time. But, despite good intentions, programming, and staff supervision, the center became a gang hangout and had to close. Determined, the congregation asked the YMCA for help in developing a more structured and controlled program that would include more values and drug education. The new program didn't reach quite as many young people, but the church was able to have a greater impact on the young people who did participate.

▶ **A master plan.** Representatives from each of the six Edmonton YMCA branches in Alberta, Canada, came together to create an "association work group on asset development" when they began to infuse their organizations and programs with the assets. Their thought and careful intentionality resulted in a master work plan on asset building. Among the activities in the plan:

- All staff are required to take two half-day trainings on the asset approach;
- Asset building is a topic in all staff meetings;
- The YMCA has taken the lead in a community's asset-building coalition; and
- The asset approach is used in training parents and guardians.

▶ **Spreading the word through youth voices.** The Colorado Summit Prevention Alliance Inspired by Assets Writing Contest gives that initiative a number of opportunities to teach and publicize assets at the same time. The first year's theme—caring—was chosen to complement the school district's implementation of a bullyproofing curriculum. The initiative's community prevention coordinator, Tara Eaton, kicks off the contest by making a presentation to a meeting of local principals and giving them contest packets—including asset information—to distribute to their schools. The Rotary Club helps judge; local businesses donate prizes. Kids receive award certificates in ceremonies at their individual schools.

Schools: Two Views

One of the most important sectors to activate is schools. It's where the critical mass of young people spends much of their time, and it's the primary venue for initiatives seeking to conduct the *Search Institute Profiles of Student Life: Attitudes and Behaviors* survey. When studying its four participant initiatives, the researchers on the National Asset-Building Case Study Project identified two distinct approaches to schools.

Schools are an up-front focus. The GivEm 40 Coalition in the Traverse Bay area of Michigan is a prime example of an effort in which schools were successfully involved as a first priority. This model makes schools a major partner in asset development from the get-go. Schools are sometimes an easier sector to work with because they're more organized on behalf of young people than other sectors like local businesses.

Schools are *not* an up-front focus. A distinguishing characteristic of Orlando's Healthy Community Initiative was the fact that the schools were not the focus of the initiative's work. The initiative members didn't want to add to the perceived burden of schools being viewed as the sole piece of community infrastructure to bring about positive youth development. So HCI intentionally sought to mobilize in nonschool sectors and sidestepped the too-common indictment of the education sector as a source of much that is "wrong" in modern society. HCI concentrated instead on building capacity in the larger community to support asset building before approaching local schools to help with the survey.

"The composition of our first invitational list was very intentional," says HCI Executive Director Raymond Larsen. "We didn't invite teachers and social workers, for example, because we know they understand a lot of the issues already and are already 'doing it.' We wanted leaders of influence in systems, association leaders and politicians. In some segments of the community, we actually started with 'white guys over 50' because that's who we needed to come to the table if we were going to start having an impact."

A third approach, noted by Karen Atkinson of Children First in St. Louis Park, Minnesota, is schools as equal partners. However you decide to include schools in your initiative, it's important to understand the pressures educators are under and anticipate potential negative comparisons across schools. It may be important to first create a strategy for emphasizing schools' strengths rather than risk negative comparisons.

To highlight the asset-building work that schools already do, many initiatives have taken a celebration approach. One good example is a project of the Asset Builders of the Summit initiative in Frisco, Colorado, called the **Summit Education Celebration.** This project started by teachers asking themselves, "How can I build assets for and with my students if I don't have assets myself?" Community members realized that school staff needed to feel valued, so they started this annual staff recognition event, which honors *all* school staff, including administrators, custodians, teachers, and bus drivers. The local Business Education Alliance cosponsors the celebration with the initiative.

Hampton, Virginia's Mobilization for Youth Initiative took another approach to engaging schools by joining forces with a local school superintendent who wanted to make developmental assets the focus of school improvement plans. One hundred students, parents, and teachers from all of Hampton's middle and high schools came together in the **CARE (Creating A Respectful Environment) Conference** to concentrate on building relationships. Each middle and high school brought a team of 10 people (four students, two teachers, two parents, and two administrators). Each team's goal was to develop a plan for creating a caring, respectful climate in its school. Each plan included strategies for promoting and improving relationships, building links between incoming students and older students, and fostering respectful peer relationships. The conference featured food, decorations, games, stories, T-shirts, recognition awards, and a theater troupe.

"The CARE Conference was very important because it gave us, the students, some authority," wrote one 8th-grade student from Jones Middle School, after the event. "It allowed us to feel wanted and needed, and we got to help the schools we attend be more caring and respectful. It is great that we get to be more involved in our school."

After the CARE Conference, individual schools quickly followed up with minievents at individual schools. The team from Kecoughtan High School decided its school needed an all-out campaign to focus on caring. A successful grant application to the local Youth Commission garnered $3,000 for its "WHO CARES!?" week, which featured giveaways, teacher-student events, and CARE-GRAMS for sale by team members.

Congregations: Tapping the Potential

"Churches, mosques, parishes, synagogues, temples, meetinghouses, and other communities of faith represent an invaluable—though often unrecognized and untapped—resource for today's children and adolescents," says Search Institute Special Advisor Eugene Roehlkepartain. Congregations have a unique opportunity and capacity to build assets in youth because they:

- Have potential for intergenerational relationships that can be sustained across many years;
- Provide opportunities for youth to understand themselves, their identity, and their world through leadership development, education, service, field trips, and other positive social activities;
- Can talk in terms of the connection between values and specific behaviors;
- Reach and work with parents, partnering with them to support their crucial role in young people's lives; and
- Have a positive public presence, with the potential for leadership, advocacy, and service on behalf of young people in society.

"Getting congregations started in some simple ways may be what's needed at first," suggests Roehlkepartain, "with a larger vision held out in front to help guide your progress." He encourages congregations to develop their own vision for asset building and then specify goals and strategies to implement that vision. He offers some tips to initiatives when they work with congregations:

- Suggest that congregations focus on areas that are consistent with their own history, values, and commitments;
- Include a mix of priorities that are relatively easy to address as well as some bigger dreams;

- Look for places where opportunities and resources intersect with identified needs;
- Find ways to enrich existing opportunities and programs; and
- Identify partnership opportunities;

> **LEARN MORE:** *Building Assets in Congregations: A Practical Guide for Helping Youth Grow Up Healthy* and numerous other resources for faith communities are available from Search Institute. See the Resources listed at the back of this book for details.

Here are a few more innovative asset-building ideas to spark your thinking:

- Hampton, Virginia's Mobilization for Youth held a developmental assets **miniconference for congregations.** The meeting spawned a faith task force and trained more than 50 local leaders in asset building.
- Youth on the Metro Council for Teen Potential and the Monroe County Asset Partner Network in Rochester, New York, **work with the local Council of Churches** to fund activities. The teens are also working with a group of faith ministers to support asset building within the city of Rochester.
- The Henry S. Jacobs Camp in Utica, Mississippi, provides a way for young people not only to celebrate their Jewish cultural heritage but to experience developmental assets as well. Sponsored by the Union of American Hebrew Congregations, the **camp** has integrated the asset framework into all curriculum and staff training. "Every camp activity can be an opportunity for asset building," says Camp Director Jonathan Cohen. "We wanted to build Jewish values and used the framework as a goal-setting tool."
- Regular monthly meetings have become a time for asset building at St. John's Lutheran Church in Boise, Idaho, when youth and seniors go beyond their Sunday night meetings to spend time with each other. Youth groups and the Fellowship Club, a group for people aged 55 and older, get together for **"fireside time."** The two groups start off doing separate activities, then come together for snacks, games, and talk. Church spokesperson Carolyn Grohn says building intergenerational relationships is especially important in Boise. "People here tend not to have extended families. This gives young people a chance to have a grandparent figure and a friend of a different generation they don't usually have access to."
- **A congregation with intention.** After attending Search Institute trainings, members of the Heritage Presbyterian Church in Glendale, Arizona, decided they wanted to start intentional asset building. They began by forming an asset team that received asset training to prepare them for their roles. "We met once a week for a long time and looked at the big picture of what was going on in the church," says Lynn Weeks. "Each team member went to a different committee in the church to determine how various areas were building assets."

Over a period of three years, the congregation promoted assets in a variety of ways. Asset team members took turns writing newsletter articles to help educate the whole church on topics such as the need for everyone to be involved in supporting youth. The church also worked hard to create a worship service that raised the level of awareness in the church about young people. One component was to decorate the church with paper silhouettes of all the children and youth; each silhouette included a heart symbol and a sentence the young person had written to describe herself or himself. Combined with music and a topical sermon, Weeks said, the service successfully focused its whole ambiance on youth.

Lessons Learned from Search Institute's Uniting Congregations for Youth Development Initiative

FROM 1995 to 1999, Search Institute conducted an initiative called Uniting Congregations for Youth Development (UCYD), which was supported by the DeWitt Wallace–Reader's Digest Fund. This initiative, which focused on seven pilot sites, emphasized enhancing the capacity of congregations of all faiths to build developmental assets. Here are some lessons learned from this initiative about engaging the faith community in asset building:

- **Stimulate and tap interest within the religious community.** A decision to form a network *must come* from the congregational leaders who would be the core of that network. If you don't already have champions within the faith community, start by finding them.
- **Focus on building relationships.** Religious leaders are much more likely to get involved in a network when they have a personal connection to someone in the network.
- **Be intentional about inclusivity.** Existing networks among congregations tend to be specific to a particular faith tradition or particular racial/ethnic community. It's important to be intentional and persistent in reaching beyond these comfortable patterns to include all members of the faith community.
- **Start with interests and strengths.** Find out what strengths and resources people in the religious community believe they have for asset building. Learn where they're interested in developing additional strength. Use what you learn to shape your efforts.
- **Stimulate, support, and encourage asset building within and among congregations.** This may involve sponsoring events for youth in which numerous congregations can participate, encouraging congregations to participate in community-wide events, offering training for congregations, or linking congregations to multisector initiatives. In each case, encourage an intentional focus on assets—then tell stories about what congregations are doing.
- **Start small.** Don't try to do everything at once. Identify concrete things you can do that will have a tangible result for the religious community. Let it grow.
- **Recognize that it will take time.** Expect a network to build slowly; give it time. It likely takes at least two years for a network to become self-sustaining.

Law Enforcement and Juvenile Justice: Redefining Success

Police departments, courts, and entire juvenile justice systems are finding ways to instill asset building into their work. "The good life for youth is not just the absence of problems," says Michael Clark, director of the Center for Strength-Based Strategies in Mason, Michigan. "A new strengths movement in juvenile justice calls all to help youth find meaningful roles in communities that will compel growth long after young people exit our court systems. We can no longer just 'fix flaws' but must do more to build strengths and assets."

Police, of course, have long been building positive relationships with young people through in-school programs like DARE (Drug Abuse Resistance Education). Moorhead Healthy Community Initiative Executive Director Barry Nelson says infusing asset building into the police department has completely changed how police in their community deal with youth daily. "They've put a lot of energy into integrating assets, from the chief to the police on the beat. Rather than just being an authority and punishing youth, the police are trying to pay more attention to building relationships. They get energy back from it because this kind of policing feels better."

Incidentally, the Moorhead HCI shares its office space with the police department in a local church rectory. This facilitates positive police relationships with youth, the schools, and minority neighborhoods in a community that has a history of racial tension between the residents and law enforcement.

In many initiatives, police departments and juvenile justice representatives are at the table as planning partners. Here are some other ideas for you to consider:

➧ The Silverthorne Police Department in Frisco, Colorado, displays "Make a difference—connect with youth/Asset Builders of the Summit" **bumper stickers** on all of its patrol cars.

The Power of One in Orlando, Florida

JUVENILE COURT JUDGE CYNTHIA MacKINNON first learned about developmental assets while serving as a member of the board of directors for Orlando, Florida's Healthy Community Initiative. Intimately aware of the problems many youth face, she also knew that it would take new strategies to have an impact on the trends she was seeing every day. She had asset information included in the bench books used by all the juvenile court's judges and hosted a "lunch-n-learn" for her colleagues to learn more about it. She decided to make a more personal commitment, too, and now tries to visit the youth she sentences to detention or programs. She shares the story of visiting one boy who couldn't believe that she not only came to see him but also remembered his name.

One way for police departments to contribute to positive youth development is to forge relationships with young people early in their lives; here, Officer Mary Jane Gay of the GivEm 40 Coalition is shown with students from Central Grade School in Michigan.

- Besides being involved as mentors or helping with after-school and weekend activities, police and court personnel often serve on **asset teams or governance groups** in the Fairborn Cares Initiative in Ohio.
- Sparked by the Assets for Colorado Youth initiative, 25 organizations are using developmental assets as a way to think about **systemic change** on the Youth Juvenile Justice Task Force in Colorado Springs.
- At least two police departments have joined forces with local youth to produce **resource booklets.** Youth and police in Jefferson County, Kentucky, distribute copies of a pocket-sized leaflet called *Partners in Making a Positive Change* to young people. The book contains information about reporting crimes, laws most often broken by youth, driving issues, and tips for getting involved. A simple booklet called *Youth and the Law: Partners in Making a Positive Community* was created by BOAST (Build Our Assets for a Safer Tomorrow) in Hanover, New Hampshire. Along with relevant laws, this booklet contains a section on youth rights and responsibilities as well as a map of the town showing young people where they can skateboard.

  The introduction to the Jefferson County resource book states eloquently: "This collaboration provided a great learning experience for both youth and officers and aided in working toward our common understanding of one another. This handbook was written to help other youth and police to reach this same understanding and to provide youth with information and resources."

▶ When working as a probation officer in Lansing, Michigan, Michael Clark decided to set aside trying to figure out why a 15-year-old boy charged with assault had grabbed a knife and gone after his sister. Instead, he refocused on the boy's interests and asked the young man what he did to blow off steam. "I work on my bikes," the teen answered. So Clark asked a local bike shop owner if the young man could sweep floors there without pay as part of his probation. The shop owner agreed as long as the teen didn't cause trouble. "The phone stopped ringing about that kid," says Clark. "His passions were touched. When I had his passions, I had everything." Eventually the teen landed a paying job at the bike shop.

Mobilizing Neighborhoods

In the same way that young people for many years have often been defined by their needs, neighborhoods are often measured by their deficits. Organizations and services spring up to address these deficits, further deepening our view that neighborhoods are problems to be fixed. In their groundbreaking work on rejuvenating Chicago neighborhoods, John P. Kretzmann and John L. McKnight assert a simple claim: each community boasts a unique combination of strengths and resources (what they call community assets, a concept that is different from but complementary to young people's developmental assets) upon which to build its future. Establishing a model for reevaluating neighborhoods, the authors write in *Building Communities from the Inside Out: A Path toward Finding and Mobilizing a Community's Assets:*

> A thorough map of those [community] assets would begin with an inventory of the gifts, skills, and capacities of the community's residents. Household by household, building by building, block by block, the capacity mapmakers will discover a vast and often surprising array of individual talents and productive skills, few of which are being mobilized for community-building purposes.

Across North America, nearly 600 community asset-building initiatives are (re)discovering and (re)building the infrastructures of their neighborhoods on behalf of young people. Some are using the Kretzmann and McKnight model for evaluating their community's resources and building on the strengths they discover. All are using a variety of activities to help neighborhoods in their community connect and support young people. Here are just a few ideas culled from those neighborhood efforts:

▶ **Connecting service.** The Adams County HC • HY Coalition in Quincy, Illinois, joined forces with the Gem City Breakfast Kiwanis Club to conduct **a musical instrument drive,** which collected 50 donated instruments. The groups then found community volunteers to teach interested youth at various neighborhood sites who might not otherwise have a chance for music lessons. The initiative also sought small grants for incentive pay for music students at Quincy University and John Wood Community College to mentor and teach the neighborhood youth.

- **Neighborhood College.** In Hampton, Virginia, neighborhood residents can attend a training program in the city's Neighborhood College to learn about asset building. The city has also infused asset building into its annual spring Neighborhood Month. And youth now serve on the Neighborhood Commission and assist in developing a youth agenda for building caring neighborhoods.

- **The Asset Banner Run-Walk-Crawl.** The community of Pittsford, New York, holds an event that includes a five-kilometer run throughout the community's neighborhoods. Members, volunteers, and staff from community organizations are stationed along the route, each of them illustrating a poster and giving out information about a different asset. After the runners take off, other individuals and families begin the five-kilometer walk. Each participant is given a list of assets to check off as he or she visits each station. To conclude the event, even babies participate by doing a five-foot "baby crawl" on a gymnastics mat.

- **Library Partnership for Youth.** The Fort Bend Community Library in Richmond, Texas, launched a unique after-school program with support from the DeWitt Wallace–Reader's Digest Fund. Called Library Partnership for Youth, the library partnered with nine community organizations, including several faith communities, to provide meaningful after-school support for young people in low-income neighborhoods. The program features career and technology exploration, technology training, homework assistance, and reading incentive programs for middle school students, as well as computer training and employment opportunities for high school students. High school students trained to troubleshoot computer problems staff the sites.

  The teens who staff the sites are an important resource and an important focus of asset building. "Youth had to be eligible for free school lunch in order to apply, and they did not have to be at the top of their class," says Molly Krukewitt. "We wanted to build self-esteem. We had as many girls as boys, and some of them were teen moms. Over three years, we had 65 young people involved and only three of them are not still with us."

- **Cultural conversations.** Project Cornerstone in California's Santa Clara Valley has emphasized building an inclusive movement by mobilizing diverse sectors of a multicultural community. They formed the **Diversity Team** to lead outreach to diverse communities as a first step toward developing partnerships with the initiative. The Diversity Team has been leading a multiwave Outreach and Listening Campaign, conducting focus groups with Latino, Vietnamese, and gay, lesbian, bisexual, and transgender (GLBT) communities, and continuing with the African American and Filipino communities, as well as youth in the juvenile justice system.

  The project's first report summarized focus group discussions about how the asset framework was useful and, in some cases, could be modified to make it more culturally meaningful (emphasizing cultural identity for youth as part of asset 34, cultural competence, for example). The report also tapped into various groups' specific concerns, provided statistics regarding each group's level of assets, and incorporated quotes from participants about the importance of certain asset categories, like Support and Positive Identity. The report concluded with a list of asset-building ideas.

> LEARN MORE: The text of the Diversity Team's first wave report is available from the group's Web site. See the Resources listed at the end of this book.

Government and Civic Engagement for and with Young People

Youth can be involved in government in many ways, from expressing opinions to trying to change state law. There are also many ways that adults can influence government at the policy and planning level to enhance the positive development of youth. Here's a selection of ideas from several initiatives:

➤ **Spreading the language.** The Fox Cities, Wisconsin, United with Youth Initiative has shared the asset framework with a number of local governments, which have now begun to incorporate new language into their goals, mission statements. and plans in ways that work for them. "One way to empower youth is to include them in the dialogue of local government," says Director Paul Vidas. "Government is mobilized, ready to get things done. It's logical to get youth involved." Adopters have taken the following steps:

- CAPPS, a strategic planning group within Appleton, Wisconsin's city government, invited the initiative to join and help direct the city's plan for connecting with youth.
- The Gang and Youth Violence Task Force of Outagamie County, a coalition interested in making the Fox Valley a safer place, included developmental assets language in its mission statement. Both adults and youth participate in this task force.

The Power of One in San Jose, California

"FIVE OF US PRESENTED A WORKSHOP at a Search Institute conference on asset building in diverse communities. Part of the workshop provided an opportunity to share my personal story as a gay youth. The following day, I was approached by a woman who shared with me that my story touched her and made her cry. I was amazed my story could have that kind of an effect. Who knows what potential I can bring to this world, how many lives I can touch with my story, and how I can make the world a better place to live in?"

PROJECT CORNERSTONE YOUTH LEADER

- The Park and Recreation Departments of Appleton and Menasha have begun using asset building as a way of training staff.
- Youth now have a seat on both the Planning Committee and the Parks and Recreation Committee in the town of Freedom. Both are paid positions with a full vote.

▶ **Changing the voice of governance.** The Colorado city of Greeley has an 11-member **Youth Commission.** The young people serve in an advisory capacity, giving direct input to the Greeley City Council regarding youth-related issues. Each year the commissioners take part in a leadership retreat at which they develop communication and role-modeling skills and learn about developmental assets. Many take part in local, statewide, and national asset initiatives as well.

▶ Fort Monroe in Hampton, Virginia, has personnel involved in initiative asset teams and provides space for local youth events. Langley Air Force Base has also provided asset training at their **Fatherhood Conference for enlisted men and officers.**

▶ In New York State, 15 counties have received strategic planning funds from the state's Office of Children and Family Services. The funds are intended to facilitate integrated county planning that will, in part, **require using the asset model as a component** for community involvement and service delivery. The state office brought in Search Institute trainers to help counties learn how to use the developmental assets framework in their plans. Counties have also been encouraged to connect with local HC • HY initiatives that in some cases assisted with trainings.

Health-Care Providers: Just What the Doctor Ordered

While the composition of each Healthy Communities • Healthy Youth initiative is different, many have tapped the local health-care community for participation and leadership. Health-care organizations have expertise and experience with young people of all ages. Like teachers, health-care providers enjoy a position of trust with youth and their families. Many work closely with schools. Health-care organizations also have a stake in the prevention of risky behaviors.

One initiative that has forged a very successful partnership with its health-care community is Healthy Nampa • Healthy Youth in Idaho. Mercy Medical Center funded the first administration of the *Search Institute Profiles of Student Life: Attitudes and Behaviors* survey in the community, helped raise more than $600,000 for asset-building projects, and donated the land for Nampa's 140,000-square-foot community center. The center also provides staff resources for many HN • HY projects, including asset training for educators and businesses.

One special project initiated by the medical center was the result of emergency room staff noticing how busy they got around noon. Staff realized many teens were getting into accidents because they had only a 25-minute lunch break. "They were racing around like mad," says Mercy's vice president of development and community relations, Lynn Borud. "They were trying to go buy a CD at the mall eight miles away and then gunning back down the road to grab a burger." Staff advocated with the high school to "close the campus" (make it a rule that students stay on school grounds over lunchtime) to increase student safety.

Other ideas for infusing asset building into health-care organizations:

▶ Ohio County Hospital in Hartford, Kentucky, became the **first local business to release employees to mentor** with Together We Care's Special Friends program. About 20 hospital associates, including the administrator, chief financial officer, and primary surgeon, have served as mentors. The hospital auxiliary has also developed its own asset project called **Prescription for Reading.** Books are purchased and given to doctors to distribute to young patients during visits. Doctors explain the benefits of reading for pleasure and give parents a "prescription" on a special prescription pad to read to their child daily.

▶ "Sometimes I've felt alone in my efforts to help youth that were struggling," writes Clarkston, Michigan, physician John Blanchard. "Now that our community has banded together through the Healthy Youth Initiative, I feel part of a larger community-wide effort to positively impact our youth." Inspired by assets, Blanchard and his colleagues have designed **a series of age-appropriate asset-based parenting brochures** to give to families when they visit the doctor's office. Starting with birth and going all the way up to age 18, the brochures describe physical growth along with important assets to provide at different stages. The content was drafted in collaboration with a local advertising writer and artist. Blanchard's office is piloting the brochures, and, once they are printed, plans are in the works to make packets of information available to other local doctors, hospitals, and the county health department.

Business: It's Not Just about Money

Don't make the mistake of only looking to businesses as potential funders. Karen Atkinson of Children First, St. Louis Park, Minnesota, offers this advice: "Businesses have fabulous resources and creative ideas. Business owners are parents, grandparents, and neighbors, and they may very well be interested in asset building. And guess what? When people get involved and committed to a project, money may follow."

Some initiatives have successfully established links between the asset framework and business by encouraging businesses to view youth as citizens and consumers in the present, who are already connected to the workforce and who need to be mentored as community stakeholders before they leave the area to pursue higher education.

The GivEm 40 Coalition of Traverse City, Michigan, after success in the edu-

Why Should Business Support Asset Building?
By Mary Scott Singer

ASSET BUILDING IS GOOD FOR BUSINESS because those of us in business have much at stake. If you are not changing the way you do business on a constant basis, ever conscious of the outside influences of our world culture, you are dying.

Because the workplace is shrinking on a global level, we are forced not only to think out of the box but also to operate out of the box. Our employees are diverse, and now our business managers must be sensitive to that diversity. Asset-rich youth provide a great pool of future leaders for our shrinking world—they value diversity in others and will make great corporate leaders.

For any businessperson reading this and thinking, "These points are valid but where do they concern me?", listen up. Making my corporation an asset-based business has impacted my bottom line. Period.

The costs of insurance rates facing business, small and large, are staggering. Add the impact of September 11 and ever-increasing health-care costs, and we have a serious shock to prepare for in the future.

Family-friendly policies have reduced my turnover to near zero and had a positive impact on profit levels. My budget for ad placement, outsourcing, and training times has been reduced to zero. Morale has remained high for the two years since the implementation of these policies.

Asset-rich youth have the added strength of valuing healthy lifestyles and avoiding violent behavior. These two factors alone can bring to the future employer the benefit of lower health-care and workers' compensation costs, a safer work environment, and the probability of well-educated workers who understand the costs of substance abuse.

Businesspeople can ask themselves a simple question: "Who was it in their young life that mentored, coached, taught, and trained them to be successful?" Then budget "payback" in your five-year goal and your annual budget. Mentoring policies will ensure that young persons learn sound business principles that will last for a lifetime.

Businesses can sponsor youth, attend events, and have asset materials available for employees as well as customers. Businesses can stand up when we see youth patronized in our places of work, and we can support parents when they need time to attend their kids' school functions. We can be a voice for what is right, and let our patrons and fellow business leaders know that asset building is virtually cost free but highly rewarding.

Vision is the key. Every decision we make to help kids in our community grow up to be productive adults is a decision to recruit well-trained future employees who have strong character.

We will invest our hearts, our time, our human resources, and our corporate policies in our future workforce. We will reap a return on our investment that will impact both our country's strength and the bottom line. And the bottom line, my fellow employers, is something we can all understand.

Mary Scott Singer is president of Venture Circle Enterprises, Inc., a manufacturing company in Orlando, Florida. She is also a speaker on asset building in her community and the mother of two.

cation sector, chose the business sector as its next place of "depth work." "We had those 'inside champions' that [Search Institute trainer] Clay Roberts so clearly talks about," says Alan VanderPaas, coordinator for GivEm 40. "Several key members of our Chamber of Commerce had been involved since the coalition's inception, and they came to us and asked what they could do to create a more intentional climate for building assets within the business community."

The result of this collaboration was the launch of the AXIS Leadership Project's four Youth Action Committees. Among these community collaborations for youth are a creative arts project, a youth-driven media project with the newspaper, and Future Focus, which brings a diverse group of the community's youth together with the Chamber of Commerce, regional school administrators, and community leaders to "guide the development of existing career and vocational programs to accurately reflect the needs of youth today."

VanderPaas credits the business community's involvement to its genuine understanding that "business as usual" is not good enough when it comes to the healthy development of our youth.

"Business leaders here are concerned about the loss of our young talent to large universities and urban centers and how that affects the long-term health of our community," he says. "It is our hope that our young people will retain a picture of their hometown as a place of inclusion, a community that cares about them and one that overtly gives them opportunities to create, develop, and produce their dreams."

Here are a few more business involvement ideas:

⏵ The Bainbridge Island, Washington, It's About Time for Kids Initiative facilitated **dialogue** between high school students, police, and local businesses to foster mutual understanding and change how adults behave toward youth.

⏵ The McDonald's restaurant in Hartford, Kentucky, seems **more like a community center than a fast-food restaurant.** The owners, Valorie and Vincent Tanner, are strong supporters of the HC • HY initiative, Together We Care. A few of the many activities centered there:

  • Students from the Screaming Eagles Academic Team (see page 82) are just one of several groups of high school students who take turns reading to preschoolers on Tuesday mornings in conjunction with the school district's Read to Succeed program.

  • Elementary school teachers can nominate students to receive the Green and Growing Award for having made the most effort to improve. They also get a certificate for a free meal at the restaurant with their families.

  • For high school dances and special events like Valentine's Day, teens can find an affordable alternative to more expensive restaurants. "We light candles, dim the lights, and act more like a full-service restaurant for a few hours," says Valorie Tanner.

In Creston, Iowa, the example of Bunn-O-Matic's commitment to asset building helped **mobilize other businesses.** One of those was the locally owned Iowa State Savings Bank (ISSB). When ISSB owners became aware of the developmental assets model and how Bunn-O-Matic had embraced it, they immediately felt that this effort fit with ISSB's strong history of supporting the health and vitality of Union County. Together with the Youth Plus initiative, the bank created the Excellence in Education monthly award program to recognize anyone in education—child-care providers, school employees, school volunteers, and students—who demonstrates a commitment to asset building.

They've also instituted a children's savings club, and young savers can go to a special kids' corner in the main bank to conduct their banking business; an employee health and fitness program, including an on-site exercise room; and work experience opportunities for high school and college students during the summer.

Sustaining Your Efforts

Engaging organizations is a crucial component of your community-wide initiative. Without the involvement of existing organizations, an initiative will face unnecessary difficulties in improving community life. It's important to keep in mind, though, that while each organization has a lot to offer, each also faces its own unique challenges. Part of your work will involve monitoring and managing the progress of organizational involvement in asset building. The asset vision can help provide a lens for setting priorities, celebrating strengths, enhancing current programs and practices, and tapping untapped potential.

"Don't put all of your eggs in one basket," says Michael Nakkula, one of the lead researchers on the case studies project. "Think about diversifying the sectors you're working with. This can be a difficult lesson to act on when one or two sectors come enthusiastically to the table and assume a strong leadership role in the initiative. While it's important to nurture the relationships with strong, enthusiastic sectors, it's critical not to lose sight of the other sectors that need to be nurtured in order for the initiative to grow and be sustained in the long run."

Some other tips to help you sustain your work in this critical area:

Clearly define your initiative's role in the community. Moorhead, for example, serves as a catalyst, clearinghouse, and brainstorming resource in addition to providing some direct services. Sometimes, an initiative acts as the catalyst for starting or seeding a program that goes on to successfully secure its own individual funding. Sort out what is needed and what makes sense in your community.

Find ways to become or remain invitational. Let people feel comfortable joining in with what you are doing, and avoid the implication that there is one right way to get involved. "We try to model asset building as we work," says former Essex CHIPS coordinator Valerie Smith. "We find any little way we can for people to contribute or get recognition."

Accept the fact that you can't do it all. You may have to practice what the folks in Traverse City, Michigan, call "strategic abandonment" to prioritize your tasks and resources. Many initiatives experience overload, and it becomes necessary to choose some efforts over others to avoid being overextended. "When you're new," says GivEm 40's Schools Coordinator Mimi Petritz-Appel, "it's important to figure out what people and organizations are going to authentically support the initiative. It's hard to let go of taking care of everybody, but you have to be clear with limited resources."

Strategic planning can help you balance the high-wire act of initiative development. Overextending yourself can be a problem, and so can being too cautious. Taking the time to put ideas, resources, and activities in the context of a longer-term plan will help you make decisions about your priorities now and still remain flexible enough to react to changes later.

Identify benefits. Unleashing new resources and commitments can extend everyone's reach and impact. Work to enhance the efforts of individual organizations by developing a collaborative commitment to asset building. By working together, by building on the strengths of each individual organization, and by encouraging organizations to enhance the asset-building qualities of their existing programs, you'll all have a broad leadership role in shaping the priorities, culture, and tone of community life.

Organizations will be more likely to get involved if they perceive that they will benefit in return from asset building. "To really maintain a collaboration," says Moorhead's Barry Nelson, "you have to make people feel there's an exchange going on. They're giving you something, but you're giving them something in return, too, something positive and constructive. That creates a real positive energy."

Ideas on the Change Pathway for Activating Sectors and Invigorating Programs

PATHWAY	TIPS/ADVICE
Receptivity: being open to change	"Search for some true believers up front," says Alaska's Derek Peterson. "Anyone willing to get their hands and hearts a little dirty, meaning they're willing to walk their talk. Heaven forbid you should wear them out with meetings. Set up time for them to connect, bond. Let them build their capacity, take small action steps, developing a language that will eventually spread out into the public. Eventually they'll also become public leaders, the voices within the system. This is how you will ultimately change your community."
Awareness: understanding possibilities	Consider adopting a theory of change to help guide your work. The Take the Time initiative in Portland, Oregon, based its work in part on "diffusion of innovations theory," as described by Everett Rogers, which helped them clearly understand how to formulate change strategies for specific projects such as mini-grants and parent support in the schools. (See Chapter 3 for more on this theory.)
Mobilization: organizing for change	The GivEm 40 Coalition in the Traverse Bay area, Michigan, brought funders and evaluators to the table sooner rather than later. Both groups helped the initiative develop, and both groups were, in turn, changed by what they learned. Moorhead brought media specialists to the table early, which helped them capture some less visible, but critical elements of their work.
Action: making change happen	The United Way of the Virginia Peninsula hosts meetings for youth-serving agencies so they can explore asset-building pos-sibilities within their programs. They've also developed a for-mat to help include asset language in their allocation process.
Continuity: ensuring change becomes a way of life	Florida's Healthy Community Initiative has found that a gen-uinely balanced, reciprocal relationship between youth and adults that authentically includes youth in decision making appears to sustain youth involvement in initiative work—a cru-cial factor for overall initiative longevity.

Activate Sectors *and* Invigorate Programs

- The involvement of many organizations and sectors in your initiative is crucial to realizing your larger vision.

- Find creative ways to involve organizations and help them identify and unleash their asset-building capacity. Play up their strengths, encourage them to develop strategies within their own spheres of influence, and help them enhance their existing programs.

- Your main role is to inspire, inform, assist, and equip organizations to become asset-building partners. This can be accomplished by:
  ‣ Showing organizations and sectors how to strengthen the asset-building potential of existing programs and make it more deliberate;
  ‣ Helping organizations mobilize their own internal capacities;
  ‣ Helping organizations create asset-friendly policies, systems, and structures; and
  ‣ Creating connections among organizations.

- Look for any avenue to infuse, connect, and expand asset building.

- Adapt asset building uniquely within sectors.

- Identify champions within sectors to further asset building.

- Find ways to help different sectors connect.

- Rally different sectors around a common vision and mission.

- Connect asset building with existing strength-building efforts in the community.

- Look for opportunities to build key bridges.

- To sustain your work with organizations, consider:
  ‣ Clearly defining your initiative's role;
  ‣ Finding ways to be invitational;
  ‣ Practicing "strategic abandonment";
  ‣ Developing a plan; and
  ‣ Identifying benefits.

CHAPTER 6

Influence Civic Decisions

I realize that changing the world sounds quite ambitious. However, I believe through the effort put forth by the conferences and events supported by the United with Youth Fox Cities youth board, this [seemingly] insurmountable feat can be accomplished. Perhaps the best way to explain this is by using the domino effect analogy. If one person is able to positively affect the life of five individuals, those people will be able to continue the effort by interacting with other individuals. I truly believe that one person can make a difference.

MALLORY BRANDT STEINBERG, YOUTH MEMBER,
FOX CITIES UNITED WITH YOUTH BOARD

UNITED WAY OF NORTHWEST MICHIGAN was the catalyst for bringing together a group of key stakeholders in 1998 to explore the possibility of launching the Healthy Communities • Healthy Youth initiative that would become the GivEm 40 Coalition. Four of the five counties in the region border Lake Michigan, and nearly half of the area's 150,000 residents live in Grand Traverse County, home to Traverse City. The area's natural wonders attract an affluent population, but many working families earn considerably less than the state's average. Economic factors, combined with the area's rapid growth, created a sense of urgency among local groups to develop collaborative approaches to meet community goals.

The group quickly saw the potential for the developmental assets framework to help them launch the kind of movement-with-a-message that would resonate regionally. Enthusiasm ran high. One of the first lessons GivEm 40 learned was that widespread recognition of asset building through good marketing did not automatically translate into the depth of understanding needed to spark change. They made the decision to temporarily abandon work in some sectors to concentrate on in-depth efforts with those ready to get on board, rather than spreading too thinly across multiple sectors.

With this strategy, an initiative is involved in day-to-day efforts to influence decisions makers and opinion leaders to unleash and unite civic, financial, leadership, media, and policy resources to act upon and solidify all aspects of its vision. GivEm 40 did this by spending time up front to bring in a selection of players to round out the initiative's partnership, including:

- Three major **funders** who committed staff time and resources to support the initiative's launch. A critical component of this participation was that the **Youth Advisory Councils** of the Grand Traverse Regional Community Foundation came in, too. The funders adopted the asset framework as the basis of their youth-related grant making.
- An early partnership with **evaluators** from Michigan State University's Institute for Children, Youth and Families and Outreach Partnership Program. The evaluators committed to learning with the initiative how to shift to measuring assets, not deficits. They helped the initiative develop its strategies and actions in ways that made them clearer and more measurable.
- An early partnership with **local media** to get them on board and fully educate them in advance of the survey *(Search Institute Profiles of Student Life: Attitudes and Behaviors)* to measure assets. The initiative forged this relationship to assuage the fears of local school administrators that their survey results would be reported in a negative way or with comparisons between schools.

Wanting to use the survey findings as a catalyst for action, the coalition spent two full years laying its groundwork, from the time it first brought stakeholders together until its original survey results were unveiled at the Rally Around Youth in spring 1999. Spending time on reaching a critical mass of commitment from funding sources, media, evaluators, and the schools paid off. All of the region's 19 school districts conducted the initial survey during the same week, the media coverage was positive, and, as a result, asset building in the school sector took off like a shot. "The schools took ownership and responsibility for the practice of asset building in their environment," says GivEm 40 Coordinator Alan VanderPaas. "This defines our long-term goal—sustainability through community ownership."

To influence civic decisions, your initiative needs to support, promote, and link the community's overall asset-building work. "This strategy is often the core work of an initiative, coalition, or organization that's supporting the community's asset-building work," says Search Institute's Gene Roehlkepartain. "Rather than seeing its role as *doing* the community's asset building, the initiative focuses on inspiring and equipping the people, places, policies, and systems of the community to engage in asset building." This means taking steps to monitor the progress of asset building, linking people together, and continually socializing new leaders and residents into the community's new vision for asset building.

Fulfilling the Vision

As your initiative continues, you'll begin to see the fruits of your efforts in the initiative itself and in the community. New people will constantly be introduced to asset building while participants will consistently be reinforced about the work and their role in it. Working collectively, everyone will keep coming up with new, creative ways to move asset building forward. Over time, the goal is for asset building to become a way of life, deeply embedded in policies, programs, and practices throughout the community.

As your initiative matures, you'll be able to see more clearly the gaps in the community's asset-building resources, and you may choose to develop the capacity to fill those gaps yourself or engage community partners who can. Ultimately, you will more clearly understand the distinction between the *actions* your initiative is taking (tactics, logistics, networking, and organizing) and the *responses* to your efforts—the asset building that is happening in the community.

What does it take to unleash and unite community supports for change? When the researchers on the National Asset-Building Case Study Project analyzed how the four participating initiatives worked to unite and unleash broader support for transforming their community, several key themes emerged. Think about these points as you do the same.

Initiatives are strategic. Initiatives that have been in operation for several years tend to emphasize careful, intentional action. They learn to exercise judgment in decisions that have potential for powerful results. They learn when to let some things go; they also learn when to extend and take risks. Bainbridge Island, Washington's It's About Time for Kids, for example, began its project with a 45-member Leadership Team fully supported by the mayor and city council. After meeting for a year, however, participation dwindled. The initiative's advisory council made a strategic decision to narrow its activities and use the limited resources available in a targeted way, concentrating on developing a focused, functional annual work plan.

Some strategic decisions to consider:

- How to use the asset framework to organize the direction of a broad range of related activities.
- How to help participants incorporate the common vision of asset building into their individual missions.
- How to consolidate and manage resources, such as raising or using existing funds and knowing when to join in or hand off to other community efforts.
- Where to start or continue building cross-sector commitment to asset-building work.
- How to institutionalize asset building across the board in order to sustain the work throughout the community in the years to come.

Initiatives consciously determine leadership. Maturing initiatives find ways to balance the different kinds of leadership needed to move their work forward. Enthusiastic individuals with a passion for asset building (sometimes called "asset champions") can be crucial in helping build key bridges early in your initiative's development, and you'll need those strong individuals throughout the life of the initiative. "If you're going to have long-term success," said Georgetown, Texas, Director Barbara Pearce at a 2000 Healthy Communities • Healthy Youth conference workshop, "someone has to be willing to take on asset building and spearhead it."

You're also deliberately cultivating leaders—both youth and adults—from organizations or groups who model the asset framework and work together to pay careful attention to the timing, action, and planning. By sharing the work, you gain the advantage of sharing the vision and preventing burnout. In St. Louis Park, Minnesota, for example, an executive team handles the day-to-day business details while a vision team handles the bigger picture. "Don't try to make one team take on all the work in your initiative as the initiative keeps expanding," advises Search Institute's Nancy Tellett-Royce. "It can derail your momentum."

Finally, you're looking for ways to cultivate shared leadership and strong partnerships so that the initiative can survive the inevitable turnover in the ranks led by what Georgetown Project organizers described to 2000 HC • HY conference participants as the visible advocates. "Leadership starts with the condition of the heart," Georgetown Police Department Sergeant Todd Turbish

Photograph courtesy of the Sage-ing Center.

Planning together and then presenting plans and ideas to decision makers, as this intergenerational pair of initiative participants from Florida's Healthy Communities Initiative is doing, shows the power of youth and adults to change their communities for the better.

told participants. "Leadership is the lifeblood of your effort. If you don't have leadership dispersed throughout your initiative, it's dead in the water."

Initiatives grasp the impact—and promote the credibility—of asset building. All initiatives face the tasks of measuring, evaluating, and documenting what they're doing. Results are vital to helping you figure out what to do next and how to sustain your initiative; the initiative itself needs to know what's working and not working. Formal and informal measures help you decide where to concentrate your resources, whether you're having a broader impact, or whether you can see evidence of orientation shifts among organizations and groups in your community toward an asset-building approach. Maturing initiatives find ways to share these good results with community decision makers to promote the initiative's credibility. You can do this through publicizing the group's collective efforts, disseminating research, and advancing credible leaders.

Challenges are met and managed. As an initiative continues, it will need to identify and overcome an ever-changing collection of obstacles, such as:

- Inevitable leadership changes.
- Becoming overextended.

- Resistance from groups who fear you will take resources away from them or who feel defensive because they think you're telling them they're not doing a good job.
- Maintaining quality control as asset building spreads.
- Shifting political climates.
- Feeling progress is minimized because some sectors or key players won't get involved or drag their feet.
- Mobility and growth of participants—including youth—in and out of the initiative.
- Resource cutbacks or old biases, either of which can lead to falling back into the habit of dealing with youth only as problems.

The Moorhead Healthy Community Initiative, for example, has been managing two ongoing challenges. One involves trying to facilitate community agreement about building a teen center. "There's been energy and motivation about doing a teen center for a long time," says MHCI coordinator Barry Nelson, "but not enough funds or a clear consensus about what the center should look like."

What Barriers Might Make It Difficult for You to Influence Civic Decisions?

1. It's difficult to get bureaucracies to change.
Try this: Focus on individuals at first, and their direct connections to young people. Once they get it personally, they will act in their spheres of influence.

2. Classification of funding in specific (especially deficit) categories gets in the way of supporting a new way of working.
Try this: Focus on how existing programs can infuse asset building into their work.

3. Participants are willing but may not understand how change happens.
Try this: We're all learning how to make community change. Keep reading and learning. Talk to fellow asset builders. Watch for indicators of progress and discuss them.

"We have many people we consider 'warriors' for our ideas," says Alaska's Derek Peterson, "but their bureaucracy doesn't allow them to act." Peterson suggests these antidotes to barriers:

- Develop impetus for change at the grassroots level.
- Teach people how change happens.
- Then recruit those at the top who can make change happen and connect them with the grass roots.

The second issue involves trying to maintain an appropriately visible role in the community. Consistent with its plans, MHCI has shifted from providing some direct services to the less visible role of supporting independent development of asset-building services by others. This sometimes results in the early contributions of MHCI being downplayed, a liability when it comes time for the initiative to secure and sustain its own funding.

Initiatives change as they go and share what they learn. There are bumps in the road as well as successes, but many initiatives turn the bumps into lessons and then share those lessons with other initiatives. Gaining knowledge and experience sheds new light on difficult processes, procedures, and other challenges. This learning goes on among youth and adults as well as new and mature initiatives.

Assets for Colorado Youth (ACY), for example, recently concluded an in-depth evaluation of its efforts to understand more clearly what makes an initiative a catalyst for transformation. ACY is distributing its summary report, *Creating Social Change,* in both written and on-line form. Some of those findings are presented throughout this chapter.

Making It Happen

As your initiative matures, you realize what a complex balancing act you are trying to maintain. As Search Institute's Field Research Coordinator Shenita Lewis phrases it in the case study project report:

> The developmental assets framework is very user-friendly, which is key to its potential adoption as an innovative approach to youth and community development. But this seeming simplicity can also be deceptive. People are often resistant to the positive orientation toward youth, and tremendous effort is required for reaching that "critical mass" GivEm 40 insisted upon. There is a paradoxical tension between the simplicity of the developmental assets framework and the complexity of consistent implementation.

All initiatives are ventures that unfold in distinctly nonlinear ways. You're seeking to balance the dynamics of what you are deliberately trying to do with the dynamics of outside forces such as changes in funding, local events, and political climate. Throw in the bumps and thrills of strategic attempts to manage taking new risks, and the path can feel pretty uncharted.

But the anxieties all these efforts produce can help lead your collective work to transformation. "As each of the initiatives in the case study has suggested in one form or another," says Lewis, "periods of uncertainty can become opportunities for reinvention. In moments of travail and anxiety, community initiatives can, with a measure of faith, see that traversing the uncharted waters of an asset initiative does indeed lead to the desired destination of a healthy community for all our youth. That's what's appealing, exhilarating, and empowering about this work."

Consider these specific objectives as you keep working toward that desired destination:

1. **Cultivate a shared vision.** Invite community members to develop, articulate, and keep alive a shared vision for an asset-rich community.

2. **Recruit and network champions.** Nurture relationships with those who champion the asset framework—people who have the passion to spread the word and help make the vision a reality. Create opportunities for these "champions" to learn from, support, and inspire each other.

3. **Communicate.** Communicate about the initiative, the vision, and what people can do by continuing to distribute information, make presentations, and tap the media to raise awareness about asset building and local efforts and successes.

4. **Strengthen capacity.** Provide or facilitate training, technical assistance, coaching, tools, or other resources that help individuals and organizations in their asset-building efforts.

5. **Reinforce and influence.** Seek to influence policies and systems in the community to support and reinforce the vision of an asset-rich community so that resources and commitments sustain the efforts long term.

6. **Reflect, learn, and celebrate.** Monitor, reflect on, and learn from current realities, progress, and challenges. Highlight and honor asset-building efforts and progress in the community.

The activities in the Assets in Action section are organized by these six tasks.

Assets in Action
Cultivate a Shared Vision
Invite community members to develop, articulate, and keep alive a shared vision for an asset-rich community.

Visions of an asset-rich community. Articulating and maintaining an asset-building vision is a task you'll come back to repeatedly throughout the life of your initiative. You started with a vision when you launched your initiative. Through mobilizing adults, engaging youth, and infusing assets into the community, use the vision to unify multiple efforts and to help hold focus as more join the effort and the initiative matures. "As we evolved through our first years in the planning stages, I thought sometimes we'd never get 'there,'" Georgetown Project Director Barbara Pearce told participants at the 2000 HC • HY conference. "But we'd go back to this vision that was driving us and then move forward again. We created our activities to contribute to that vision."

In its final report as a Jostens Our Town grant winner, the initiative described how it used its vision to develop activities, starting by articulating this "Imagine Georgetown" vision: "Imagine a community where no child is hungry, hurt, alone or rejected and where all children believe they are loved, respected, and treated with dignity."

Then the project looked at what resources already existed in the community to fulfill this vision and depicted them by drawing circles on a page. The first thing initiative members noticed was that there were few connections between circles of resources. "We've really worked to bring circles together around specific issues so that now we're moving in clusters of circles," says Pearce.

She cites as one example bringing six organizations together to address the fact that children who received free and reduced-cost lunches during the school year had no such support in the summer. "No one was willing to do it alone," said Pearce in the final report, "but with six groups doing it, it became a more reasonable task."

The groups collaborate on a summer enrichment program called Kid City that not only feeds kids but also offers summer-long activities. The program is managed through a combination of several paid Parks and Recreation staff and lots of congregation volunteers. "Lots of good things happened and it wasn't just the children we touched," said Pearce. "It was the fact that all of these groups were coming together and sharing a model for collaboration."

Youth and vision. GivEm 40 in Traverse City, Michigan, has successfully mounted several large-scale **youth-driven events** as a way of sharing the vision and generating enthusiasm. In addition to its initiative launch, the Rally Around Youth, which attracted over 900 people (half of whom were youth), young people have been involved in putting on the Youth Summit on Violence Prevention and the Choose to Lead Conference.

The Youth Summit on Violence Prevention involved 500 students and faculty from 20 high schools. Young people learned about how to be asset builders with their peers as the best way to combat violence and were encouraged to fill out a pledge card with their personal commitment to build an asset in their community or school. The summit also ran a Youth Action Marketplace that featured 18 active youth organizations and offered 14 different breakout workshops, most led by young people, with ideas about how to build safer, stronger communities for young people.

The **Choose to Lead Conference** centered on youth effecting change within the school environment. Eight hundred students from a five-county region and 100 administrators, teachers, and community leaders came together to talk about ways to help their schools become more caring and connected places. Choose to Lead teams are now working in almost every middle and high school in the region.

SOMETIMES AN EFFECTIVE WAY TO COMMUNICATE *an initiative's vision is through the sharing of common or symbolic stories that help people understand the emotional or historical value of the work.*

The police department in Georgetown, Texas, did some thinking about what sort of symbol best described its initiative's vision and and leadership. Here's what Sergeant Todd Turbish told 2000 HC • HY conference participants they came up with:

"We picked up on the mascot of the Georgetown High School—the eagle—and did some research. The eagle is known for its vision, its courage, its strength, but more importantly, it's known as one of the greatest animals in the wild. It will spend more time with its young than any animal in the wild. When it teaches an eaglet to fly, it pushes it out and flies under it so that when the eaglet can't fly anymore and falls, the parent catches it on its back and supports and carries it. An eagle is the only animal in nature that can fly above a storm. When nature brings a storm into its environment, the eagle will fly above the storm in the sunshine until the storm is over. Children and youth look to us as leaders. They expect us to lead, to influence them so that their lives are full."

Recruit and Network Champions

Nurture relationships with those who champion asset building—people who have the passion to spread the word and help make the vision a reality. Create opportunities for these "champions" to learn from, support, and inspire each other.

The importance of asset champions. Assets for Colorado Youth (ACY) has emphasized identifying and equipping asset champions as one of its key strategies. ACY defines asset champions as "messengers who intentionally promote assets, successfully engage others in asset building, and advocate for youth—especially in forums where youth voices might rarely be heard." An examination of the role of asset champions in ACY's efforts found that these individuals play a significant role in the wide recognition and support of the asset framework. "The presence of asset champions contributes to the unfolding of asset building within communities and organizations," concludes the *Creating Social Change Summary* completed by Omni Institute for ACY.

The evaluation found that individuals who emerge as asset champions exhibit six key traits:

1. A deep sense of commitment and connection to the community;
2. A social conscience;
3. A magnetic quality that draws people together on behalf of youth;
4. Legitimacy as a social change agent and a messenger;

5. A heightened awareness of teachable moments; and
6. The ability to apply assets in ways that help individuals connect the asset message to their everyday lives.

Ultimately, asset champions were found to demonstrate a sustained commitment to and passion for assets and often serve as a hub for asset-building networks.

Asset roundtables. The Time for Kids initiative in Tarrant County, Texas, home to Fort Worth, sponsors bimonthly developmental assets roundtables as a way to share ideas, enthusiasm, and resources. Participants have an opportunity to come together to discuss how they are furthering the assets in their particular environment, and the roundtables have become a popular venue for discussing the best practices for increasing assets in all aspects of life. To facilitate discussion, each roundtable usually focuses on one area of the community.

During one meeting that focused on how congregations are furthering assets, one of the invited speakers included a young man whose African American Baptist church had developed a mentoring program for at-risk middle school children in the community. The program was based entirely on assets. Teachers of the young people later reported a marked increase in positive behavior and interest in schoolwork. The church hoped to expand the program to include a computer lab.

Communicate

Communicate about the initiative, the vision, and what people can do by continuing to distribute information, make presentations, and tap the media to raise awareness about asset building and local efforts.

The Power of One in Rochester Hills, Michigan

MURPHY EHLERS from St. Luke's United Methodist Church in Rochester Hills, Michigan, shares this story in his own words:

"A young man in 10th grade was caught with marijuana at school. They had a zero tolerance policy and when caught for the second time, he was suspended for a semester. Both his parents worked and could not quit their jobs [to stay home to keep an eye on their son]. The dad called me at church; he was very upset. Staying home and sleeping would have been just what this young man wanted, and who would supervise him? So I offered to pick him up every day on my way into church, and he did custodial and lots of other work. One of the senior men taught him how to strip furniture and more. I spent lots of time talking with him and when the semester was over, he was drug free and ready to go back to school with a healthy outlook on life and relationships."

The most important thing to remember about communicating the work of your initiative is to never stop. Do it often and in as many ways as you can think of. Then do it some more. Because this particular task is both vital and ongoing, this section includes a wealth of ideas for you.

Case study in communication. Portland, Oregon's Take the Time initiative was launched as a state-government-inspired campaign within the Commission on Children, Families, and Community of Multnomah County to measure youth wellness instead of deficits. The initiative, one of four studied in the National Asset-Building Case Study Project, began in 1997 with paid staff and an 18-member steering committee of youth and adult volunteers. Their work started, as does the work of many community-improvement efforts, with a conventional launch and media campaign in the community. However, the launch and campaign did not result in the expected flood of volunteers to the initiative. The Portland organizers paused to step back and rethink their strategies.

First, the staff and steering committee decided to tackle a deeper understanding of how change takes place. "Portland decided to view the developmental assets framework not so much as the model of community change, but rather as 'the what and the why,'" says Search Institute's Field Research Coordinator Shenita Lewis.

Prompted by both diffusion-of-innovations theory and Malcolm Gladwell's best-selling book *The Tipping Point: How Little Things Can Make a Big Difference,* the initiative adopted the premise that change is disseminated person by person in relationships in a series of stages similar to Search Institute's change pathway.

Young people were instrumental in launching a drive to transform the entire community's media culture.

"Their work emphasizes listening, rather than 'preaching' the developmental assets," continues Lewis. "It also honors the individual's, program's, or sector's existing 'system.'"

Two very successful tactics formed the centerpiece of Portland's strategies. The first was the awarding of minigrants of $200–$500 totaling $100,000 to more than 200 organizations and individuals. Many of the grants went to support school-community partnerships using the asset framework. One example, the Middle School Outreach Project, expanded its reach into the community by targeting parent involvement. Other minigrants went to community art and gardening projects, and to groups promoting intergenerational and cross-cultural activities.

The minigrants were then highlighted in the second prominent initiative tactic: an ambitious new media campaign. Young people were instrumental in launching a drive to transform the entire community's media culture. "If a teen goes into a store and the security guard starts following him around, it's because the guard thinks the teen's going to shoplift," says former Youth Advisory Board Cochair Jessica Weit. "The guard got that mind-set from the media.

Deciding to target the media was huge, but we felt it affected even the simplest things in the everyday lives of teens."

Weit and other teens were invited by an editor at Portland's daily newspaper, the *Oregonian,* who happened to be evaluating their youth coverage at that time, to come up with ideas for making the paper's coverage of young people more balanced. A summerlong partnership between the young people and the editor led to the newspaper's assigning a full-time reporter to cover youth issues exclusively, starting a weekly feature on youth issues called "The Zone," and expanding the paper's coverage of youth events beyond sports, proms, and crime.

Initiative staff also persuaded many of the county's major media outlets to become partners on the asset-building team. Their efforts resulted in 2 million dollars' worth of donated ad space, sponsorship, and television and radio coverage as well as help from a hot advertising agency in Portland called NERVE, Inc., which donated $300,000 of its time through advertising, a Web site, and promotional advice. The media strategy was all part of the initiative's design to help move people from knowledge to action.

Consistent and oft-repeated messages are vital to launching and sustaining an asset-building initiative. As Portland learned, just informing people does not guarantee that they will take action. To fully embed asset building into a community's policies, programs, and organizations, an initiative must repeatedly promote and raise awareness of asset building in a variety of redundant and overlapping ways.

This task starts with cultivating and reinforcing a shared vision of contributing to the healthy development of young people. This may involve the judicious use of media and promotion tactics to do the following:

- Consistently remind people about asset building and their role in it;
- Constantly introduce new people to assets; and
- Embed asset building in policies and practices throughout the community.

Communications breakthrough. The Take the Time Initiative of Multnomah County (Portland), Oregon, established a free lending library of asset-building resources to provide follow-up for educators and others who "get all fired up" after coming in contact with the initiative. Leveraging Search Institute's in-kind support through Take the Time's Jostens Our Town Award, the initiative purchased an extensive collection of books, videos, and other learning materials to share with educators, youth, parents, mentors, and other caring adults. Among the available materials was the initiative's own booklet, *Building Assets in Schools: Moving from Incidental to Intentional.*

After a four-year effort, the booklet and lending library, combined with initiative workshops, finally helped catalyze support within the Portland Public Schools for becoming full partners with the initiative. One important result—a highly successful asset training called the Principal's Academy attended by more than 100 school administrators.

Media-savvy young people. Because young people today are growing up with many media options, they can be significant, savvy partners in coming up with creative ways to promote messages and opportunities. So infuse asset building into your promotional efforts. Rather than turning promotional activities over to a committee of adult "experts," urge the adults to seek out and join with a group of young people to share the work and the learning.

"I think young people get excited by events," says Ian Rataczak, a former youth member of the Colorado Springs initiative's Youth Assets Council. "Asset building needs to be continuous, but you need signature projects to help people get involved." Rataczak was instrumental, for example, in planning a daylong Teen Town Hall. "We look for ways to give youth a voice to make them feel they're being heard by each other as well as community leaders."

Expand your concept of "the media." Activate and leverage a wide variety of communications channels to get your initiative's messages out repeatedly: meetings, conferences, focus groups, networking, trainings, organization newsletters, and congregation bulletins. Remember: you're looking for both formal and informal channels for getting the message out. Keep an eye out for unusual channels, too; some initiatives, for example, always make sure they have a float in local parades or put their messages on bus signs.

Karen Atkinson of Children First, St. Louis Park, Minnesota, offers three good reasons to include a focus on the use of other organizations' printed vehicles and meetings: credibility is inherent in others sharing the message; consistency of message is enhanced when the same message is heard across sectors; and it's cost effective, often free!

There are also the media, of course—newspapers, television, radio, cable, and the Web. Carmen Patent with the Nebraska Asset Building Coalition has specialized in developing asset-oriented media strategies. She advocates developing media partners to help you learn how to spread the asset message and offers these tips:

1. *Consider writing a media plan before you start.* "We wouldn't have been able to grow and coordinate as well without one," says Patent. "I share it with everybody." You don't need money to do this, either. Portland and other initiatives have found volunteers with media and marketing experience who willingly help develop plans.
2. *Remember the asset message comes first.* Sometimes radio and television will want to treat your message like a commercial, but that's not really what you're doing. You're providing a positive message for families first.

What Barriers Might Make It Difficult for You to Promote Asset Messages and Opportunities?

1. Little or no budget for communications.

Try this: Short asset messages can be placed in congregation bulletins and parent newsletters sent home by the schools.

2. No experience in media, public relations, or marketing.

Try this: Every community has someone with some expertise in these areas; consider asking a high school or college journalism or marketing class to take on your initiative as a class project.

3. Too narrow a focus on traditional media as the only outlet for messages.

Try this: A study of an asset awareness campaign launched across Colorado found that ad placements in local weekly papers generated more calls than did ads on the network TV affiliates.

3. *Network with your media partners.* You have to be in touch with them all the time. You have to meet their needs and deadlines, too, in order to develop trust.

4. *Keep your messages personal.* It's what makes us unique. Don't be afraid to project messages that ring honest, genuine, and caring.

5. *Be willing to adapt and grow.* Keep track of what you do as you go. By evaluating how your messages are spread, shared, or transmitted to others inside and outside the initiative, you can calculate your successes and adjust your communications strategies when necessary. You'll learn along the way.

Become "media fierce." Develop a working understanding of the role of the media in your initiative, including how the media shape people's perspectives on youth and how to use the media to enhance the initiative's work. Portland is one example here, and another comes from Boise, Idaho. The HC • HY Initiative of Ada County brought a variety of media representatives to the table; together, they decided that building healthy youth was an aim that called for modeling cooperation. An unprecedented level of cooperation among all five TV stations, the *Idaho Statesman* newspaper, and *Boise Family* magazine resulted.

Boise Family ran coinciding asset information, and the *Idaho Statesman* has developed a weekly youth page that is written by high school and middle school students. Along with a feature-length article, the page includes regular departments:

- My Best Shot—favorite snapshots;
- Kudos—recognizing good deeds;

- Making a Difference—volunteer profiles;
- Get Involved—volunteer opportunities; and
- Successful Assets—what adults and young people can do to build a particular asset.

The three network affiliates, the Fox affiliate, and an independent station have sometimes "roadblocked" their public service announcements so that each station airs the same script at the same time. "Together, we can make our community the best place in the nation to be young!" is one message Boise viewers heard one evening on whatever station they tuned in. And viewers saw the asset philosophy in action: each station's anchorperson paired with a youth to deliver the announcements together.

Seep information into other channels. Many initiatives find logical, creative, and cost-saving ways to combine getting the message out by embedding asset-building information in community directories, catalogs, calendars, and reports. Some representative examples include:

- **The Get Connected Youth Directory**—High school action team members on the Mason City, Iowa, HC • HY initiative produce a **directory** for their peers full of information and resources on health, cultural events, legal issues, crisis agencies, volunteer opportunities, and things to do. They gather all the material and distribute up to 2,000 copies to schools, service providers, and other community groups.
- **Parks and Recreation Guide**—The Parks and Recreation Department in Clarkston, Michigan, provides space every year for the HC • HY Coalition for Youth to produce a four-page **insert about asset building.** The guide goes out to 10,000 households.
- The It's About Time for Kids Initiative on Bainbridge Island in Washington State **piggybacks** its information at no extra cost through a Glaser Foundation quarterly newsletter that goes to every resident on the island.
- The Central Bucks 40 Asset Project in Doylestown, Pennsylvania, **collaborates** with its local hospital to insert information about developmental assets into paychecks and new parent packets.
- **Team television**—The Youth Asset Team involved with the Kanawha Coalition for Community Health Improvement in Charleston, West Virginia, has partnered with a local television station to produce **weekly segments** titled "Building Dreams, Building Futures, Building Kanawha County Youth." Every Tuesday evening, an asset is highlighted and viewers are shown how to help build that asset. One segment involved high school theater students and local business people participating in a program called "Role Models— The Good, the Bad, and the Ugly."
- **And more television**—The Youth Service Bureau, the YMCA, and others collaborate on providing a unique television experience for young people in

Fort Wayne, Indiana called **Team TV.** With training and access to equipment provided, the Youth Communication Network of local young people produce their own high-quality television shows and a Web site centered on youth issues. Among their many activities, young people produce a monthly forum broadcast live on community TV, create Web casts, and recruit young people to be media representatives from community groups like congregations, schools, or other youth organizations. Check out what they do at www.ymca-teamtv.org/start.htm.

▶ **Public service announcements**—PSAs are a very popular way of getting the asset message out, and young people love getting involved in their production. Many radio and television stations welcome these 10- to 30-second spots and will often help local groups produce them. One aspect of Traverse City, Michigan's GivEm 40 media partnership has been PSAs **featuring local youth speaking** in their own words to share the key messages of the initiative. A local high school video class also produces PSAs on school climate.

Carmen Patent of the Nebraska Asset Building Coalition takes PSAs one step further in her **Growing a Healthy Community media campaign.** To reach listeners in her 22-county "community" in northeastern Nebraska, she persuaded local radio stations to let her do a two-minute asset "spot" each day coupled with a 30-second PSA produced by the station. She's even brought in students in grades 1 and 2 to help her do some asset segments that became local favorites.

▶ **Web sites**—Web sites are a very popular venue for publicizing asset building, particularly because they can be updated at any time. They're also popular because many initiatives have plenty of youth interested in designing and maintaining the Web sites—an asset-building activity in and of itself! A sampling of initiative Web sites includes:

- www.cary-youth.org—The Web site for C.A.R.Y. (Creating Assets, Reaching Youth) in North Carolina gives basic information on assets, upcoming events, and even parenting tips.
- www.takethetime.org—Portland, Oregon's site focuses on showing adults in the community who aren't necessarily parents how to build assets for and with kids. They constantly cull stories from the community to refresh their content.
- www.project-aim.org—Youth have developed the Web site for Assets in Motion in Prairie Village, Kansas, as well as produced a video and designed the initiative's brochure. The site advertises its bilingual trainings on asset development, mentoring, and personal and organizational asset mapping.
- www.buildingyouth.com—Warren, Pennsylvania's site includes a history of the initiative. The timeline (beginning in 1997) documents the people and sectors involved, as well as numerous awareness-raising and promo-

tion events and activities; its an invaluable resource for new and established initiatives.

Coordinate marketing strategy. The statewide Assets for Colorado Youth (ACY) initiative is one of several initiatives that have brought together a variety of appealing and consistent elements into a multileveled, coordinated marketing strategy. Among ACY's many activities:

ASSETS
for Colorado
YOUTH

- The development and use of a recognizable **logo.** The logo, often paired with a tagline about what ACY does, clearly communicates that the initiative's work involves young people;
- The publication of a quarterly **newsletter,** free to interested readers, which reports on current projects, community awards, new trainings, evaluation results, and best practices;
- The dissemination of ACY's **annual report on CD-ROM;**
- A **Web site** (www.buildassets.org) that reinforces ACY's asset-building priorities of providing information and training for educators and parents as well as distributing resources and materials in Spanish and English on cultural diversity;
- A series of **original publications and materials**—many in Spanish and English—including *The Spirit of Culture* and *Parenting with Purpose;*
- Consistent use of the newsletter and Web site to **market** printed materials and trainings;
- An internal emphasis on **storytelling** that allows initiative participants to constantly gather the results of asset building for circulation among ACY's materials, trainings, and events; and
- The hiring of a marketing and communications **specialist** to coordinate the initiative's promotional activities.

Put artists to work. The Asset Development Network in San Luis Obispo County, California, supports its many youth task forces, situated in various communities, in finding creative ways to get the message out:

Resources to Help You Promote Asset Building

NOT EVERY INITIATIVE HAS A COMMUNICATIONS TEAM or the ability to connect with a publicity expert. If you're a small initiative, or even a solitary person who wants to promote asset building through presentations and the media, two ready-to-use resources available from Search Institute can equip any asset champion to become a one-person dynamo in spreading the asset message:

Get the Word Out: Communication Tools and Ideas for Asset Builders Everywhere is like a mini-media campaign in a single book. Section one provides background information and basic principles for deciding on core messages and communication strategies. It also includes worksheets to help you identify goals, audiences, vehicles for message communication, and follow-up steps. Section two provides inspiration and learning from the real success stories of five HC • HY initiatives. Section three is a compendium of ideas you can use to create your own success. And the core of the book is a large section of ready-to-use materials: articles about the assets, press releases, sample letters to the editor, public service announcement scripts, awareness-raising handouts, and more. And as a bonus, all the ready-to-use materials are available for purchasers of this resource to download from Search Institute's Web site for easy adaptation to your unique needs.

Speaking of Developmental Assets: Presentation Resources and Strategies is a three-ring binder of complete resources for making presentations to almost any audience about the developmental assets and asset building. A basic brief presentation script is followed by two outlines for adapting the script to longer speaking opportunities. And other tabbed sections of the binder provide information on customizing the message to the needs of specific audiences, answers to frequently asked questions, ready-to-copy handouts, and transparencies for the presentation. This resource also provides a password with which you can download from the Search Institute Web site a PowerPoint presentation to adapt for any speaking opportunity.

> **LEARN MORE:** For more information on these resources and related trainings available from Search Institute, see the Resources listed at the end of this book or visit www.search-institute.org.

- Teens with the **Grover Beach** South County Youth Coalition Youth Asset Team petitioned the city for permission to paint bus stop benches with asset messages. The city couldn't authorize painting the benches but was so impressed by the teens' presentation, they offered them mural space in a community park instead. The plan is for new artwork to incorporate one asset a month over a period of several years.
- A brand-new skate park in **Cambria** will soon showcase youth artwork with asset messages incorporated into ramps and on five 4'-x-8' billboards

attached to fencing. This project is a collaboration between the Cambria Coalition for Youth and Cambria's Community Center.

- ▶ The **Paso Robles** Youth Task Force helped design a series of asset banners that welcomed residents and visitors during the community's Cultural Heritage Days. The 2'-x-4' green-and-yellow vinyl banners had tips on both sides like "You can encourage, you can listen" and will be reused for other upcoming events.

Sustain your communication efforts. Promoting the asset message is just one important aspect of a complex series of maneuvers all initiatives are trying to juggle. You are trying to educate those around you and encourage them at the same time to take their newfound wisdom to the next step—action on behalf of young people. You're also challenging the status quo of public perceptions about young people and trying to engage the forces that often shape those perceptions, the media, as allies to create and sustain a new vision.

Some final ideas to keep in mind as you move forward in your efforts to promote asset building:

Make it personal. All the awareness raising you do won't go anywhere if people don't think about how it applies in their own lives. Getting local, credible voices involved in all aspects of your message promotion helps make those personal connections that most people will find meaningful. Nebraska's Carmen Patent, for example, likes to recruit recognized people from the community to do her two-minute asset radio spots. "When our school principal goes on the radio and talks about wanting to have a great school," says Patent, "that means something to that community."

Make assets your priority. "We've remained wary of using any marketing approach that places high importance on image and flashy messaging, sound bites and media frenzy," says GivEm 40's Mimi Petritz-Appel. "Marketing is important because it helps to create the excitement that generates interest. Initiatives must keep the message in rotation. Yet, we keep it secondary to the meaningful work of asset building, of demonstrating that it is not necessarily *what* you do but *how* you do it."

Many resources are available to you in the community and among your volunteers to promote asset-building messages, policies, practices, and opportunities. While you may not have a lot of financial resources to develop a media plan, it is possible to gather a "kitchen cabinet" of local experts to help you come up with one. Such a plan can then become a useful tool in garnering funding to achieve some of your communications strategies. With the involvement and insight of youth in particular, you are likely to discover the unique concerns of your community and be able to address them in ways that have a long-lasting effect.

Strengthen Capacity

Provide or facilitate training, technical assistance, coaching, tools, or other resources that help individuals and organizations in their asset-building efforts.

Share Shop asset trainings. Youth and adults working on the HC • HY initiative in Brown County, Wisconsin, have been busy developing a number of venues in which to share information and successes, starting with local asset trainings called Share Shops. The trainings provide a forum for community members to brainstorm how to use the 40 assets in their everyday lives to create positive change. In cooperation with school districts, the members of the Brown County Teen Leadership also participate in five daylong trainings that take place during the school year. Youth learn how to network and collaborate with organizations and individuals. Local governments, businesses, and the community are very involved in this project, which is modeled after a successful adult training.

Coaching congregations. The HC • HY of Lehigh Valley, Pennsylvania, provided training and technical assistance to its United Way to help design a special asset-based funding initiative. The funding initiative supports faith communities to develop or expand after-school programs with asset-based curriculums. Faith communities are asked to operate their programs between 3 and 6 p.m., complete an asset-building checklist for congregations, identify strategies for building four to six assets, and demonstrate positive outcomes for participating children and youth. At least ten communities of faith have begun asset-based after-school programs using this funding.

Asset-building neighborhoods. The Colorado Springs Assets for Youth initiative works with the Pikes Peak Area Rotary and the Colorado Springs Parks and Recreation Department to host asset-building discussion groups in neighborhoods. The groups used a Search Institute resource, *Taking Asset Building Personally*, to ground the discussions. (See this book's Resources section for details about the resource.) Starting with six groups, weekly 90-minute discussions were held over six weeks that focused on how neighborhoods could improve youth's perceptions that fewer than one in three adults care about them. Each group was assisted in creating and adopting an action plan to implement at least one change in the neighborhood and its local school.

Technical assistance. Take the Time in Multnomah (Portland) County, Oregon, provided technical assistance and materials to four local organizations to help them more fully incorporate asset building into their practices:

- *Commission on Children, Families and Community* (the initiative's parent organization), which increased youth participation and redesigned meetings to make them more youth-friendly;

- *Camp Fire Boys & Girls,* which launched a new initiative of its own that pairs adults with youth and emphasizes relationship building, reciprocity, and mentoring;
- *Portland Impact,* which developed a model for "family coaching" in which adult-youth teams visit families to assist them in using their strengths to find solutions to challenges they face; and
- *FamilyWorks,* a community and family service center, which held a series of events designed to give youth a voice in redesigning the organization to be more youth-friendly.

Reinforce and Influence

Seek to influence policies and systems in the community to support and reinforce the vision of an asset-rich community so that resources and commitments are in place to sustain the efforts over the long term.

A long-term plan. Since its launching in 1999, the Healthy Community • Healthy Youth of Ada County initiative in Boise, Idaho, has had a clear understanding of the time it will take to embed assets in the community. Starting with an ambitious vision that states "our community will become the best place in the nation to be young," the HC • HY initiative has developed a strategic plan that seeks to:

- Align resources, initiatives, and commitments of service providers, agencies, and the philanthropic community to advance our mission (to increase developmental assets in the lives of all young people);
- Use the data on community young people's levels of assets to prioritize needs, mobilize action, policy making, and resource allocation;
- Track outcomes to build shared accountability for results; and
- Engage community members from all sectors and walks of life to ensure that their choices at home, work, play, and worship support positive youth development.

HC • HY leaders envision a 20-year plan for a paradigm shift to the assets philosophy. The goal is that the formal HC • HY initiative will eventually become unnecessary and "disappear" as the community aligns itself with asset building.

So far, the initiative has produced some solid results, including the involvement of more than 200 organizations. By emphasizing collaboration and coordination among all sectors in the community, the initiative has influenced a wide variety of participants and reinforced asset building on many levels. Among its outcomes:

- Positively influencing strategic plans, activities, and curriculum development within the city of Boise, the Boise and Kuna School Districts, the United Way of Treasure Valley, the Boise Family YMCA, and St. Luke's Regional Medical Center, among others;

- Successfully supporting youth membership on key commissions and boards for the city, United Way, YMCA, Big Brothers Big Sisters, Boys & Girls Clubs and many others;
- Unifying regional media on behalf of assets (see page 135–136);
- Offering a consistent vision to youth as they develop their own projects such as a multigenerational café, an education skit troupe, writing school curricula, and producing films; and
- Influencing the Idaho state legislature to allocate $300,000 to the Children's Trust Fund for statewide asset building.

Citywide action. Since 1996, the city of Bellevue, Washington (a large suburban city just east of Seattle), and the Bellevue School District have collaborated on the It's About Time for Kids initiative. Since conducting the *Search Institute Profiles of Student Life: Attitudes and Behaviors* survey the first time, the two institutions have incorporated asset building within the city and schools as well as partnered with other organizations in the community. An awareness of asset building helps drive the city's budget process, and the youth-led Youth Link Board and Bellevue Youth Council contribute to setting priorities and directing funds for youth activities.

An awareness of asset building helps drive the city's budget process, and the youth-led Youth Link Board and Bellevue Youth Council contribute to setting priorities and directing funds for youth activities.

In 2000, Bellevue students once again took the survey. The results were used in two ways. First, the city and school district cosponsored a daylong Community Summit to release the results. The summit featured guest speakers and community leaders, a youth-produced video highlighting survey results, and facilitated workshops on key assets in which participants were encouraged to implement a short-term asset-building project. Half the attendees of the several hundred participants were youth and school staff who received release time from the district. Participants received free registration and a wealth of asset materials produced especially for the event.

Second, initiative staff (who are city employees of the Parks and Community Services Department) conducted focus groups with youth to discuss the survey results and find out why they thought some asset levels were lower or higher than others. Staff talked with a total of 114 middle and high school students in seven different groups from a cross section of the city's public, private, and alternative schools, as well as one after-school club and a faith-based youth group. Among the results, staff learned:

- Youth believed that the number of youth using tobacco decreased from 9 percent to 5 percent because of the effectiveness of antismoking television ads (especially the "TRUTH" ads) and school DARE programs.
- Youth said younger students have more assets than older students do because they have more adult support.
- Youth suggested that adults could *demonstrate* they value youth more by being more polite and showing respect for young people as well as spending more time with them.

The city and school district are using the results of the survey, summit, and focus groups to determine the next set of steps in the ongoing asset-building work in Bellevue.

Vision at the civic level. Many initiatives channel the natural enthusiasm young people have for civic engagement by experimenting with different kinds of asset-building plans with local governments. The San Luis Obispo Youth Task Force approached its city council in 1998 with the idea of implementing a **Youth Master Plan,** which would set aside money every year to be used for asset-building programs in the city. Network Cochair Richard Enfield says it was actually a pretty easy sell. "When teens that are really together go to a government body and do a good job of presenting their case, it's less of a hard sell than you might think." The city now sets aside $15,000 a year for asset-building grants of up to $5,000. Some projects have included a Friday night basketball program at the YMCA, support of environmental clubs, and video productions. Youth help select the grant recipients.

Hampton, Virginia's Mobilization for Youth has worked with its city government to incorporate asset building into the city's **strategic and neighborhood plans.** Various city officials serve on initiative leadership teams, and the Employee Council has developed an asset project creating volunteer opportunities for any city employee. Asset information is distributed through the city newsletter and local television programming. Assets are also the focus of the city's Youth in Government program, which recognizes hundreds of youth who volunteer in city departments.

Cool happenings in Alaska. What's the first thing that comes to mind when you think of Alaska? Ice? Polar bears? Oil?

If Derek Peterson has his way, the United States' northern-most state will soon be known as much for its human resources as for these natural ones. Since 1995 Peterson has been the director of child/youth advocacy for the Association of Alaska School Boards (AASB). He came to the position with a passion for asset building and the idea that the AASB was a "sleeping giant" ready to be awakened to the idea of building developmental assets. With a fantastic network of political leaders, state and federal agencies, school staff and officials, and everyday heroes now in place, his goal is for Alaska to be recognized as the best place in the nation to raise children and youth.

The history of AASB's commitment to a strength-based approach precedes Peterson. In 1991 the board of directors created the Child Advocacy Committee and charged it with "promoting parental, public, and social service commitment to the shared responsibility of educating all children in public education." This was no small assignment, especially in a region as diverse and geographically spread out as Alaska. But the results have been breathtaking.

Peterson spoke in October 2002 with asset-building champions from Oklahoma, Arkansas, and Nevada. He was quick to remind these leaders that it's too early for his team to measure their success in terms of increased assets. Indeed, the hope is that they will be able to show evidence of change in fifteen years. Yes, years. That's practically a lifetime by today's funding standards. In the meantime, though, Peterson points to other indications that their work is well on its way to becoming part of the culture of Alaska: the $14 million (including funds from the American Indian Education Equity Act) that has been secured to support a statewide Initiative for Community Engagement (Alaska ICE); the more than $35 million that has been leveraged in order to infuse asset building into every school in Alaska; the gubernatorial candidates who in their campaign speeches each made statements about the power of developmental assets; the eleven school districts that have measured assets (some of them multiple times) using the *Search Institute Profiles of Student Life: Attitudes and Behaviors* survey; the eight regional asset-focused conferences that have been held; the support and buy-in from local media; the worldwide distribution of 125,000 copies of the book linking assets to the stories and values of Alaskan Natives; and the relationships, partnerships, and shared commitments that have been forged.

Above all else, the intentionally collaborative nature of the effort may be the key to its success. For the first six years that Peterson was on board with AASB (www.aasb.org), the goal was not to raise money for their own work but rather to advocate and work on behalf of like-minded agencies and organizations. In that same vein, all Alaskan asset-building trainers have a standard rule: they never tell people what assets are . . . they ask them what kids need. These listening-, service-, and support-based approaches create an environment in which everyone owns the framework and begins to accept responsibility for making change happen. As Peterson explains, "If you asked any group [in Alaska] about assets, they would all say they introduced it and I would agree." The result, he says, is that "we're embedding the story of assets into Alaska's story."

While the amount of money Alaska ICE has been able to secure and leverage is impressive, Peterson says it's only the beginning. He envisions a statewide initiative that spends $2.1 billion per year. In other words, he hopes that eventually every dollar spent in Alaska will be directly related either to building assets for and with children and youth or to supporting the systems, services, and structures that do.

Sharing resources, philosophy, and results. The Summit County Asset Builders of the Summit initiative in Frisco, Colorado, has forged a strong partnership with its county department of Youth and Family Services to support AmeriCorps Promise Fellows in spreading the asset philosophy through their service plans. Promise Fellows help develop and promote activities based on a specific asset every year such as figuring out new ways for youth to feel valued by the community. Some of their results include:

- Developing a youth advisory board, which drafted its own strategic plans and also collaborated with violence prevention efforts in the community;
- Helping youth create a series of public forums so that youth opinions could be gathered on topics such as "Do Summit youth want a teen center?" and "What is life really like after high school?"; and
- Working with youth to approach local businesses to create a Summit County Youth Discount Card, which provides discounts at local theaters, fast-food restaurants, ski and snowboard stores, recreation centers, and other local businesses.

Promise Fellows also worked with the local Rotary Clubs to collect and distribute over 1,200 books to low-income families in a FIRST FIVE book drive.

Promise Fellows have worked extensively with the early childhood community to develop a kit for providers, explaining the asset philosophy and offering tips on how to use assets in early childhood programs. Promise Fellows also worked with the local Rotary Clubs to collect and distribute over 1,200 books to low-income families in a FIRST FIVE book drive. Extending the commitment to reading for pleasure, Promise Fellows also recruited more than 30 senior citizens to read weekly in local preschool centers through the READ IT! (Reading Efforts Are the Difference for Infants and Toddlers) program.

Leveraging resources. When Pennsylvania's Warren County initiative received its Jostens Our Town grant, it used the funds to leverage resources and excitement in the community to extend the impact of its work. Here are some examples that any initiative can use of how this HC • HY initiative leveraged funds to accomplish multiple tasks:

- Hired a young adult majoring in media and communications who prepared a new set of reproducible media materials.
- Developed a media campaign using these materials. One strategy was to get the materials into business, school, congregation, and organization newsletters. Another strategy was to get the materials into communications media, newspapers, shoppers guides, and cable TV community pages. Because the initiative provided the materials, media outlets ran them for free.

- Leveraged the media campaign into more donated advertising on placemats, poster boards in businesses, billboards, trade magazines, and business newsletters.
- Tapped volunteers to hang banners in various towns, get local governments to issue proclamations, and recruit 4-H volunteers to hand out asset information cards.
- Collaborated with county commissioners in a Year of Respect campaign involving 50 partners who passed on messages of respect to coincide with the schools' antibullying campaign.
- Used Jostens Our Town funds as matching money for a state health improvement development grant to award minigrants to organizations that would promote, design, or enhance asset building. A panel of teens from across the county reviewed the proposals and awarded the funds.

"Our steadfast strategies of constantly keeping the initiative and asset building before the public has served us best," says HC • HY Coordinator Sue Collins. "We want to give the consistent and constant message that our youth require daily involvement in their lives from all of us. No effort is too small."

The Mayor's Youth Summit. St. Louis Park, Minnesota's mayor sponsors an annual youth forum, planned by young people, to which people from all over the community are invited. The forum includes groups that typically serve youth within the city, such as parks and recreation and schools, as well as interested adults from the community. High school students, who have received advanced training, present a slate of issues of concern to them and facilitate the discussions. Past forums have focused on school safety and the need for good places for teens to spend after-school time. There's only one rule for adult participants—they can't talk. Their job is to attend each session and listen. Ideas are distilled for a report back to the mayor. One forum resulted in the city conducting a feasibility study for a new skate park.

The policy and practice of diversity. Seattle, Washington's It's About Time for Kids initiative conducted focus groups in several communities of color to discover what kind of written materials parents would use. This activity promoted the asset message on a variety of levels. First, the initiative's outreach to diverse communities was a demonstration of its walking its talk. Second, a new audience was exposed to the concept of developmental assets. Third, the initiative got valuable information about how to customize materials in ways that would make them relevant and useful to diverse communities. And finally, new relationships were started between the initiative and communities.

The initiative quickly discovered that at least 40 percent of the Cambodian community couldn't read in their own language or in English, but parents were hungry for practical tips on how to enrich their children's everyday lives. The

Tipsheet #10
Host a Link 'n' Learn Meeting

ONE EFFECTIVE WAY TO PROMOTE the asset message is to hold a Link 'n' Learn meeting. A Link 'n' Learn meeting provides a forum for those involved in community initiatives to network and share lessons learned. Participants are both learners and teachers at a Link 'n' Learn meeting. The hope is that all participants have every opportunity to ask questions, get answers, and share ideas about assets and the HC • HY movement.

Link 'n' Learns are designed to bring participants' expertise to bear on group problem solving. What has made the event so successful is that all aspects of it, even the mealtime activities, strive to promote networking and mutual support among participants who have not met before.

Although one person or one organization can plan and host a Link 'n' Learn meeting, some rich and useful ideas can be generated by hosting a planning committee for the event, either in person or via conference call, email, or satellite. Consider having geographic representation from other communities in the region you plan to target.

In general, a Link 'n' Learn meeting uses three learning techniques:
1. Presentation on the asset framework, community mobilization, or a related topic;
2. Formal networking opportunities with other communities on specific topics related to implementing the asset framework in their community; and
3. Informal networking opportunities to share ideas, such as during breaks and at meals.

Potential Link 'n' Learn sharing session topics include:
- Discussing the administering of and/or data from surveys;
- Building and strengthening local HC • HY initiatives with regard to a specific phase or strategy, such as getting started, mobilizing adults, sharing your message, engaging youth, involving all generations, strengthening youth-serving programs, or financing your initiative;
- Maintaining established HC • HY initiatives; and
- Community celebrations.

You don't need a fancy or expensive facility to host a Link 'n' Learn meeting. An economical facility helps keep down costs, making the event charges more reasonable and giving more participants access. Many planning committees have preferred such settings as a school, congregation building, or community center because these are often where the real work of asset building happens in their community. Such facilities also seem more welcoming to many people.

Search Institute has found that Link 'n' Learn meetings can be a powerful tool for community initiatives in your area to inspire and equip asset builders by learning promising strategies from your neighbors and peers. And don't forget—you can hold a Link 'n' Learn more than once. Some initiatives hold them regularly to keep ideas flowing.

> **Learn more: For the basics on how to plan and conduct a Link 'n' Learn, including sample agendas, materials, evaluation, and planning checklists, go to www.search-institute.org/linknlearn/index.html.**

initiative designed simple tip sheets that were then distributed to "natural leaders" in neighborhood congregations and businesses. By making sure tips were in the hands of the community's trusted leaders, ideas were circulated even though the tipsheets couldn't be read by everyone.

Conversations for Kids. Assets for Colorado Youth (ACY) convened a group of policy leaders to identify strategies for applying principles of positive youth development to address youth violence issues. The jumping-off point for the Conversations for Kids forum was a Youth and Violence study of 1,012 Colorado youth commissioned by The Colorado Trust. The study concluded that young people who had supportive relationships with their parents, teachers, and friends were much less likely to be either victims or perpetrators of violence. ACY brought together participants representing state government, state education and health agencies, violence prevention and policy organizations, juvenile justice, and foundations to discuss the policy implications of the report.

The group analyzed community needs and the political landscape and framed a youth development agenda. Among the recommendations were ideas for more effective involvement of youth in policy issues as well as broader and deeper coordination of services to prevent youth violence. This was just the first of ACY's planned series of community conversations about helping children thrive.

Reflect, Learn, and Celebrate

Monitor, reflect on, and learn from current realities, progress, and challenges. Highlight and honor asset-building efforts and progress in the community.

Community council. The South Bend, Indiana, Healthy Communities Initiative of St. Joseph County participates in the Families Council, which is made up of representatives from local youth- and family-serving agencies. The group was originally formed in partnership with the local congressional delegation to respond to federal "No Child Left Behind" legislation. "The events of 9/11 took most of our local funding," says HCI Director Marilyn Eber, "so now we're concentrating on studying what's already going on in our community and what we can do with available resources."

The group was able to work with a local college student to research existing resources and found that many agencies serving families weren't even aware of what other agencies were doing. Since the initiative is aimed more at teens, the Families Council concentrates its efforts on generating resources for families with young children. One specific outcome is the Backpack Program. The council teamed up with social workers to make sure underserved children in the community got new backpacks full of everything needed to start off the school year. "We incubated that project for a year and got really good community support for it," says Eber. "One of the local TV stations picked it up, and we reached a lot of kids that way."

Using stories as tools. Both the Georgetown (Texas) Project and Connecticut Assets Network are experimenting with a way of gathering stories by using a tool called journey mapping. Developed by Barry Kibel, journey mapping is based on the multiple stages of the hero's journey outlined by Joseph Campbell in *The Hero with a Thousand Faces*.

Youth participants keep on-line journals of their involvement in asset building, documenting meetings and activities as well as writing stories of their experiences. Young people and initiative organizers are trained in how to assign and tabulate a point system Kibel developed that documents movement through the "journey" of the initiative and to note built-in benchmarks.

In Connecticut, the costs of access to the on-line journey mapping system are shared by five entities. Journey mapping provides a way of collecting the anecdotal and quantitative material initiatives need to make their case and learn about their own progress.

Capturing success. To celebrate its fifth anniversary, Assets for Colorado Youth gave Outstanding Asset Builder awards to groups who use innovative strategies to mobilize their organizations and communities using asset building. Some of the awards went to:

- School districts, elementary schools, and preschools for embracing and embedding assets in their communities.
- The Colorado Statewide Parent Coalition for infusing assets into parent advocacy programs.
- The Community Justice Division of the Denver District Attorney's Office for using assets to give youth positive opportunities.
- The Teen Pregnancy Prevention Initiative for using asset building in its clearinghouse for youth involvement.

ACY also publicizes the awards in its quarterly newsletter and sends out press releases to the local media.

Teen power. Celebration events are created by many initiatives. Roswell, New Mexico, put on a celebration called "Teen Power! ¡El Poder de Juventud!" It included an exhibit of audio self-portraits installed in personal stereos, a "low-rider" bike show, youth art traveling on city buses, and murals decorating the Roswell Museum and Art Center, the hospital, and a local printing company.

Using Link 'n' Learns to Reflect, Learn, and Celebrate. Many initiatives use Link 'n' Learn meetings, but here's an example of how a community uses the format to accomplish a variety of tasks. The Healthy Community Coalition in Park River, North Dakota, held a daylong event advertised as a combination Link 'n' Learn and Youth Empowerment Summit. Cosponsored by the coalition, Park River School, and the Walsh County Tobacco Free Coalition, the event was funded in part by North Dakota Region IV Children's Services Coordinating Committee. The event's goals included opportunities to:

- *Reconnect*—network with youth in other schools and communities who build assets for and with youth;
- *Renew*—understand the concept of developmental assets and apply the categories of developmental assets to your own experiences and perceptions;
- *Rejuvenate*—empower youth to carry the asset-building message back to their schools and communities and plan an asset-building project for their school; and
- *Rejoice*—celebrate asset-building strategies and actions that are working in other communities.

The day included team-building games, a creative-thinking exercise, and lunch.

Sustaining Your Efforts

Fully realizing the transformation of a healthy community with and for our young people is a task that is at once simple and complex. Together, we are all moving toward that vision. Yet no single type of change or technique alone will accomplish the goal of having a society in which all young people are valued and have the experiences and relationships they need to thrive.

"One of the most important things to remember is that you don't have to have all the answers," says Children First Coordinator Karen Atkinson. "Your job is to be a catalyst. You lay out the story and the philosophy, and people will come up with their own answers. In fact, they'll far exceed whatever a coordinator or executive committee could come up with."

In analyzing its work as a statewide initiative, Assets for Colorado Youth (ACY) has clearly identified several key strategies for any asset initiative to consider as it continues its asset-building efforts. "Colorado's experience suggests that a critical role for statewide organizations in promoting assets is to establish credibility as a messenger," says ACY's *Creating Social Change* summary, "to guide individuals and organizations in how to apply the framework to their specific contexts, and share success stories from the field."

Further, ACY's evaluation identifies these six major catalyzing forces that have been important to the organization's ability to facilitate the spread of the asset message:

1. **Leadership** in innovation and engagement of diverse sectors and communities;

2. Organizational and cultural **innovations** in applying the asset framework;
3. **Asset champions** who serve as local messengers, engage communities in asset building, and advocate for local youth;
4. **Relationship building** between individuals and organizations on behalf of youth;
5. **Funding** to support training, convening of asset builders, and the development of asset-related projects; and
6. **Youth engagement** in asset-building organizations.

You can adapt all of these lessons to your unique community and your initiative's efforts to effectively engage individuals, communities, and organizations and create bridges from awareness to action. In case you're feeling a little overwhelmed by the magnitude of the tasks and strategies, remember that strong, healthy relationships within your initiative are also a fundamental element of success. It's never wasted time to just talk with your colleagues, partners, and volunteers, even if it means delaying a few initiative tasks until next week.

"When we talk," says Alaska's Derek Peterson, "let's talk about the individual people, families, teachers, classrooms, congregations, and groups that are building relationships with youth and making a difference in their lives. Let's not spend our short time concerned about 'the initiative.' Let's share true stories, let's give names of people—not their titles or associations, and let's pat each other on the back and say, 'Keep up the good work!' "

Ideas on the Change Pathway for Influencing Civic Decisions

Search Institute is currently involved in a collaborative effort with the Donald W. Reynolds Foundation to develop and support three statewide initiatives in Arkansas (Raising Arkansas Youth), Nevada (Raising Nevada), and Oklahoma (Healthy Communities • Healthy Youth: Oklahoma). The following tips come from these three initiatives.

PATHWAY	TIPS/ADVICE
Receptivity: being open to change	To generate enthusiasm and initial buy-in, potential asset builders in these three states are offered scholarships to attend the annual HC • HY conference. "Conference attendees get so excited about asset building, they tend to step up for more training opportunities," says Search Institute Partner Services Manager Kristie Probst.
Awareness: understanding possibilities	Each state hosts the *Essentials of Asset Building Training of Trainers.* So far, about 80 people in all three states have been taught how to deliver asset-based training back home. "Equipping teams of trainers builds additional capacity to engage leaders, professionals, parents, and citizens in implementing asset-building strategies," says Probst.
Mobilization: organizing for change	Trainers delivered information and strategies to more than 4,800 participants in one quarter. "The three states are initiating broad and deep outreach into various environments and settings that have the capacity to positively impact youth through asset-building philosophies and practices," says Probst. Some of the groups that received training included the YMCA, Boys & Girls Clubs, school district staff, county probation employees, mental health associations, local service clubs, businesses, and a program for new mothers.
Action: making change happen	**Arkansas** has created an information manual for new initiative members and is focusing on engaging everyday citizens in congregations. **Nevada** has developed some mutually agreed-upon strategies for moving asset building forward regionally with statewide coordination where it makes sense. **Oklahoma** envisions a positive youth development center housed at the Oklahoma Institute for Child Advocacy that can serve as a clearinghouse and support center for statewide activities.
Continuity: ensuring change becomes a way of life	The statewide initiative coordinators help disseminate information about their projects to community-level asset-building initiatives in their respective states as well as organizations and systems. The initiatives in Nevada and Arkansas are also seeking nonprofit status to ensure the existence of their coordinating roles.

Influence Civic Decisions

- **Work to unite civic, financial, leadership, media, and policy resources** to act upon and solidify all aspects of the asset-building vision.

- **Take steps** to monitor your progress, link people together, and continually socialize new leaders, decision makers, and residents into the community's vision for asset building.

- **Be strategic:** emphasize careful, intentional action.

- **Determine leadership:**
  - ▶ Balance the need for "asset champions" with the need for effective teams.
  - ▶ Cultivate leaders from different organizations who share the vision and work so that people don't burn out.
  - ▶ Maintain shared leadership and strong partnerships to help survive turnover.

- **Document and share your results:** look for formal and informal ways to demonstrate your credibility in the community.

- **Identify and overcome challenges:** Be tolerant of unresolved issues as you learn how to balance competing interests or marshal resources to solve a problem.

- **Act as a catalyst** to unleash and unite the community on behalf of asset building.

- Use these six tasks to **gain an overview** of your efforts:
  1. Cultivate a shared vision.
  2. Recruit and network champions.
  3. Communicate.
  4. Strengthen capacity.
  5. Reinforce and influence.
  6. Reflect, learn, and celebrate.

PART THREE

Keeping It Going
and Growing

CHAPTER 7

Over the Long Haul: Sustaining Your Initiative

People say, "We've been doing this forever, why do we need a coalition?" If we stay with a bunch of isolated, disparate efforts in the community, obviously the sum total of that is not producing the results we want for our children. If we don't have more of a community road map, we're just going to get the same kind of result.

BECKY BEAUCHAMP, GIVEM 40 COALITION

TRAVERSE CITY, MICHIGAN

IN THE SPRING OF 1992, Carl Holmstrom, then superintendent of the St. Louis Park Public Schools in Minnesota, gave the speech of a lifetime. Talking to the city's largest Rotary Club on the subject of "Are the Public Schools Working?" the surprised Holmstrom found himself facing a standing ovation at the end of his thirty-minute presentation. "It's the only time a speech of mine ever got a standing ovation," Holmstrom later told educator and author Robert Ramsey for his book *The Children First Story: How One Community Partnership Is Learning to Put Its Children and Families First.* "It felt good."

Schools were working successfully where the partnership between the home and the school was working, he said, but he feared the partnership was in jeopardy as more and more families were becoming stressed and dysfunctional. When families failed, Holmstrom observed, kids were lost and the entire community suffered.

But what Holmstrom added and emphasized, and what eventually brought the audience to its feet, was that as long as children are at risk in the city and in our society, *the problem was bigger than the school district.* He challenged *the whole community* to invest more—not just more money, but more of our time and of ourselves as well—in children and youth.

The next day, retired businessman Wayne Packard met with Holmstrom. Packard and his wife offered Holmstrom a sizable cash donation to do something about the issues he'd described. Holmstrom was reluctant at first, uncertain of how to use the funds. Packard persisted, however, and within a month, a second philanthropic entrepreneur and active Rotarian, Gil Braun, offered to match Packard's contribution. Holmstrom decided to form a committee, composed largely of school staff members, to figure out how to spend the money to address the issues of children and families. He originally called the new panel the At-Risk Families Committee.

The committee was able to build on work already done by a school district study group that had been analyzing why increasing numbers of students weren't succeeding in school. The new committee aimed to identify some working strategies that would empower the community to help *all* students succeed in and out of school.

Adopting a new name—Children First—the committee drafted its first mission statement ("to build a community which puts children first in order to create a better tomorrow for everyone") based on the belief that it takes an entire village to raise a child. After a bit of "spinning their wheels," as one initiative participant phrased it, on how to proceed, Children First linked up with Search Institute. Peter Benson, Search Institute president and researcher, joined Holmstrom's committee and, writes Ramsey in his detailed account of Children First, "things have never been quite the same in St. Louis Park."

Today, Children First can say it is the oldest asset-building initiative. But if you ask Children First's Coordinator Karen Atkinson to share exactly what makes an initiative mature, she'll chuckle before she answers. "I don't think you ever feel mature in this work. We were the first, so we must be mature, but we're always learning new things."

Joy and Hard Work

"Launching and sustaining a community asset-building initiative is not for the fainthearted," says Search Institute's Nancy Tellett-Royce. "It's both joy and hard work." By carefully tending the seeds of your garden—and doing your best to respond to the inevitable, unpredictable changes along the way—you hope to see your garden mature. As the improvements you have nurtured among adults, youth, organizations, sectors, and systems come to fruition, you begin to identify ways in which asset building is becoming integrated into all aspects of the community's life. You can stand back and see the ebb and flow of the movement that your initiative seeks to grow.

But it's not just the garden that matures; the gardeners mature, too. Helen Beattie of Hardwick, Vermont, describes the changes she has seen in her region's HC • HY initiative since its inception in 1995:

> Our initiative matured in a very vivid way. We had funding and leadership in the beginning to carry consciousness and mobilize people. Now the initiative is part

Tipsheet #11
Lessons Learned from Children First: What Works to Sustain Passion and Momentum

Successful changes, even small ones, can prompt continued dedication and zeal. Positive results spur renewed effort that will outlast the coming and going of charismatic individuals. Children First has built into its initiative several other forces that help keep it going, including:

1. Rotating leadership.
Leadership of the initiative's Executive Team and Vision Team regularly rotates among its five lead partners (representatives from city government, schools, businesses, congregations, and health-care sectors). This brings new energy, a different style, a fresh perspective, and different priorities to the table. It also helps generate new excitement and regenerate old passions.

2. A fluid vision team.
Membership on the team is open to everyone in the community, so a continuous flow of fresh faces and fresh ideas helps pump up enthusiasm—especially from young people. The constant infusion of different people helps the team remain dynamic and creative.

3. Success stories beget more success.
Sharing good news, examples, and success stories has always been a priority within the initiative. Stories plant seeds and serve as inspiration and catalyst. Stories about ordinary people doing extraordinary things help convince others that anyone can be an asset builder.

4. Living up to its reputation.
Since St. Louis Park was the first community to translate the developmental assets into community action, many other communities and groups have looked to Children First as a model. Responsive to the pressure to live up to their reputation, initiative participants don't pretend to have all the answers but find the high expectations can be a source of renewal.

5. Institutionalizing the initiative.
Over time the Children First philosophy has become ingrained in the institutions of the community. This formalization of the initiative's principles provides another guarantee of a continued life for Children First.

> **LEARN MORE:** See the Resources listed at the end of this book for how to order *The Children First Story.*

Edited excerpts used with permission from *The Children First Story* by Robert Ramsey of the fabric of the community and many pieces live on in that fabric. The initiative is almost silent but present in the lifeblood in the way that things work. We don't have to remind the local newspapers to seek youth voice, for example. They just do it on their own. The initiative percolates at its own rate and that provides a readiness when something comes up so we don't have to always start everything from scratch.

Eventually every initiative will face the question of how to help the community maintain its commitment once the newness has worn off. You will no doubt struggle to manage growth, turnover, and shifting political and fiscal considerations as well as how to effectively evaluate your efforts—all while keeping the other plates spinning! You not only can see what you've been able to accomplish so far, you also begin to understand the real implications of trying to maintain the initiative's work over the long haul. "We're so used to having things happen so fast," says one initiative coordinator. "You introduce something and it's supposed to take over, but changing the focus takes time."

To sustain an asset initiative, it's important that the initiative remain healthy and vibrant. But time alone does not define a sustainable initiative. Nor, oddly enough, does success. "In the asset-building world, there are so many warm and fuzzy ceremonies," says GivEm 40's schools asset development coordinator Mimi Petritz-Appel. "But in and of themselves, that's not shifting the culture. To go deep takes discipline because there are so many endless opportunities to go wide quickly. There's that constant temptation to do quick fixes."

While mature initiatives continue to address the tasks of engaging adults, mobilizing youth, activating sectors, invigorating programs, and influencing civic decisions, a new emphasis on continuity requires you to develop strategies for sustaining momentum, energy, and progress. Sustaining your initiative is about learning to address the challenges of continuing and deepening the commitment to asset building so that it becomes an integral part of the identity of individuals, organizations, and your community. Change and revision—and the anxieties that go with charting new territory—are just as much a part of continuity as is sustaining a particular course of action.

When the researchers on the National Asset-Building Case Study Project analyzed how the four participating initiatives succeeded in sustaining their efforts, they found that each of them:

- Keeps things focused on the simplicity of assets so that people do not feel overwhelmed.
- Makes little things count because small efforts are necessary and move things forward.
- Spares no opportunity to disseminate materials and information about its work.

Connecting the Dots

THE GIVEM 40 COALITION in the Traverse Bay area, Michigan, has developed an integrated strategy for achieving its key goals, including social marketing, transforming sectors, raising awareness, and developing innovative programs. The basis for the entire strategy is strong leadership, a youth cadre, and, ultimately, community ownership. "Nothing stands alone and everything is connected," says initiative coordinator Alan VanderPaas. "It would not be effective to present a sector strategy without knowing how to connect the dots." The initiative has learned that several things must occur in unison as coalitions build an asset-rich community:

1. People come to new understandings: "Business as usual is no longer acceptable when it comes to the health of our youth."

2. People replace their old ways of doing things with new practices and behaviors: "Community members ask youth for their opinions on matters that affect them and have youth representation in community roles."

3. Cultural shifts occur to support our new understandings and behaviors: "We have observed that not only is the language of assets being heard wherever we go, but also cooperation and collaboration in the community have created a new set of norms that are supportive and respectful of youth."

4. Social structures in the community support asset-building champions: "When local human service agencies present applications for funding with developmental assets language, it not only demonstrates the depth of a coalition's efforts but also shows that practitioners and funders alike are in agreement that asset building is an effort worth making."

GivEm 40 is compiling key learnings and pivotal strategies collected from mature asset-building initiatives into a publication called *AHA! Assets Have Arrived.* When completed, the report will be made available to other initiatives.

Fulfilling the Vision

Sustaining and supporting an asset-building initiative is about trying to achieve a new norm in our culture. We start our efforts because we are dissatisfied with the status quo and want to use the developmental assets framework to make our communities better places for young people. Then we attempt to create and implement a vision of a community in which asset building eventually becomes natural and normal. Each of us individually commits to the message of asset building and we join with others to do the same in larger arenas.

That new norm of long-term social and community change will take years to achieve. But one of the markers along the way toward that new norm is the increasing number of maturing asset-building initiatives.

"It's a mature initiative when we start seeing more people promote the positive stuff," says Colorado's Brenda Holben. "The word 'assets' just doesn't mean money. It has put us all on a level playing field that makes us all responsible for raising kids. We finally have a majority of people that have a common language and framework."

Maturing initiatives still face challenges, albeit different challenges from when they first started. "We're the knowledge center," says Orlando's Healthy Community Initiative Executive Director Raymond Larsen, "and our communities own their asset building, but we're still learning. How do you build firewalls around these microinitiatives so that if one falls, they don't all fall? And how do you weave all this together to create social change?"

Supporting this kind of positive community change requires that many initiatives dedicate themselves to learning and sharing what it takes to identify and achieve sustainability. Many have, in fact, begun working in networks across states or provinces as one way of sharing information and experience. (See a list of network contacts on Search Institute's Web site: www.search-institute.org/communities/partner.htm.)

The tips in the next section include ideas gathered by Search Institute staff from initiatives across North America, supplemented with thoughts and ideas from the case study project and from interviews with initiative participants and trainers.

Eight Tips for Sustaining Your Initiative

Tip #1: Approach community change as a dynamic, unpredictable process.

Communities are like gardens, in which unforeseen factors always have an impact on what you can do and how you can do it. Communities and gardens also grow in a nonlinear manner; sometimes you work and work with no visible results and then the flowers bloom all at once. Sometimes the garden will be expanding and growing; other times it will appear dormant. This is normal; it's part of the dynamic process of change.

The Georgetown (Texas) Project is not the only initiative to have experienced what it calls a "major upheaval" in local politics, which resulted in drastic budget cuts and even the loss of its city-based offices. "Our survival as an organization was in doubt for a period of time," said Director Barbara Pearce in the project's final Jostens Our Town award report. The group's solution was to retrench and keep going. By building on the strengths of its successes so far, the initiative was able get some new local grants to replace the funds it had lost. The project also created the Got Hoops? Get Assets! Intergenerational Basketball Tournament when the mayor declined to support the Youth Advisory Board's request for a skate park. In a unique twist on the sport, 100 adults and youth participated on the same teams. The event was so successful, plans are under way to make the tournament an annual event.

Multnomah County (Portland), Oregon's Take the Time initiative also dealt with big budget cuts when its parent organization, the county's Commission on Children, Families and Community, reallocated resources. To adapt to these changing circumstances, the initiative's strategy was to build on its strengths, leverage existing resources and opportunities whenever possible, and, finally, cut the losses and change course when mandated by external forces beyond its control. Despite being unable to finish some projects, the initiative has gathered lessons learned into informational materials that it circulates as part of its ongoing communications strategy.

All initiatives run into challenges along the way, and it's important to keep an open mind and be flexible as you figure out how to respond. "Don't be afraid to revisit old ideas," advises Search Institute's Nancy Tellett-Royce. "We've all been in situations where we've become an 'old timer' in a group. Someone brings in an idea that we've tried before and it gets shot down. This often happens when the idea comes from a young person. Don't say, 'We tried that and it didn't work.' You could say, 'Here's what we might run into, what could we do?' Explore the variations, the possibilities. If you squelch someone offering an idea, he or she might assume the initiative is a closed shop. And sometimes youth come up with solutions or variations that the group had not thought of before."

"In our initiative, some of the players have changed over time," wrote Warren County, Pennsylvania's Sue Collins in her initiative's final Jostens Our Town grant report, "but the changes have resulted in new blood and some reorganization of our initiative steering group, interestingly at a time when we have been reflecting upon and evaluating our efforts so far. Identifying a task force to give some thought and direction to the initiative resulted in defining ourselves as a partnership rather than an advisory board, which more correctly defined our goal of spurring others to build assets rather than programming. That emphasis on commitment to community building, not programs and money, is what really sets us apart from other things happening locally, especially for youth."

Tip #2: Give it away.

"We're not in charge of what happens, that ripple effect of getting the message out," says former Essex CHIPS Coordinator Valerie Smith. "We're trying to reach people heart-to-heart and balance that with programming. If someone gets it and runs with it, great!"

To "give it away" means empowering people in the community to implement the developmental assets framework in ways that make sense to them. Pay attention to *their* personal and organizational interests to help determine where to invest the initiative's energy, and allow them to celebrate their successes as their own.

Tipsheet #12

Phases of Community Change Checklist

This checklist created by the HC • HY initiative of Warren County, Pennsylvania, can help you see your initiative through the lens of the change pathway and begin to record the actions you are taking in regard to each phase of the pathway.

I. Receptivity

Recognize and acknowledge that our young people's situation is not what it needs to be—and that things really could be better.

☐ We know what motivates and concerns people in our community.

☐ We have shared information on the current realities of young people in our community.

☐ We have identified individuals with interest in asset building and enlisted them as allies in getting others interested.

Activities, audiences addressed, other evidence:

_____

_____

_____

II. Awareness

Provide information to help individuals and organizations think differently so that they are motivated to try out new behaviors.

☐ We have convinced people of the benefits of changing the way they interact with youth and recognize their own capacity to make a difference in the circumstances of youth.

☐ We have spread the word about what asset building can do for youth.

☐ We have framed asset building into the priorities of individuals and organizations that we want to involve.

☐ We have influential people of every age involved in the movement.

☐ People feel "expected" to be involved.

Activities, audiences addressed, other evidence:

_____

_____

_____

III. Mobilization

Articulate a shared vision for asset building, develop an action plan, and begin connecting with allies through formal and informal networks.

☐ We have developed a shared vision for asset building.

☐ We have an action plan.

☐ We have formal and informal connections with our allies.

☐ We have connected asset building with existing strength-building efforts in our community.

☐ We have young people as partners in planning and networking.

cont.

- We encourage personal and public commitments to asset building.

Activities, audiences addressed, other evidence:

_____

_____

_____

IV. Action

Support a wide range of asset-building activities and start new ones to fill in the gaps in our community's capacity to build assets.

- We have infused asset building into existing programs.

- We encourage people to move from one-time, short actions to more sustained involvement with young people and asset building.

- We have sponsored activities that connect and strengthen isolated efforts.

- We provide learning and networking opportunities.

- We support asset champions so that they continue to grow and don't burn out.

Activities, audiences addressed, other evidence:

_____

_____

_____

V. Continuity

Keep commitment and engagement strong as the newness wears off, as commitment deepens, and other ideas come along, so that asset building becomes integral to the

identity of who we are as individuals and as a community.

- We recognize and celebrate asset-building action in ways that reinforce commitment.

- We have convinced organizations and individuals that asset building is an indispensable part of who they are and what they do.

- We monitor progress and identify opportunities for deepening commitment as well as look at problem areas.

Activities, audiences addressed, other evidence:

_____

_____

_____

VI. Please reflect on where we have been and where we are, based on your answers above.

VII. Please reflect on where you think we should go next. For example, address some thematic issues such as youth sports; broaden our focus more intentionally on mobilizing organizations or communities that are not currently on board.

At the same time, to continue to motivate participants and to persuade funders of your good work, balance "giving it away" with clear documentation of the initiative's role in your community's positive change. Granted, this is not always an easy balance to achieve. Moorhead's Healthy Community Initiative, for example, found it had done such a good job of supporting the autonomous development of some of the services it had launched that its own contributions of innovating and networking were becoming less visible to the community. With the transition to a new executive director, the initiative has entered a new period of self-assessment that could help reframe some of its work in the community.

One way to maintain the visibility needed to garner funding and maintain participation is to remember to publicly celebrate initiative successes and keep accurate records of your activities. "It's a critical piece to keep track internally of your successes," says Nancy Tellett-Royce, "to not lose track of your history. This will help you be strategic as you continually develop your initiative." Two tipsheets are included here (the initiative activities and events log and the group memory exercise) to assist you.

Tip #3: Combine planning and doing.

Good planning is a critical tool for supporting the asset-building movement, but avoid spending so much time planning that energy and enthusiasm wane in the absence of action. You'll likely have both planners and activists on your team; honor both roles. Think of planning as stepping with the left foot and doing as stepping with the right foot, then integrate your planning and doing so that the contributions of both planners and doers are clear.

"One of our biggest challenges was going from just providing information to actually implementing assets," says Maureen McKasy-Donlin with Colorado Springs Assets for Youth. "CSAY found it absolutely necessary to create or be involved with tangible projects through which individuals, organizations, and/or businesses could implement assets. It wasn't enough to merely offer information. We had to model asset building and then celebrate our implementation."

That challenge comes as no surprise to Search Institute's Nancy Tellett-Royce. "What I love about this work is that it's a conundrum," she says. "It's as easy as saying 'hi' to the kid next door, but it can be as complex as analyzing how to move adults from new understandings to new behaviors to habitual activity on behalf of young people. It's appealing *because* it's both simple and complex. Your role is to attract different people to those different tasks by remaining invitational. Keep inviting and informing. Keep circulating ideas. Find ways to revisit your vision and mission, but just keep going!"

Tipsheet #13 *Initiative Activities and Events Log*

Type of Activity or Event (name and date)	Relationship to Initiative Goals	Number of Participants	Funds Raised (for or during event)	Promotional or Learning Materials Developed	Asset-related Successes, Challenges, and Knowledge Gained

From *First Steps in Evaluation: Basic Tools for Asset-Building Initiatives*, by Thomas H. Berkas and Kathryn L. Hong. Copyright © 2000 by Search Institute, Minneapolis, MN; 800-888-7828; www.search-institute.org.

Constructing Group Memory in Your Initiative

This exercise, compliments of Derek Peterson with the Alaska Initiative on Community Engagement (Alaska ICE), can help you capture or recapture your initiative's history and successes. "One of the hurdles facing initiatives is turnover among participants," says Peterson, the director of child/youth advocacy for the Alaska Association of School Boards. "New, talented people are recruited and expected to 'fill in.' But the 'old timers' and the 'new timers' are not quite involved in the same initiative. This is a simple exercise that I have used to get people to learn from themselves and their own experiences."

The Historical Record

Every initiative for positive community change has a past, present, and future. You will be much more effective at setting priorities and making a case for promoting the developmental assets framework to others if you can recall where you have been.

Typically, each member of a team knows only a chunk of it. This exercise helps focus your attention on the forces that brought you together in the first place, and on exactly "what were we and those other crazy people thinking back then" when everyone first set out to change the community for youth.

With large blank paper taped to the wall, mark out a timeline across months or years, so that everyone can see the chronology from the initiative's beginning to the present day. Then ask people in the meeting to consider and answer the following questions:

- How did this initiative begin?
- What was it like at the beginning?
- What was the original purpose?
- Who got you (us) all together?
- What were the founders of the initiative trying to produce?

Usually a few people will begin talking and sharing memories of dates. As each person shares information, record the event on a sticky note and post it on the timeline. (Of course, you will move the notes as needed.)

- What happened next?
- When?
- Whose idea was that?
- Why did you do it that way?

Your purpose is to move through time adding new episodes and events to the wall. You may want to draw lines on the timeline, showing trajectories of particular successes, problems, people, teams, and projects.

As people begin to understand the significant milestones you are looking for, you can ask more in-depth questions to help them bring out the stories of their efforts:

- What happened between this date and that date?
- Who left? Who joined?
- What was needed at this juncture? What crossroads did you face?
- Why the period of inactivity here? What was happening?
- What were the biggest barriers you had to overcome? When?
- What problems were the most tiresome and irksome? When did they arise? When did they finally go away?

cont.

- When did you celebrate? Why did you choose that time? How did you celebrate?
- When was the initiative the most fun? The most rewarding? When did you most enjoy being involved? Why?
- When did you least enjoy being involved? Why?
- What were your breakthrough moments? When? Why did they occur then?
- What went smoothly? Why? When?
- What went poorly? When? Why?
- Did individuals make a difference? What were the characteristics of those who did?

- What were the characteristics of those who did not?
- Who were the champions? Who were the barriers? What were the characteristics that distinguished them?

Before long, you'll uncover aspects of the original purpose that had been forgotten or lost in the day-to-day efforts of making change happen. After this exercise, teams will have a keener sense of their common purpose and be asking themselves, "Have we completed our mission? What shall we do next?" You may want to use the timeline as the basis for a written history of your initiative or for a "sustainability plan."

Tip #4: Pay attention to renewing and broadening the leadership.

Leadership focuses on the strategies and organizing principles that guide an initiative. Effective leadership must respond to the constantly changing environment and needs to be as informal and flexible as possible. Effective community leadership is not institutionalized through formal positions. In nurturing long-term change, an initiative continually seeks to cultivate new leadership for the initiative and to broaden the role of local leaders by identifying and supporting asset champions throughout the community who can guide and inspire the community change movement.

Leadership is an area that will be uniquely adapted to the needs of your community's initiative. Various initiatives are using various models, including vision teams, nonprofit boards, and combinations of youth-adult partnerships. Your leadership needs will be determined in part by whether you have a coordinator at the helm, what tasks that coordinator performs, and whether that coordinator is paid or not. This again is one of those areas that can't be reduced to a "one size fits all" model. There are some useful ideas to keep in mind, however:

▶ **Look for catalyzing leadership.** "It's critical to bring together the cast of characters from your town or community that can serve as the best catalyst for the work," says Vermont's Helen Beattie. "Start with a strong student leadership piece and look at who other important players are in your town and how they can be part of shaping the vision together in a way that's different from what they've done before."

- **Cultivate shared leadership.** "Shared leadership is a prime example of community ownership," says trainer John Linney of Impact Associates, who has been a part of the El Paso, Texas, initiative. "Sustaining your initiative will come, in part, from people knowing they have a role to play."
- **Strengthen the capacity of your initiative.** "A mature initiative is bigger than personality and can handle some of its initiators moving on," says Alaska's Derek Peterson, "but you have to have enough capacity within the initiative to get others on the wagon to carry on."

One way to cultivate shared leadership and strengthen capacity at the same time is to form partnerships with other organizations. "Partnerships are critical to the long-term success of any initiative," says Rick Phillips of Community Matters, a California training organization that specializes in community building. "Trying to develop partnerships can seem a bit daunting at first, but nothing is more powerful in addressing community issues than an effective partnership."

Phillips offers these "plain truths" to help you think realistically about what it takes to forge working partnerships:

- *Partnerships are challenging* to manage and to master because everyone comes to the table with different experiences, conflicting styles of leadership, uneven levels of commitment, and different levels of experience with collaboration. So the "solution" of forming a partnership to address an issue can itself become the new "problem." While few automatically have the skills to manage all these issues, what it takes to build a partnership can be learned.
- *Partnerships are built on two pillars: form and process.* Form is about how the partnership is organized. Process is about how the people in the partnership interact and treat each other. If either pillar is allowed to grow weak, the partnership will collapse, so it's important to find ways to develop and strengthen both structure and relationships.
- *Partnerships are easier to start than to sustain.* Many collaborative projects are sparked by a crisis, funding concerns, or a dynamic personality. They begin with high hopes, but all too often commitment wanes, meeting attendance drops off, and initial enthusiasm gives way to doubt and frustration. The key to maintaining an effective partnership is similar to what you are doing to build an asset initiative—maintaining a positive focus based on strong relationships.
- *Partnerships go through stages of development.* At each stage, the partnership requires different things from members, is marked by different developmental milestones, and has an increased capacity for achieving results. For example, trust must be built slowly and deliberately at the initial stage. This trust increases members' commitment to contribute the resources that equip the partnership to carry out its activities, and if successful, trust expands. Even-

tually, trust is high enough to support the purposeful conflict required for creative problem solving and high-level partnership performance.

"Addressing today's complex issues requires a multisector, comprehensive approach," says Phillips. "Taking the time to nurture a strong partnership allows you to bring all the players to the table, forge a shared vision, and develop a clear plan for working in concert on a common problem."

> LEARN MORE: Find more tips and ideas about partnerships and other elements of building a community initiative at the Community Matters Web site, www.community-matters.org/index.html.

Tip #5: Money is not the central focus.

Funding, lack of funding, changes in funding, and how to garner and manage funding are issues with which all initiatives are dealing. Money pays the bills, and an infusion of funding can certainly help support the work of an initiative. Indeed, at a meeting of the four initiatives that participated in Search Institute's National Asset-Building Case Study Project, the two main subjects on the minds of participants were youth engagement and money.

But money alone does not create long-term stability, and the efforts to raise funding can actually sap the human resources and spirit that sustain effective community change efforts. And sometimes outside infusions of financial resources can diminish local ownership and also set up dependencies that challenge sustainability. Instead of investing tremendous amounts of time and energy in raising money, focus on what resources are needed and creative ways to tap resources that already exist within the community.

You can approach funding and resources in as many different ways as there are initiatives. Whether you decide to seek grants on behalf of partners, as Moorhead has, or decide, as Orlando has, to seek no funds directly for your own initiative, managing resources involves thinking strategically. "It's always important to look ahead on funding," says Nancy Tellett-Royce. "If you are receiving grants and you have one now, what's next? Do you have multiple funders? When you get your grant, that's the beginning of your communication with your funder, not the last conversation. The continuing dialogue between you and your funders is about how to fuel a vision and measure successes. By engaging them and keeping them informed as you go, you build in sustainability."

For initiatives involved in seeking grants, one of the biggest issues involves trying to reconcile the long-term nature of community change with funders' needs for short-term outcomes. The researchers on the National Asset-Building Case Study Project specifically examined funding challenges among the four participating initiatives and found several themes that contribute to success:

- Ideally, get funders to the table early.
- Actively engage funders in the initiative.

- Work with funders to fund a vision rather than just a program.
- Support and celebrate funders as trendsetters in the asset movement.

GivEm 40 in the Traverse Bay area of Michigan has been especially successful at incorporating these elements into its work. "The strong relationship between the initiative and the funders allowed not only for the growth and maintenance of the initiative, but also for joint planning on developing activities," says Karen Foster, one of the lead researchers on the case study project.

It's important not to underestimate the skills required to raise money for an initiative. "Some people are really good at the personal, charismatic 'ask'; others are good grant writers. You may need both, and those skills may not come all bundled into one coordinator," says Nancy Tellett-Royce. "Coordinators need a cadre of people who fill in the skill sets they don't have. This actually strengthens the initiative because more people become committed to your success."

Not all initiatives get funds, however, and some initiatives specifically decide not to seek funds. "We seek hearts and time, not pocketbooks," wrote Warren County's Sue Collins in the initiative's Jostens Our Town final report. "Any of our efforts can be modeled by other communities with volunteers and a little cash support or a copy machine. We do recognize the need for a paid coordinator capable of seeing and directing the big picture, but too much staff time and money becomes a program."

"You don't need money to build assets, but you have to change attitudes about money," says Alaska's Derek Peterson. "In some communities, people are spending more time searching for funding than they are working to build assets. The rhetoric they use is, 'If we don't get funding, this asset-building initiative is dead.' This is hogwash. Individuals, families, neighborhoods, schools, and communities have been building assets for centuries. Just because one loses funding doesn't mean that the work of caring for youth stops."

Tip #6: It's all about relationships.
Growing a strong community is about building healthy relationships between diverse people and across generations. Whether it's accomplished through informal or formal organizations, the work of the initiative needs to be viewed as helping to connect the community with and around its young people. Healthy relationships are shared: people sharing what they have and receiving what is offered. They are also multileveled, dynamic, and challenging to our assumptions about each other. Remember that the focus on relationships is not only essential for building developmental assets with and for young people, it also provides the strength that will build and sustain the members of your initiative.

One of the basics of relationship building is to continually invite people, and that's just as important for adults as it is for young people. "An initiative really runs on some level of youth interest and involvement," says Tellett-Royce. "It's

How to Engage Youth Meaningfully

These tips come from the keynote address by Will Gaines, sophomore at the University of Minnesota, at the Search Institute 2002 HC • HY Conference "Youth as Change Agents" Assembly.

WHEN YOUTH AND ADULTS connect positively, change works. But it's very important how they connect. When it's real, when there's trust, respect, responsibility, and honest partnership, the bond becomes as important as what they are trying to accomplish. Here are some key points for authentic youth engagement:

1. Process is very important. Be open and inclusive to youth as equal partners from the beginning to the end of the campaign or project.
2. Take time to really listen:

   - Don't rush meetings.
   - Allow time for real sharing.
   - Keep inviting all to share.

3. Finishing a planning meeting on time is not as important as everyone feeling they are part of the decisions made so that they feel valued and heard.
4. Building relationships of the youth and adults working together is very important. Be interested and interesting. Take time to socialize and learn about others' interests. Each individual is important.
5. Take action. Work on projects together. Trust will come from working together. "Hands-on" projects are a great way to build relationships.
6. Everyone is of equal value. Offer support and skill-building opportunities.
7. Create opportunities to experience responsibility and making a difference.
8. Reach out to unconnected youth. Just *ask* them to be involved and make it possible for them to participate in adult partnerships.
9. Show you care.

easy to get a core group, but they might graduate in two years. You have to continually cultivate youth engagement. Even when you're humming along, you still need to think about how to get new students involved. That may mean stretching the adults' definitions of the age at which youth can be involved. Children First has a quartet of grade 6 students who've really jolted the adults into seeing much more talent at much earlier ages. And eventually, they'll take over, and *that's* sustainability!"

You're not just trying to build relationships among the adults or between young people and adults, you're also building relationships among the youth involved. Heather Shill joined the leadership team of Vermont's Essex CHIPS as a freshman in high school but has stayed on through her senior year because other youth have been involved to share the work. "When you have a personal dedication, that's good, but you can't sustain your interest without peers," she told workshop participants at the 2002 HC • HY conference. "It's too difficult. I've been on committees all alone and it didn't work. In CHIPS, there are tons of supporters with the same goals."

Tip #7: Good evaluation is rooted in good planning, which is rooted in good evaluation.

Evaluation, like funding, is a large issue that sparks widely varying opinions. The current trend in evaluation mirrors the trends in youth engagement and funding—incorporate it sooner rather than later. Evaluation has typically been done after the project is over by a team not always connected to the work. More initiatives are successfully experimenting with having researchers and evaluators come to the table at the beginning of the planning process to help shape the course of the initiative's work in ways that can be effectively measured.

At its core, evaluation is an opportunity to reflect on whether you're doing what you set out to do. Establishing measurable goals and a procedure for evaluating your progress at the outset will allow the kind of systematic reflection that can simultaneously inform your actions in moving toward those goals. Keeping the end in mind will help sharpen and focus your efforts in nurturing asset-based community change.

The next tipsheet is a tool from Search Institute's *First Steps in Evaluation: Basic Tools for Asset-Building Initiatives* to help you begin identifying how your asset-building effort is developing. (See the Resources listed at the back of this book for more on planning and evaluation.)

Tip #8: Trust the community.

Community change is messy—after all, it's hard to garden without getting your hands dirty. At times it may seem complicated or even totally out of control. Your best plan is to do all you can to nurture positive change and then trust the community to shape the asset-building movement in ways that reflect its own spirit and identity.

"Our work is all about trusting and building trust with others," says Nancy Tellett-Royce. "You have to be willing to trust that, at their core, people want to do good things for kids. You may disagree with how people go about it, but an asset-building initiative provides common language grounded in research and a forum for people to talk about that higher purpose. Caring about kids shouldn't be owned by any particular faction. That's why engaging multiple sectors is really important. Kids are beyond being somebody's issue—they're everybody's issue. The more voices you have at the table, the stronger you'll be once you work through the differences you might initially have or agree to table those that interfere with your shared goals."

Here's a good example of how trust—and patience—can help see you through the "messiness" of asset building. This story comes from Carla Beach, coordinator for the HC • HY of the Abingtons in Clarks Summit, Pennsylvania:

I moved to this community in 1994. At that time the school board had been "taken over" by candidates whose primary focus was on not raising taxes, sort of a taxpayer revolt. Education was secondary to them. I was shocked and appalled. I'd never seen anything like it before.

I believed that this had to change, and that I would do my part, whatever that might be. I volunteered in the schools, helped raise money for the PTAs, the normal kind of stuff, and always gave moral support to others whose goals were similar to mine. Four years ago there was this "new 40-asset thing" that our local ministerium and some visionaries in the school district administration had collaborated on. I got involved with that, too. Lots of other people were out there doing their part to make the community better—some making major commitments and grand gestures, others doing some small parts that were no less important.

Fast-forward, although it didn't always seem that fast, and now it's eight years since I moved here. Because of the collective efforts—large and small—of so many people in the community, changes have occurred in our community that didn't seem even remotely possible when I first arrived. We have a school board that not only supports education, but last March proclaimed our school district an "Asset-Building School District." The changes all happened incrementally, one person at a time. Sometimes it happened so slowly that it's only in looking back that I can see that there were quantum leaps forward when at the time I thought we were moving at a crawl.

Anyone can look at your own community and see the changes. It doesn't matter whether you were personally the catalyst or whether the changes are part of the ripple effect of the work you do. I'm confident you can have a positive impact. When you get tired or discouraged, take some time to pat yourself on the back, take yourself out to lunch, take a nap, or do whatever you need to do to recharge your battery, and then get back in the trenches. We all have more work to do, and we need to do it together!

Uniting Head and Heart

Among the many stories of asset building in different sectors that Robert Ramsey captures in his book about St. Louis Park's Children First Initiative is this one related by a food service employee, Dolores Therres, at her retirement:

> One day I was leaving my ticket room and a young lady came running down the hall to get a lunch ticket—she was late. I told her, "Honey, don't run. I'll wait for you." She started to cry. I asked her why and she said, "Nobody's ever called me 'honey' before, not even my mother." With that I put my arm around her and gave her a hug. I went back to the office and had a good cry.

"Vignettes like this," writes Ramsey, "are powerful reminders that the best of Children First is often made up of unhistoric acts performed by unlikely heroes."

So it goes with our work toward positive community change. Community asset-building initiatives are complex and adaptive ventures, subject to periods of uncertainty and improvisation. These periods of uncertainty can become

Asset-Building Community Mobilization Grid

Who Members of initiative leadership team

What This tool is designed to help your leadership team identify how its community-level asset-building effort is developing. You can use the information this tool provides for planning your initiative's activities and to assess how your initiative is evolving.

When/Where Distribute copies of the tool to the initiative leadership team and ask them to return the completed copies to the evaluation team.

Tallying You may first want to have the members of your initiative's leadership team join the evaluation team for an initial discussion to clarify their views and responses. Then use the tally sheet provided to record where people think your initiative is today. For summarizing, you may discuss each item to achieve consensus and then circle the appropriate response, or use the comments and responses to create a "word picture" describing where your initiative is on each item. To use this tool to assist in planning, brainstorm and record potential steps your initiative can take to move toward more advanced efforts in each of four main mobilization categories: philosophy, leadership team, asset-building efforts, and evaluation.

Asset-Building Community Mobilization Grid

For each numbered item, circle the phrase that most accurately describes your initiative today.

PHILOSOPHY	INITIAL EFFORTS		ADVANCED EFFORTS	
1. Focus on developmental assets	Community leaders/members begin to ask about assets	Assets introduced to community, which is starting to talk about them	Assets used for planning youth activities and/or programs	Building assets is integrated into youth activities and/or programs
Comments:				
2. Youth targeted for outreach efforts	Emphasis only on vulnerable or "at-risk" youth	Mostly on "at-risk" youth, though some for all	Equal rhetoric for all, though still emphasizes "at-risk" youth	All youth in the community are equally emphasized
Comments:				
3. Time frame	Less than 1 year	1–2 years	3–5 years	More than 5 years
Comments:				

PHILOSOPHY	INITIAL EFFORTS		ADVANCED EFFORTS	
4. Vision/mission statement(s) about assets	Whether oral or written, shared by very few people	Although written, only a few are aware of them	Substantial awareness of them across the community	Beginning to be the consensus of the wider community
Comments:				
5. Initiative's goals and objectives	Still vague	Clear enough to be written down	Real enough to be assessed	Findings from assessment being used in planning
Comments				

LEADERSHIP TEAM

6. Total number of members	Fewer than 5	5–10 consistent members	More than 10 members	Leadership decentralized
Comments:				
7. Community representation	Less than ¼ from community	At least ⅓ from community	At least ½ from community	At least ¾ from community
Comments:				
8. Reflects community's diversity	Homogeneous	Some diversity represented	Most diversity represented	All diversity represented
Comments:				
9. Number of youth on team	None	Less than ¼ of team	Up to ⅓ of team	Over ½ of team
Comments:				

ASSET-BUILDING EFFORTS

10. Speaking and/or training being provided	1–2 times per year	3–4 times per year	5–6 times per year	More than 6 times per year
Comments:				

ASSET-BUILDING EFFORTS	INITIAL EFFORTS		ADVANCED EFFORTS	
11. Number of sectors involved[1]	1	2–3	4–5	More than 5
Comments:				
12. Collaboration across sectors	None	1–2 sectors collaborating	3–4 sectors collaborating	5 or more sectors collaborating
Comments:				
13. Public awareness or communication efforts	Minimal efforts under way	Several efforts per year	Systematic efforts that reach most members of community	Systematic efforts that reach all members of community
Comments:				
14. Volunteers involved	Fewer than 10	Fewer than 50	Fewer than 100	More than 100
Comments:				
15. Funding of initiative	Less than $5,000 per year	$5,000–$9,999 per year	$10,000–$50,000 per year	More than $50,000 per year
Comments:				

EVALUATION

16. Of effort's implementation	None	Some informal efforts	Oral discussions of findings	Written evaluation report
Comments:				
17. Of effort's outcomes	None	Some informal efforts	Oral discussions of findings	Written evaluation report
Comments:				

1. Where "sectors" are education, business, religious, health, government, youth organization, media, etc.

Asset-Building Community Mobilization Grid

Use tally marks to record responses for each item, then write the totals for each response category at the bottom of the box.

PHILOSOPHY	INITIAL EFFORTS		ADVANCED EFFORTS	
1. Focus on developmental assets	Community leaders/members begin to ask about assets	Assets introduced to community, which is starting to talk about them	Assets used for planning youth activities and/or programs	Building assets is integrated into youth activities and/or programs
Totals:				
2. Youth targeted for outreach efforts	Emphasis only on vulnerable or "at-risk" youth	Mostly on "at-risk" youth, though some for all	Equal rhetoric for all, though still emphasizes "at-risk" youth	All youth in the community are equally emphasized
Totals:				
3. Time frame	Less than 1 year	1–2 years	3–5 years	More than 5 years
Totals:				
4. Vision/mission statement(s) about assets	Whether oral or written, shared by very few people	Although written, only a few are aware of them	Substantial awareness of them across the community	Beginning to be the consensus of the wider community
Totals:				
5. Initiative's goals and objectives	Still vague	Clear enough to be written down	Real enough to be assessed	Findings from assessment being used in planning
Totals:				

Philosophy: Our initiative

Next Steps

LEADERSHIP TEAM	INITIAL EFFORTS		ADVANCED EFFORTS	
6. Total number of members	Fewer than 5	5–10 consistent members	More than 10 members	Leadership decentralized
Totals:				
7. Community representation	Less than ¼ from community	At least ⅓ from community	At least ½ from community	At least ¾ from community
Totals:				
8. Reflects community's diversity	Homogeneous	Some diversity represented	Most diversity represented	All diversity represented
Totals:				
9. Number of youth on team	None	Less than ¼ of team	Up to ⅓ of team	Over ½ of team
Totals:				

Leadership Team: Our initiative

Next Steps

ASSET-BUILDING EFFORTS	INITIAL EFFORTS		ADVANCED EFFORTS	
10. Speaking and/or training being provided	1–2 times per year	3–4 times per year	5–6 times per year	More than 6 times per year
Totals:				
11. Number of sectors involved[2]	1	2–3	4–5	More than 5
Totals:				
12. Collaboration across sectors	None	1–2 sectors collaborating	3–4 sectors collaborating	5 or more sectors collaborating
Totals:				
13. Public awareness or communication efforts	Minimal efforts under way	Several efforts per year	Systematic efforts that reach most members of community	Systematic efforts that reach all members of community
Totals:				
14. Volunteers involved	Fewer than 10	Fewer than 50	Fewer than 100	More than 100
Totals:				
15. Funding of initiative	Less than $5,000 per year	$5,000–$9,999 per year	$10,000–$50,000 per year	More than $50,000 per year
Totals:				

Asset-Building Efforts: Our initiative

Next Steps

2. Where "sectors" are education, business, religious, health, government, youth organization, media, etc.

EVALUATION	INITIAL EFFORTS		ADVANCED EFFORTS	
16. Of effort's implementation	None	Some informal efforts	Oral discussions of findings	Written evaluation report
Totals:				
17. Of effort's outcomes	None	Some informal efforts	Oral discussions of findings	Written evaluation report
Totals:				

Evaluation: Our initiative

Next Steps

opportunities for reinvention, however. There's no doubt that thousands of youth and adults are together charting the new territory of transforming our society *with* and *for* young people.

We continually seek to fuse the knowledge of our heads with the direction of our hearts as we explore together. We don't have all the answers, nor is the work done yet. But the joint commitment of youth and adults to our shared vision of the future is evident every day in small acts of asset building, like the one described above, and in the work of the increasing number of asset-building initiatives.

Over the Long Haul: Sustaining Your Initiative

Eight Tips for Sustaining Your Initiative

- Tip #1—Approach community change as a dynamic, unpredictable process.

- Tip #2—Give it away.

- Tip #3—Combine planning and doing.

- Tip #4—Pay attention to renewing and broadening the leadership:
  - Look for catalyzing leadership.
  - Cultivate shared leadership.
  - Strengthen the capacity of your initiative.
  - Learn about what it takes to build an effective partnership.

- Tip #5—Don't make money the central focus.
  - Get funders to the table early.
  - Actively engage funders in the initiative.
  - Work with funders to fund a vision rather than just a program.
  - Support the development of funders as trendsetters in the asset movement.

- Tip #6—It's all about relationships.

- Tip #7—Remember that good evaluation is rooted in good planning, which is rooted in good evaluation.

- Tip #8—Trust the community.

Nourishing the Spirit of the Community Change Leader

Good seed makes a good crop.

IF YOU'RE READING THIS BOOK it's likely that you are, in one manner or another, a leader of community change. That puts you in very good company.

Throughout North America and beyond, passionate, principled, and dedicated people like you are undertaking the daily task of working to improve the condition of our communities and the circumstances in which our young people develop. Increasingly, these individuals are finding hope for their efforts in the field of positive youth development. For many such leaders of change, the work described in this book, using the developmental assets framework of Search Institute, has become central to what they do and, more deeply, who they are.

As longtime Search Institute trainers and consultants, we recently met with 18 such leaders of change—friends whom we've met over the past several years in this work across the United States and Canada—for a lightly facilitated conversation of what nourishes their spirit as community change leaders. We took our cue from Margaret Wheatley in her book *Turning to One Another: Simple Conversations to Restore Hope to the Future*, in which she encouraged people who care deeply about the same things to talk with one another. We wanted to learn from these leaders, to hear their experience of the relationship between the inner life of mind and spirit and the outer life of action and service. Our goal was simply to understand what sustains this group of energetic, long-term leaders for change—what keeps them going—in whatever way they would define that part of themselves we chose to call "spirit."

Inspiring Stories Refresh Our Spirits

OFTEN, IT IS THE STORIES WE HEAR from the people we come across that inspire us and keep our spirits up. Keith Pattinson, regional director of the Boys and Girls Clubs of British Columbia, offers this story to audiences as a way of inspiring them and reminding them that they, too, have the capacity to change the lives of young and older people, simply by taking a few minutes to become significant in the lives of others.

At an evening community workshop I conducted several years ago, an audience of approximately 200 moms, dads, grandparents, and folks generally interested in the well-being of young people embarked on the task of identifying significant people in their lives. At the point they divided into pairs to share their stories, I noticed a middle-aged woman break into tears and leave the room. She returned at the conclusion of the exercise and participated in the balance of the evening.

She was one of six to eight folks who lined up at the conclusion of the event to talk with me personally, a part of workshops I always enjoy because it gives me a chance to learn what works (or doesn't work) from a participant perspective. She opened our discussion by saying I must have been wondering why someone would break into tears and walk out in the middle of my workshop. I assured her (somewhat flippantly) that it happens often and I understood the sentiment well. In response, she asked if I'd be interested in learning what happened. Here's her story as I recall it.

She told me that when she was 13 years old, she lived with her mom and dad and attended grade 7 in a junior high school where she had earned honour roll status. Things were great at school but a challenge at home due to her dad's addiction to alcohol, a hardship made bearable by the consistent love, encouragement, and support she received from her mother.

Things began to change for the worse at home as she entered grade 8, and within months she came to understand that her mother's battle to deal with her father's drinking had led to her addiction to prescription drugs. In her words:

> That realization was the beginning of the end for me, and as I neared the end of that year at school, the only subject I was passing was English. I remember because it was in February of that year that our English teacher gave us an assignment to write a story or poem about ourselves. I thought long and hard about it and decided maybe if I told people what was going on in my life, someone would listen and maybe tell me what I should do. I spent hours on that poem because it gave me a chance to share something important to me and gave me hope someone would listen.

She went on to tell me that she was devastated when the students' corrected work was returned to the class a week later. Her poem had earned her numerous comments in red ink: poor punctuation, bad grammar, poor spelling, and a failing mark. All this led to an accelerated decline in her attitude and behaviour at home and school.

It was several months later when an announcement over the school's public address system summoned her to the principal's office. She recalled shuffling down the hall thinking to herself, "This is all I need on top of everything else that's going wrong in my life; now I'm going to get kicked out of school."

On entering the principal's office, she candidly asked him why she was there. He responded, "Maria, it's about your poem." Assuming the worst, she told him she was sorry, that she'd apologized to her teacher and her parents but she'd forgotten to apologize to him.

Her principal told her it was *his* turn to apologize to her. He said that he had been doing a review of classroom work a few months ago and come across the poem she had written, and that it was one of the most powerful and moving poems he had ever read. He went on to explain that there was a province-wide writing competition taking place at that time, and he had, without asking her permission, submitted her poem as part of the competition. He explained that it had been wrong for him to do so secretly, but having read her poem, he was concerned that the last thing she needed was another disappointment if the poem didn't receive some recognition.

The principal handed her a book published as a result of that writing competition, explaining that her poem, printed in a place of honour, had been given the highest recognition in the entire province.

He went on to tell her that he now better understood what was happening in her life and was giving her the book to keep as a reminder that she could achieve any goals she set for herself. He told her as well that he believed in her and that he and all the teachers wanted her to know that from now on they'd be there to help in any way they could.

She recalls leaving the principal's office five minutes after arriving there, bouncing down the hallway saying to herself, "I can be anything I want!" The adult Maria told me that night that within a year she was back on the honour roll, and graduated from high school and university with honours, all because one man took five minutes to tell her that he understood, that she was okay, and that he and others would be there for her.

She closed our discussion by telling me she broke into tears in the middle of the workshop because for the first time in over 40 years she realized she couldn't even remember the name of the man who had changed her life in a matter of minutes.

Why did these 18 people say yes to our invitation? A sampling of their responses reveals both positive motivation (whether personal or professional) and a sense of "weariness" from the rigors of this work:

"My real work is nourishing the spirits of others, and we tend to attract kindred spirits in this work. Assets work resonates with everything I've ever believed. I appreciate being able to actually talk about the inner life as part of this work."

"I am 'up to here' in community change work and I need to talk with others about it."

"In our community work, we hit plateaus, and we need to find ways to keep the movement moving, as well as to keep leaders going 'inside.'"

"Adapting the assets work to one's local culture is a challenging and satisfying opportunity. I need to be renewed in that work."

As a means of organizing our conversation, we chose to use the metaphor of a seed. Loosely borrowing from our former biology teachers, we described the protection seeds enjoy by virtue of their shell, the seed coat; the nourishment provided by the endosperm that feeds the living embryo of the seed; and the central "kernel" that contains the complete DNA necessary to create the future plant in its full form.

Together we explored how each of us, in our efforts to influence positive community change, has a similar central core that represents the essence of who we are, what we do, and why we invest in this work. To sustain that essence, we each identified what nourishes our spirit—practices, people, places that feed our continued investment in social change that matters deeply to us. And finally, we discussed the "seed coat"—ways we protect ourselves from the challenges to our continued investment in these efforts.

The dialogue was rich. For a brief few hours, we set aside *what* we do and *how* we do it to spend time contemplating *why* we find ourselves led to this work and, more important, the critical nature of something we don't fully understand—a deeply rooted part of us that cannot be ignored.

For some of us, a central part of our being is our love of helping young people develop—a strong sense of mission in community-based youth development. Our ways of nourishing our spirit were wide ranging—mentors to help us along, a religious community or a spiritual guide, renewal through the arts, stories of hope, being around positive people, family members who believe in what we are doing.

Acknowledging that keeping the spirit viable for leadership can be a challenge, we noted that we need to deal with the politics of change, negative impacts of the culture on young people, loss of a sense of community, and—just as important—imbalance in our own lives.

To protect our vitality, we engage in such practices as solitude, meditating, being in nature, exercising, getting adequate rest, listening to our inner voice and trusting its messages.

While the differences in perception and description were sometimes significant, the most powerful dynamic was the heightened sense of passion evident in this group of dedicated change agents as the conversation unfolded. Our commitment was reinforced as we found support in others who are on the same journey. We came to see that what Margaret Wheatley described at Search Institute's national conference in November 2002 was true. Like a grove of aspen trees, we are all connected at our "roots."

This notion of feeding the spirit of community change leaders seems often overlooked as we rush to understand "how to do this." As you consider all that this book has to offer, take a few moments to sit in silence, reflecting on that part of yourself that leads you to this work. How will you nourish that "spirit," however you define it for yourself?

It really is a critical question, since it is our hope that five, ten, or fifteen years from now, you will *still* be part of a vibrant youth development movement, nourished by those people, places, and activities that help you stay true to who you are and able to reinvest in this desperately needed work. The young people of today and tomorrow need you and thousands more like you involved in the effort, so sustaining yourself is essential. What we found in our conversation with like-minded friends who are attuned to this part of their life experience is that it matters . . . deeply. We left our conversation uplifted, recommitted, and renewed. Our spirits had been nourished.

Be well.

TIM DUFFEY AND I. SHELBY ANDRESS

RESOURCES

The following list of selected resources—both from Search Institute and from asset-building initiatives—is organized by the chapters of this book to make it easy for you to find resources on the topics most relevant for you.

Unless otherwise noted, the resources below (and many more) are available from Search Institute through our online catalog at www.search-institute. org. For more information or to receive a printed copy of the complete catalog, please call 800-888-7828. For complete information on all the Search Institute trainings and workshops offered through Vision Training Associates, see the Search Institute Web site or phone 800-294-4322 (pricing for trainings and workshops varies by number of participants).

Check the Search Institute Web site periodically for new surveys, trainings, and resources, too!

Part One
Vision, Preparation, and Planning

Introduction: The Vision for Asset-Building Communities

- ▶ **The Asset Approach** A great handout for sharing the power of assets with others, this 8-page booklet introduces adults to the power of using the developmental assets in their daily interactions with young people. Packets of 20, $7.95
- ▶ **An Asset Approach to Positive Community Change** Designed to share with leaders in your community or organization, this 8-page booklet shows you how you can work together for and with young people to create an asset-rich community. Packets of 20, $7.95
- ▶ **All Kids Are Our Kids: What Communities Must Do to Raise Caring and Responsible Children and Adolescents** by Peter L. Benson. This book presents the original, comprehensive vision of using the developmental assets to guide work toward building healthy communities. $28
- ▶ **Healthy Communities • Healthy Youth booklet** This 20-page informational booklet paints a comprehensive yet easy-to-understand picture of the asset framework and its implications for community building. $2.95
- ▶ **Building Communities from the Inside Out: A Path toward Finding and Mobilizing a Community's Assets** by John P. Kretzmann and John L. McKnight. A book and 2-video set by two respected researchers and innovators in the field of community

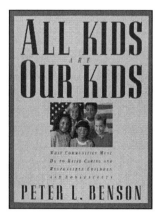

ALL KIDS ARE OUR KIDS

WHAT COMMUNITIES MUST DO TO RAISE CARING AND RESPONSIBLE CHILDREN AND ADOLESCENTS

PETER L. BENSON

change. Together, the book and video set walk you through six different focuses on "asset-based community development" that show how a focus on strengths helps communities rebuild. Book 376 pages, videos 101 and 111 minutes. Set $99.95

▶ *Training: Starting and Supporting Asset Building in Communities* A workshop on successfully launching and supporting a Healthy Communities • Healthy Youth initiative to promote asset building in your community. 1 day. Call for pricing.

▶ Benson, P. L., & Saito, R. N. (2001). The scientific foundations of youth development. In P. L. Benson & K. J. Pittman (Eds.), *Trends in Youth Development: Visions, Realities, and Challenges*. (pp. 135-154). Norwell, MA: Kluwer Academic Publishers. This chapter offers an expansive and comprehensive view of youth development and the science needed to undergird it. Examines four primary settings in which youth development principles are applied and in which youth development can and does occur—programs, organizations, socializing systems (schools, family, neighborhoods, etc.), and community. Availability: libraries or publisher.

Chapter 1. Beginning the Process of Change

▶ *Developmental Assets: A Synthesis of the Scientific Research on Adolescent Development* by Peter C. Scales and Nancy Leffert. This foundational volume examines more than 800 scientific articles and reports on adolescent development that tie to each of the 40 developmental assets. 304 pages, $24.95

▶ *The Spirit of Culture: Applying Cultural Competency to Strength-based Youth Development* by María Guajardo Lucero. Written by an asset champion who is the director of Assets for Colorado Youth (ACY), this work includes individual essays on personal cultural identity as well as worksheets and training materials for use in cultural competency workshops. 52 pages, $23 (Available from Search Institute or from ACY at www.buildassets.org)

▶ Mannes, M., Benson, P. L., Kretzmann, J., & Norris, T. (2003). The American tradition of community development: Implications for guiding community engagement in youth development. In R. M. Lerner, F. Jacobs, & D. Wertlieb (Eds.), *Handbook of Applied Developmental Science: Promoting Positive Child, Adolescent, and Family Development through Research, Policies and Programs; Vol. 1, Applying Developmental Science for Youth and Families: Historical and Theoretical Foundations*. (pp. 469–499). Newbury Park, CA: Sage Publications. Youth development involves taking into account the complete context of adolescents' lives; recognizing that youth grow up in a number of interrelated and overlapping community socializing systems; affirming the fact that each and every member of the community has something at stake and therefore a role to play in youth development; and imploring communities to provide the supports and opportunities to foster healthy development. Availability: libraries or publisher.

Chapter 2. Getting Started: What Needs to Happen First?

◗ *First Steps in Evaluation: Basic Tools for Asset-Building Initiatives* Worksheets for planning, goal setting, and reporting, and other basic tools for assessing progress and guiding improvement of your initiative. 111 pages, $13.95

◗ *Making Evaluation Integral to Your Asset-Building Initiative: Employing a Theory of Action and Change* by William Mesaros. This report can be viewed online or downloaded free at www.search-institute.org/research/knowledge/MakingEvaluation Integral.html.

◗ *Search Institute Profiles of Student Life: Attitudes and Behaviors* This student survey measures the levels of 40 developmental assets in your community's young people. The resulting report provides a "snapshot" of your young people's assets and can help you plan where to focus your initiative's first activities. Pricing varies by number of students surveyed and type(s) of report requested. Call 800-888-7828 for details on this and other survey instruments available from Search Institute.

◗ *Training: What's Up with Our Kids?* An introductory presentation on the 40 developmental assets using your students' data from the *Search Institute Profiles of Student Life: Attitudes and Behaviors* survey. 1½ to 2 hours. Call for pricing.

Part Two
Making It Happen: Five Action Strategies for Your Asset-Building Initiative

Chapter 3. Engage Adults

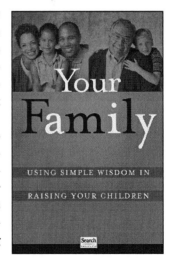

◗ *Your Family: Using Simple Wisdom in Raising Your Children* This compact booklet helps parents and other caregivers reflect on their important role in bringing good things into the lives of their children. Introduces the concept of developmental assets through a discussion of the eight asset categories and what those eight categories of development mean for children. Packets of 20, $13.95

◗ *Taking Asset Building Personally: Planning Guide and Personal Action Workbook* Help yourself and others get personal with asset building using facilitated small-group discussions. Guide includes step-by-step instructions for starting supportive groups, while individual workbooks include information on the assets and numerous worksheets and activities for reflecting on intentionally building assets in daily life. Guide and 6 workbooks, $69.95

◗ *Grading Grown-Ups 2002* A summary report based on data collected from thousands of interviews with youth and adults about how adults are—or are not—positively influencing the development of children and adolescents. Packaged in an easy-to-read, graphically appealing 12-page booklet. Packets of 10, $7.95

- *Tag, You're It! 50 Easy Ways to Connect with Young People* Research shows that most young people don't have enough caring adults in their lives, and that many adults don't know what to do to be there for the young people around them. Hence, this book filled with 50 simple acts of caring to reach out to children and youth. 148 pages, $7.95

- *Pass It On! Ready-to-Use Handouts for Asset Builders* Everyone in your community has an impact on kids, but is it a positive one or a negative one? This collection of reproducible handouts provides you with the means to bring inspiration and practical suggestions to everyone from grandparents and store managers to bus drivers and teachers. 176 pages, $22.95

- *Training: Everyone's an Asset Builder* A workshop introducing asset building into the personal and professional lives of attendees. Learn how to strengthen your intentional asset-building efforts. 4 hours. Call for pricing.

- *Helping Kids Succeed—Alaskan Style* Includes asset-building ideas from more than 100 Alaskan villages, towns, and cities, with all their cultural diversity. More than 125,000 copies in circulation. 190 pages. You can order a copy of this book from Alaska ICE at www.AlaskaICE.org or from Search Institute at www.search-institute.org.

- *What Kids Need to Succeed: Proven, Practical Ways to Raise Good Kids* by Peter L. Benson, Judy Galbraith, and Pamela Espeland. The book that first brought developmental assets to the general public's attention. More than 500,000 sold. Filled with more than 900 examples of actions that can make a difference in young people's lives. 224 pages, $5.99

- Simpson, A. Rae, & Roehlkepartain, Jolene L. (2003) Asset building in parenting practices and family life. In Lerner, R. M., & Benson, P. L. *Developmental Assets and Asset-Building Communities: Implications for Research, Policy, and Practice.* (pp. 157–193). New York: Kluwer Academic/Plenum Publishers. The authors summarize current research on parenting adolescents and correlate what is known with the framework of developmental assets. Includes several theoretical frameworks focusing on raising awareness about the importance of parenting during adolescence, shifting negative perceptions about parenting and adolescence, and providing tools for raising healthy teenagers. Availability: libraries or publisher.

- Roehlkepartain, E. C., Scales, P. C., Roehlkepartain, J. L., Gallo, Carmelita, & Rude, S. P. (2002) *Building Strong Families: Highlights from a Preliminary Survey from YMCA of the USA and Search Institute on What Parents Need to Succeed.* Chicago, IL: YMCA of the USA. Reports on a 2002 poll of U.S. parents. Findings include the following: Most parents surveyed are going it alone; many parents interviewed lack a strong relationship with a spouse or partner; a majority of parents surveyed feel successful as parents most of the time; most parents polled face ongoing challenges; and many things these parents say would help them as parents are easy things others can do. Accessible at www.abundantassets.org.

- Scales, P. C., Benson, P. L., Roehlkepartain, E. C., Hintz, N. R., Sullivan, T. K., Mannes, M., & Grothe, R. (2001). The role of neighborhood and community in building developmental assets for children and youth: A national study of social norms among American adults. *Journal of Community Psychology, 29* (6), 703–727. Examines the roles of unrelated adults in the positive socialization of children and youth; reports on a national survey that reveals that there is a gap between what adults consider important and what they actually do to construct positive, intentional relationships with children and youth. Availability: libraries or publisher.

Chapter 4. Mobilize Youth

▶ *Me@My Best: Ideas for Staying True to Yourself—Every Day* This 16-page booklet introduces the developmental assets framework in a youth-friendly way, encourages young people to explore what the categories mean to them personally, and inspires them to find and build upon their own strengths. Packets of 20, $9.95

▶ *Get Things Going! 50 Asset-Building Activities for Workshops, Presentations, and Meetings* There's nothing like a game or activity to break the ice at meetings, and this book offers a refreshing collection of asset-related icebreakers, mixers, and closings. 73 pages, $14.95

▶ *Building Assets Together* by Jolene L. Roehlkepartain and *More Building Assets Together* by Rebecca Grothe. Fresh, creative activities to do with groups of young people to help build assets and to help them learn about building assets for themselves and with their peers. 128 pages each, BAT $22.95, MBAT $26.95

▶ *Step by Step! A Young Person's Guide to Positive Community Change* This spiralbound workbook is loaded with action ideas and examples for young people who want to contribute to making their world better but don't know where and how to begin. 96 pages, $19.95

▶ *Involving Youth in Your Organization* A booklet created in Mason City, Iowa. To request a copy, email Mason City Youth Task Force Director Mary Schissel at mcytf@masoncity.net.

▶ *The Power of an Untapped Resource: Exploring Youth Representation on Your Board or Committee* Find this free resource on youth engagement online at www.aasb. org/Publications.html.

▶ *Succeed Every Day: Daily Readings for Teens* by Pamela Espeland. Snippets of insight for teens to contemplate and appreciate; each day's passage includes a quotation and an affirmation to carry them positively through the day. 388 pages, $10.95

▶ *What Teens Need to Succeed: Proven, Practical Ways to Shape Your Own Future* by Peter L. Benson, Judy Galbraith, and Pamela Espeland Use this book to let teens know they've got the power—the power to look at their lives, celebrate the good parts, identify the problem areas, and shape their own success. 272 pages, $14.95

▶ *Assets Happening Here* Produced by and for teens, this video cneters on the real lives of three young people to introduce assets in a way that engages teen viewers. 17 minutes, $24.95

▶ Search Institute offers a number of trainings specifically for young people and adults together, including Youth Service, Leadership, and Empowerment Workshops. Call 800-294-4322 for details.

Chapter 5. Activate Sectors and Invigorate Programs

▶ *Outreach and Listening Campaign Report by Project Cornerstone's Diversity Team* This first wave report on using the asset framework in a community "outreach and listening" campaign is available at www.projectcornerstone.org.

Youth Organizations

▶ *Walking Your Talk: Building Assets in Organizations That Serve Youth* Author Neal Starkman's interviews with youth workers and youth program directors across North America result in a compendium of asset-based methods, activities, and stories to help organizations become more intentional and successful in asset building. 184 pages, $29.95

▶ *In Good Company: Tools to Help Youth and Adults Talk* by Franklin W. Nelson. This hands-on workbook includes 8 sets of tear-out sheets with introductory and get-acquainted activities perfect for adults and youth in one-on-one mentoring relationships. 48 pages, $6.95

▶ *What's Working? Tools for Evaluating Your Mentoring Program* by Rebecca N. Saito. Assess your mentoring program's goals and progress with tools based on the developmental assets developed by Search Institute; includes surveys, focus group questions, and interview protocols. 136 pages, $24.95

▶ *Martin's Good Things* A read-aloud book for use by parents or mentors with preschool and elementary school students, this tale tells of young Martin and how he learns to recognize the important things he has in his life, including a loving family and helpful neighbors. 28 pages, Packet of 10, $14.95

▶ *When Parents Ask for Help: Everyday Issues through an Asset-Building Lens* by Renie Howard. Help the parents and other caregivers of adolescents take a fresh, new look at the tough, everyday issues they face with this resource of reproducible handouts. Includes handouts on topics such as body image, conflict, risky activities, jobs, homework, chores, dating, and more. 144 pages, $24.95

▶ *The Possible Dream: What Families in Distressed Communities Need to Help Youth Thrive* A research report that offers strategies for reaching families in distressed neighborhoods and strengthening the systems that support them. 48 pages, $12.95

▶ *You Can* and *In Our Own Words Posters* Decorate your walls with these colorful, eye-catching posters. *You Can* highlights the eight asset categories, explaining in one short sentence the meaning of each. *In Our Own Words* is a set of eight posters, one for each category, that feature phrases and words that 17 young people used to describe what those categories of development mean to them. Great as conversation starters. *You Can* poster, $7.95; set of *In Our Own Words* posters, $32.95

Schools

▶ *Powerful Teaching: Developmental Assets in Curriculum and Instruction* Shows education professionals how to infuse the assets into their curriculum and instruction and highlights research-based instructional strategies that are consistent with asset building. Includes examples from language arts, social studies, mathematics, science, health education, and visual arts. 304 pages, $34.95

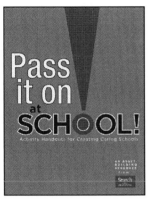

▶ *Pass It On at School! Activity Handouts for Creating Caring Schools* Draws from proven ideas and tips from educators and students. Use the handouts again and again to find new ways to take advantage of "asset-building moments" throughout the school day and throughout the school community. 208 pages, $24.95

▶ *The Power of Parents: Parent Engagement in Schools and the Developmental Assets* by María Guajardo Lucero and Patsy Roybal. This book describes how the developmental assets framework offers school communities a powerful resource for strengthening relationships between parents, school staff, and students. 56 pages, $20

▶ *Great Places to Learn: How Asset-Building Schools Help Students Succeed* by Neal Starkman, Peter C. Scales, and Clay Roberts. A powerful, positive guide to infusing assets into any school community. Learn the reasons why building assets is important to young people's education and strategies to put that learning into action. 216 pages, $29.95

▶ *"You Have to Live It": Building Developmental Assets in School Communities video* This inspiring video lets you see and hear for yourself how students, teachers, principals, and school staff are building assets at school. Use it for instruction, use it for inspiration, and use it to get others on board! 27 minutes, $24.95

▶ *Ideas That Cook: Activities for Asset Builders in School Communities* by Neal Starkman. Cook up lasting results with kids by using this collection of energizing projects from educators in all 50 states. 168 pages, $26.95

▶ *Training: Building Developmental Assets in School Communities* A workshop to describe the connections between the assets and student achievement. Learn how to initiate, increase, and strengthen the asset-building efforts that already exist in your school. 1 day. Call for offerings and pricing.

▶ *Training: Change of Heart: A Student and Staff Retreat* An exciting two-day retreat for students and school staff to begin the process of fostering a more supportive school climate. 2 days. Call for pricing.

🔹 Scales, P. C., & Taccogna, J. (2000). Caring to try: How building students' developmental assets can promote school engagement and success. *NASSP Bulletin 84* (619), 69–78.

🔹 Scales, P. C., Blyth, D. A., Berkas, T. H., & Kielsmeier, J. C. (2000). The effects of service-learning on middle school students' social responsibility and academic success. *Journal of Early Adolescence, 20* (3), 332–359.

Congregations

🔹 *Building Assets in Congregations: A Practical Guide for Helping Youth Grow Up Healthy* and *A Foundation for Success: Congregations Building Assets in Youth (a 30-minute video)* Together, this book and video provide tools, examples, stories, and ideas from numerous faith traditions on how to integrate asset building with the life of a religious institution. Book 176 pages, video 30 minutes. Set $29.95

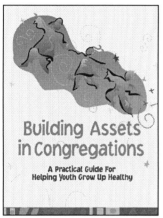

🔹 *Networking Congregations for Asset Building: A Tool Kit* Find the tools and strategies you need to bring together the congregations in your community for asset building. 205 pages, $24.95

🔹 *Prescription for a Healthy Church: Ministry Ideas to Nurture Whole People* by Jolene L. and Eugene E. Roehlkepartain. Written for Christian congregations, this book contains a wealth of ideas on strength-based youth ministry that can be easily adapted for other faith traditions. 160 pages, $17.99

🔹 *Training: Integrating Assets into Your Congregation* A training for congregations of all faith traditions who want to learn how to re-envision congregational life and youth work from an asset-building perspective. 4 hours to 3 days. Pricing varies.

🔹 Roehlkepartain, E. C. (2003). Making room at the table for everyone: Interfaith engagement in positive child and adolescent development. In D. Wertlieb, F. Jacobs, & R. M. Lerner (Eds.), *Handbook of Applied Developmental Science: Promoting Positive Child, Adolescent, and Family Development through Research, Policies, and Programs; Vol. 3, Promoting Positive Youth and Family Development: Community Systems, Citizenship, and Civil Society.* (pp. 535–563). Thousand Oaks, CA: Sage Publications. This chapter proposes engaging the faith community by developing interfaith, community-based strategies that tap, strengthen, and broaden congregations' shared commitment to young people's healthy development. Availability: libraries or publisher.

Chapter 6. Influence Civic Decisions

🔹 *Get the Word Out: Communication Tools and Ideas for Asset Builders Everywhere* Features ready-to-use materials, including asset articles and press releases, sample letters, and success stories. 192 pages, $44.95

- *Speaking of Developmental Assets: Presentation Resources and Strategies* This kit is packed with scripts, outlines, transparencies, handouts, and stories to make it easy for you to tell others about the power of assets. 202 pages, binder, transparencies. $195
- *Developmental Assets and Asset-Building Communities: Implications for Research, Policy, and Practice* This new resource extends the scholarly base for understanding the connection between young people's healthy development and the development of healthy communities. 244 pages, $55

- *Training: Sharing the Asset Message* Learn how to effectively deliver a variety of asset-building and asset-promoting messages to multiple audiences. 4 hours. Call for pricing.
- *Creating Social Change* report from Assets for Colorado Youth. Available at www.buildassets.org.

Part Three
Keeping It Going and Growing

Chapter 7. Over the Long Haul: Sustaining Your Initiative

- *The Children First Story: How One Community Partnership Is Learning to Put Its Children and Families First* by Robert D. Ramsey. Order by calling 952-928-6075 or emailing: atkinson.karen@slpschools.org or mailing: Children First, 6425 W. 33rd St., St. Louis Park, MN 55426.
- *Vision to Action Planning Retreat* An intergenerational planning retreat designed to help asset-building initiatives create a community-wide mobilization strategy and action plan. 1½ days. Call for offerings and pricing.

INDEX